To Mary Peray
    with gratitude and
our best wishes

Phyllis Kaeostaun

Hv. Bunny Austin

A MIXED DOUBLE

By H. W. Austin

BITS AND PIECES
LAWN TENNIS MADE EASY
UNDER THE HEAVENS

*

By Phyllis Konstam

HE WAS NOT THERE
(A Play)

A MIXED DOUBLE

H. W. 'Bunny' Austin
and Phyllis Konstam

1969
Chatto and Windus
LONDON

PUBLISHED BY
CHATTO AND WINDUS LTD.
42 WILLIAM IV STREET
LONDON, W.C.2
*
CLARKE, IRWIN AND CO. LTD.
TORONTO

FIRST PUBLISHED JUNE 1969
SECOND IMPRESSION AUGUST 1969

SBN 7011 1446 0

PRINTED IN GREAT BRITAIN BY
WILLIAM LEWIS (PRINTERS) LTD.
CARDIFF

CONTENTS

ILLUSTRATIONS

7

ILLUSTRATIONS

A MIXED DOUBLE

CHAPTER ONE

I

Bunny

THIS is the story of an adventure, an adventure which I met at the height of my tennis-playing days. As I clung precariously to the top of the lawn tennis tree, I often used to wonder where I would go from there. As far as tennis was concerned, there was only one way, and that was down.

I could, of course, capitalise on my position and turn such success as I had earned into cash.

But I had only one life to live. What, I wondered, was the greatest thing I could do with it?

Very soon I was to find out—clearly and without doubt. For when an adventure greater than Wimbledon or the Davis Cup presented itself, I knew it was the game for me. And that game, which absorbs every energy and satisfies every longing, becomes no less playable as the years go by.

From the first I knew it would be a battle. I went into it with my eyes open. I have not been disappointed. I have been accused of being a Fascist and a Communist, a pacifist and a warmonger, of running away from the war and of going on fighting it after others have stopped. I have been thrown out of the All England Lawn Tennis Club at Wimbledon and have only once in the last twenty-five years been asked to a tennis occasion. Yet during these same years I have been the guest of Presidents and Prime Ministers and have felt the warmth of the affection of the so-called ordinary man on five continents.

It has been a fascinating life, taking me to more countries than tennis ever did—and taking me far deeper into the real lives of their inhabitants. I have, through it all, been privileged to work with some of the most remarkable men in our generation. I marvel at my good fortune.

Since this adventure is open to all, I have decided to tell my story, to put down the facts as they are and were, and not, as often they have been, "twisted by knaves to make a trap for fools".

The story is also my wife Phyll's story. When I first encountered our adventure she had already written her name in the
bright lights of theatre and film stardom. Her reaction to it
was different from mine. She will tell you about it, for we are
writing this book together.

But let me start at the beginning

II

My origins are lost in the smoke and fire of the Irish revolution.
Somewhere mingling in the soil of Ireland lie the records of my
family history. Almost all is forgotten. Just a few salient facts
remain.

My grandfather came from Ireland. That is certain. He
went into trade, and he went broke.

I was not born at the time but this was the decisive moment of
my unborn life. My father was seventeen. He was a great sportsman. Rugger, cricket, tennis, golf, snooker, billiards–there
was no game indoors or out he did not play and love. At seventeen he was playing cricket for the Surrey Second XI at the Oval.

When my grandfather went broke, the shock of his financial
loss incapacitated both him and his wife. My father, the
youngest of a family of three boys and two girls, became the
family breadwinner. First he went goldmining in Costa Rica
and still only seventeen, armed with a huge revolver, was foreman of the miners. But the cost of mining the gold was more
than the value of the gold mined, and my father returned to
London. He became the secretary of a circus, worked in the
Bank of England and finally joined a firm of jobbers on the
Stock Exchange.

But his heart always lay with sport. His own ambitions
foiled, he dreamed of the day when he would have a son who
would fulfil all the sporting ambitions frustrated in his own life.

One day he saw one of the beautiful daughters of Mr Cock,
who lived in the old manor house which had become a part
of the London suburb of South Norwood. She was fourteen.
"That is the girl I am going to marry", said my father. And
Wolf, as my father was always called, since Wilfred was too
anaemic a name for so aggressive a young sportsman, waited

patiently for twelve years until the mining market on the Stock Exchange boomed and he could afford to marry.

Two daughters were born and then at last the son for whom his ambition longed. No sooner had I made my entrance into the world than my father snatched me away from the doctor's arms to make sure I was all of one piece. Satisfied, he gave me into my mother's care until I should be old enough to throw, stroke, hit or kick those spherical objects known variously as cricket, tennis, golf and foot balls.

III

It was a summer evening in 1912. On the laburnum tree outside my nursery window at the top of our Victorian home a song thrush sang merrily, calling to a neighbour up the road.

It was past the time when I was usually asleep. Nanny— Fat Nanny, as we used to call her because of her ample size— had said good night and left me to sleep; but this was a night when sleep was impossible. It was the night of the great decision. An event was afoot which was going deeply to affect my life.

In other lands that night other events were afoot destined, too, to affect everything I did. An exiled Russian with a bearded face and hate-filled heart was planning how he could one day upturn the world. Across the Channel in Germany a proud Emperor with a withered arm and imperious moustache, was scheming schemes by which he hoped to humble the proud majesty of his cousin King George of England. Somewhere in Austria lived a young man of twisted heart and mind who in later years was to spawn diabolical schemes and stand at last as the epitome of all that is evil in mankind.

But as I lay in my bed on that bright summer's evening and listened to the song thrush singing outside my window, only one thing concerned me. My elder sister Phyllis had been made a junior member of the local tennis club. My sister Joan had insisted, too, on being allowed to join. And now I, aged six, had put in my plea. Tonight my parents had promised me to give me their decision. Would they or would they not allow me to join too?

13

How I longed to play! How many hours I had sat watching my father and his friends! The game held a magic for me, inexplicable but inescapable. For hours with racquet and ball I would play against the nursery wall. The rocking horse was my net, the wall a series of Wimbledon champions. Mrs Lambert Chambers was my most deadly rival. She was a famous name, the greatest of the ladies. If the wall returned the ball and I missed it, that was a point against me. If I could hit the ball between the wall and rocking horse, that was a point to me. In this way Mrs Lambert Chambers and I waged deadly struggles. Little did she know how often she had to bow to defeat at my hands!

My parents were indulgent. Various pictures on the nursery wall regularly lost their glass, splintered by an errant shot. The whitewashed wall itself was, where I played, an uneven colour of grey. Wet days were my usual days of practice when the weather was too bad for outdoor enjoyment. The window behind me was open to the fresh air. Mother never allowed any of us in any room however cold without an open window. But, alas, when Mrs Lambert Chambers returned the ball too promptly and I missed it, it would leap through the window and had to be retrieved, wet and muddy, from the garden. The game, however, had to go on, and balls were scarce. The white wall grew an ever darker grey.

But this evening a new vista had opened up. If only my parents allowed it, I would play a real game on a real court. True, I was only six years old, but if I could wallop Mrs Lambert Chambers, why shouldn't I beat my sisters too?

Suddenly I heard footsteps on the stair. A stocky man with greying hair and a bristly moustache, my father, came into the room.

"Mummy and I have decided you can join the club."

The magic words had been spoken. It was as if paradise itself had dropped into my lap. Of course, I said nothing. What was there to say? Words were not invented, and certainly not possessed by my six-year-old vocabulary, to express the magic of that moment.

My father left me, and I lay in bed wondering whether I was dreaming or awake. The crucifix which my sister had given me and which I treasured greatly looked down at me from the wall above my head. Under the gas lamp, hanging on the wall by the window, I could see the Apostles' Creed which I had learned by heart even before I had learned to read. But my imagination was not with these things but with the game that I would play, with the way the grass courts would feel underneath my feet and with the magic of a ball being struck.

It was with joy in my heart that I lay in my bed that night, and it was with joy in my heart, as the sun set and the lamp-lighter came with his pole to light the lamps along the road outside, that I eventually went to sleep.

IV

It was August 1914. For the third year in succession the family were on holiday at West Runton, a little village in Norfolk that lies between the towns of Sheringham and Cromer.

We stayed in a cottage on the far side of the common, past the Links Hotel and the golf course where my father used to play. Most days my sisters and I, in green jerseys and sandshoes, and accompanied by an older cousin, Doris, walked down to the sea. The way lay over the common, past the little pond where we used to sail our boats before breakfast, over the main road, now become dangerous with motor cars (and stinker buzzers, as my father called the motor cycles) dashing along at twenty miles per hour, and down by the dusty hedge-lined lanes which ran between the cliff-top fields. Finally, with a great burst, we would rush down the incline which had been cut through the cliff and, with a last jump, spreadeagle our-selves on the sand.

This day in August seemed much like any other day as, our morning on the beach over, we prepared for the mile-long walk back to our cottage. Slowly we climbed the incline between the cliffs and walked along the dusty hedge-lined lanes towards the dangerous main road. Just before we reached it, a girl came towards us on a bicycle. She braked and alighted.

"Have you heard?" she said. "War has been declared."

Suddenly the summer morning grew tense. I was still only seven years old and I did not understand the fateful meaning

15

of these words. But I knew from the disturbed faces of the grown-ups with me that this news was a solemn thing.

We crossed the main road in silence. Then my cousin Doris spoke. "It may be only a rumour," she said, but then as if dismissing this thought, "Tod and Ken will have to go."

Tod and Ken were Doris' two big brothers, both of them well over six feet tall. I did not know them well, but at Christmastime they gave me half a crown. They had big stamp collections which made me envious and once they made an exciting 'marble railway' by which marbles ran all the way from the top storey of their house to the bottom. One day I hoped to grow up and be like Ken and Tod.

But now, said Doris, they had to go. Where would they go, I wondered? I was old enough to grasp that war, whatever it was, was very solemn, but I did not realise at that moment its urgent meaning. The day would come, however, when I would not be able to remember a time when there was no war, when the whole of my life seemed to have been lived against its background.

But on that summer day, though the occasion was to remain forever photographed on my mind, I had other things to think about. Lunch called; and in the afternoon perhaps we would go up to the Roman Camp and play trains in the bracken, or go to the 'heights' and slide down their grassy slippery sides. Soon after that solemn and disturbing meeting with the girl on the bicycle my sisters and I were back in holiday mood again.

v

The sirens wailed and soon the air was filled with the drone of the high-flying Gothas. A moment later came the intermittent boom of the lone gun at Elmer's End.

There was a stir in the house and my father came into my bedroom. Another raid. We were going downstairs to sit under the dining room table.

It had been written in the papers that the safest place in a raid was under a good stout table. Our dining room boasted an extremely good stout oak table guaranteed to take the weight of the house should it collapse. So downstairs we went, my mother and father, my two sisters, myself, fat Nanny and Tim the dog. My mother and father managed to get under the table. So did my two sisters and myself. But the problem arose when it came to fat Nanny.

"I'm all right, Mummy dear," she assured my mother, "I've got my head under."

With Nanny's remark, the ridiculousness of the situation began to strike. My sister Joan, who never knew the meaning of fear, began to giggle. We all began to giggle. "Let's all go back to bed," suggested my father.

We all squirmed out from under the table. My father was much happier upstairs anyway. He liked to sit by the bedroom window and watch what was going on – the puff of the shells among the high-flying planes. Sitting by an open window watching the raids he felt most safe.

We scrambled up the stairs again. Suddenly from the top of the house there came a piercing scream. Kathleen!

Kathleen was the latest addition to our family, a cook. She was a young woman, probably about thirty, though to my eight years anyone over the age of sixteen or so seemed to be of immense antiquity and could simply be classified as 'old'!

Following the scream, my mother and father, lighted candles in hand, rushed to the top of the house to the maid's room. They found the room in darkness.

"Are you all right?"

A faint whimper came from Kathleen. They found her half fainting on the floor, an upturned candle beside her.

What had happened?

"I don't know," she groaned, "I'd just got out of bed. No more than a few seconds. Suddenly there was a crash. I'd put the candle on the end of the bed. Suddenly it went out. I don't know what has happened."

My father looked at the bed. Square on the pillow was a large round piece of metal, exactly where Kathleen's head would have been if, moments before, she had not got out of bed. Above her pillow was a neat round hole in the ceiling through which the metal had fallen. It was the fuse of a shell that had been fired from the gun at Elmer's End.

The broken slates of the roof had, of course, to be mended. But the hole on the ceiling remained, a memento of the air raids of the First World War, until in the Second World War our home was destroyed altogether.

VI

The fields sloped awkwardly on either side; it was hard to get the ball away. Moreover, being wartime, the outfield had been turned over to hay. The balls which the fielders failed to stop were held up in the stubble or halted by a stook.

I made thirty-seven runs, and practically all of them in singles.

It was hard going, it seemed to me. Long before my innings was over I began to ache, and when at last it was over, I had hardly an ache-free muscle in my body. On an ordinary field, my teammates assured me, I would have made a hundred.

It was Saturday, and I was only a weekly boarder at my preparatory school. This was the day I returned home to enjoy the good food provided by my family, to make up for the sparse and meagre fare which was dished out the rest of the week. Wednesday was a particularly horrid day–soup, thin as water, with an ugly suet dumpling floating in it, or rather, heavily submerged. You would attempt to cut it in half with your spoon, and it would stick to it and refuse to be removed. How to finish the soup with a dumpling sticking to your spoon was a problem.

This, the first course, was followed by 'satin cushions'. Satin cushions was a misnomer. There was nothing satiny about these treacle tarts. The pastry was cooked as hard as rock and you had to cut through it with your fork, and your fork would curl up and look at you with a disdainful smile as if saying, "Poor fool, a mere fork's no good. What you need is a hatchet."

How hungry we used to get at school! Two slices of bread and margarine was hardly a sustaining supper for young and growing boys. We used to sneak lumps of sugar and nibble them when we got to bed to assuage our hunger. The younger masters used to take pity on us, and sometimes when lights were out, would creep in with chocolate.

It was a relief to go home for the weekend, and escape not only the food, but the headmaster, a terrifying man with black hair, a black moustache and a dark mien, who raved at us like a lunatic during Latin hours, and was not unknown to hurl at your head ink pots, pens, pencils, India rubber and anything else that came to hand. Not only was Wednesday soup and 'satin cushions' for lunch, but it was Latin compo–a day to be dreaded.

This Saturday there was even more than the ordinary excitement of going home. The family were on a picnic. I would ride home on my bike and then ride out to join the family where they had gone. But I wondered as I rode home if I could do it. That innings of mine, joyful as it was and glad news for my father, seemed to have stiffened me up all over. I debated long when I went home: should I go on the picnic or go to bed? I decided on bed.

When I did not turn up at the picnic my parents came home. How had I done that afternoon? I told them of my score and the difficulties under which I had made it. Why had I not come to the picnic? I told them I was tired and achey.

My mother took my temperature. It was 104°.

There followed those hazy, unhappy days of a high fever; the soft tread, and the soft reassuring voice of the doctor, the loving attentions of my mother, the sponge baths, so cooling in the heat of the fever and the summer days.

At last there dawned that morning when I was allowed a poached egg for breakfast.

And soon health returned and the following Monday, only nine days since I was stricken with the 'flu, I was able to return to school, and with all the school present, to receive my First XI colours from the headmaster.

VII

"Your daughter, in my opinion, is good enough to play in the Junior Championships."

The speaker was Mr A. D. Prebble, a Wimbledon player and a great friend of my father. He would often come down to play with my father on the local courts. He and Dad would play against the Australian S. N. Doust and another excellent player, M. R. L. White. They would play for the dinner following the game and they had titanic struggles which I followed with goggle-eyed excitement.

Mr Prebble had watched the development of my sisters and me since the earliest beginnings. Following the announcement by my father that I had been allowed to join the junior club with my sisters I had played enthusiastically every day that the summer weather would allow. While I was still at the local kindergarten I would dash out of school at twelve o'clock when the morning lessons were over and play for an hour before lunch. After lunch I would be back on the courts again for the rest of the afternoon.

My chief opponent at that time was a girl who went to the same kindergarten. She was one of the seven daughters of the local vicar. I regularly beat her six-love, but that did not affect the enthusiasm of either of us.

In the holidays my sisters would be free from school. Fierce contests took place. At the end of the summer all of us would compete in the Junior Tournament. Each match consisted of eleven games. The first year I beat my sister Joan ten to one. She threw her racquet at my head!

In succeeding years I waged deadly battles with Joan. They were breath-taking struggles, with never more than a game between us.

Then the day came when Mr Prebble made the announcement to my father that sister Joan was good enough to play in the Junior Championships of Great Britain. We were astonished! Neither of us had thought of playing in tournaments outside our own club. To us the great players of the day were gods and goddesses. We even looked with awe on the champions of our own club and eyed each other with envy if one of us was invited by the grown-ups to play with them on the senior courts. A girl or a boy who played in the Junior Championships must, we imagined, be a kind of junior god or goddess. Could my sister possibly be one of them?

The Junior Championships that year were played in Eastbourne. My sister, highly excited and slightly bewildered, departed with Mr Prebble. Silence fell. At the week's end a

CHAPTER ONE

telegram arrived, "Am arriving with Junior Champion." It was from Mr Prebble. Sister Joan had won the Championship.

VIII

"My son has as much chance of beating Dearman as I have of beating Tilden." My father spoke firmly and my father knew.

The young fellow who was speaking to my father was, however, not convinced. "Your son beat me," he said, "and I know how good he is. He can beat Dearman."

I was fourteen years old. It was my first tournament. It was the Surrey Junior Championships. I had entered to keep my sister company.

I was very small. For all my fourteen years, as the papers said, I could only just see over the net. Dearman towered above me. He was the Schoolboy Champion, crowned at Queen's Club.

My father said I could not win. My late opponent said I could. I agreed with my father and had absolutely no expectation of winning, or even of gaining a set. I was glad to make a match of it in the first set. I was delighted to win the second—I could congratulate myself I had done well. When I won the match, I was no less amazed than my father, my opponent and all the audience. Tiny little Wilfred Austin had beaten the Schoolboy Champion!

I did not sleep that night—I was too excited. In the final I was beaten. But I had made my mark. With my sister I too had arrived on the tennis map. Much to my amazement, in spite of all my dreams, it really seemed that I was good—as good as other boys who played the game. Even better. Could this boy, who had done so well, I wondered to myself, really be ME?

IX

During my years at my preparatory school discussions took place as to where I should go when I left. My father wrote round to various schools all over England. Eventually he received a charming handwritten letter from a housemaster

21

called J. F. Carter of the Orchard House at Repton. My father was so taken with this letter that he decided this was the House and the school for me. So not long after my success in the Surrey Junior Championship I found myself, a very small boy, arriving for my first term at Repton School.

My father's evaluation of Carter's letter was abundantly justified. When I left school he wrote expressing a certain gratitude for me "not least because it is through him that we have become acquainted with his parents and developed with them, if I may say so, one of those friendships that help to enrich life."

Carter had served in the Boer War and, when I went to school, had only recently returned from the First World War. He was a fine all-round sportsman. One of his games was golf. During the winter holidays my father and I, Carter and the school doctor, Hodson, and Bryan Valentine, my best friend at school, who was later to play cricket for England, often went away together for a week's golfing holiday.

I was as fortunate in my first study holders, Jack Spilman and later his younger brother, Dick, as I was in my house-master. Jack was also a keen tennis player and we often played with Carter and other masters on a strange black cinder tennis court in a yard behind one of the houses, the only hard court which Repton had at that time. One of the masters I played with was called Hayward. He was a very tall fellow, well over six feet, and was the housemaster of the Mitre. A friend has since told me he met Hayward one day looking very perplexed. He turned to him. "You know," he said, "an extraordinary thing has happened to me. I have just been beaten at tennis by a little shrimp called Austin!"

The little shrimp was considered too small to carry a rifle. And so during my first winter I spent the hours of OTC parades being coached at cricket by Carter on a concrete and matting wicket he had laid down on one of the fields. And I was taught the art of hitting a straight ball with a straight bat instead of sweeping it round to square leg which had been my dangerous but enjoyable habit up till that time.

I had much reason to be grateful for my years at Repton even though during my first term some of the masters had scared the daylights out of me. There had been, for example, one of the form masters, a man with a round bullet head who would fix you with his piercing eyes and boom at you in a thunderous voice, "Have you learned your lesson?"

"Yes, Sir."

"Well, stand up and prove it."

By the time you got to your feet any thoughts you might have had had gone out of your head.

Then there was the master who took me for Latin. He used to rub his hands together between his knees and in a high-pitched voice say to me as he tried to din a little Latin into my thick head, "You coot, you miserable coot. You get nought –write it out."

The maths master used to keep a bottle of disinfectant in his room which he would sprinkle over any boy who had failed to have a cold bath that morning. And he used to keep a large, round lump of India rubber which he would throw at the head of any boy who failed to add successfully in what he called 'mental arithmetic at high pressure'.

The French master shut you in the grandfather clock at the back of the classroom if your knowledge of the French language failed to come up to standard. Unfortunately even this aid to learning somehow failed to induce the French language to take possession of my anxious brain.

I had not enjoyed studying under any of these masters and it was with considerable relief when, having passed the School Certificate at the end of my second year, I moved into the Fifth Form and specialised in modern languages. After one year, however, it became apparent that in the master's opinion there was little hope for me as a specialist in any language, so I transferred to the history section. And for the last two years I studied under my own supervision in the school library.

There were two comfortable armchairs in the library, most conducive, I felt, to the study of history, but sometimes during warm summer days it was hard to keep awake. One day I fell asleep and woke to find the piercing eyes of the headmaster fixed upon me. I felt uncomfortable but fortunately there was nothing the headmaster could do. He went into the Sixth Form room and I went back to sleep.

In school hours he was a fierce man, was the headmaster, but out of school hours he was charm itself and greatly loved by all Reptonians. So was his wife. Dinners with Mr and Mrs Fisher, to which as house prefects you were automatically invited, were the greatest fun. Mr Fisher laughed heartily and, it seemed, genuinely at your poorest jokes and had the gift of making you feel absolutely at ease. So did Mrs Fisher. She was a warm and gracious lady and she, too, was greatly loved by all Reptonians. Mr Fisher was later to become Archbishop of Canterbury.

Repton in recent years has had a hold on the archbishopric of Canterbury. I was at school with the present incumbent (I believe that is the word). I remember A. M. Ramsey lumbering around the Mitre when I went there to see his tennis-playing housemaster.

Another Archbishop with Repton associations was William Temple, headmaster of the school from 1910–14. Later he became a close friend of Phyll and myself. He frequently invited me to dine with him at Lollards' Tower in Lambeth Palace where his great laugh boomed forth, shaking the ancient rafters. One summer when he was Archbishop of York he invited us to stay with him at Bishopthorpe. He had a mind like a filing cabinet and could remember by heart not only whole pages of books he had read but schoolboy conversations from the years when he was headmaster. He liked to play tennis and had an old sweater knitted by his mother. It was full of holes but he delighted to wear it.

I have mentioned B. H. Valentine as being my best friend. We went in first together for the school cricket eleven; I played right half at soccer to his inside right; we were in the school Fives team together and we won the Schoolboys Lawn Tennis Doubles Championship at Queen's Club. As our housemaster's name was Carter we were known as 'Carter's Little Liver Pills'.

Bryan arrived at school a year later than I. He arrived with a great sporting reputation, a cricket bat several sizes too big for him and an engaging and irrepressible friendliness which broke down every barrier. He transformed the House which, among the boys, had strict levels of seniority into a true democracy.

Bryan, brilliant at sport, was not quite so successful in the classroom. The important occasion of a cricket match saw him at his best. But on the important occasion of an exam he was at his worst. In one geography exam he scored nought. "The central plain of Scotland," he is reported to have written, "is called a plain because it is so hilly," and "They grow wheat in Dublin because of the pigs."

One year there was an epidemic of mastoids. Bryan got one and was taken away for an operation. After the operation, to the school's intense delight, it was discovered that the surgeon had written, "I had great difficulty in operating on Valentine's mastoid as I was unable to locate his brain."

Bryan may not have been at his best in school work or at exams, but he was not only a brilliant bridge player but in later life he became an excellent businessman.

He was a joyous cricketer. One wishes today one could see more of his like in the county elevens. He was restless for runs –too restless. It was one of my jobs when I saw a certain gleam in Bryan's eye to have a chat with him and calm him down. Otherwise Bryan would be leaping down the pitch, head in air, with the intention of knocking the ball for six. Too often he would miss it and be stumped.

The first time he played for Kent Second XI he was 49 at tea-time. His friends gathered round him. "Now, Bryan," they advised, "when you get back in, just play the first over quietly and then go for your fifty." Bryan nodded obediently. After tea he walked out to resume his innings. The first ball was bowled. He leapt halfway down the pitch and was out by yards!

Another friend was Dyson, a short, stocky boy of immense physical strength. One Easter holiday I went on the Broads with him and two other friends. When we boarded our yacht there was a high wind blowing. Dyson, who liked to go all out in everything he did, refused to take in a reef. Not until we nearly capsized four times did he at last consent to do so.

It was early April and for the week we were there we met only one other yacht. We lived off a tinned food called 'Frisky Bunnies', and eggs. The four of us ate 126 in the week. I went home fitter than I had ever been!

One evening Dyson and I went out in the dinghy and sailed down Hickling Broad. It is two miles long. We had a following wind and went bumping along merrily over the choppy waters. Then we turned to sail back to our yacht. It is not easy to sail close to the wind in a dinghy. As we slowly went back and forth across the Broad it gradually grew darker. The wind grew stronger, the Broad rougher and as we swung around on each tack we began to ship water.

Dyson enjoyed all this immensely. Danger was the breath of his life. He sought it out on every occasion and as the water came on board and the night grew dark Dyson chortled merrily. Personally I was not so amused. I began to wonder if we would ever get out of the Broad and, even if we did, how we could ever find our yacht again. It was pitch dark except for the stars. Many channels reached out from the Broad. Down which was our yacht anchored? I need not have worried. We did not capsize and when at last we reached the end of the Broad, Dyson with unerring instinct chose the right arm and about two a.m. we found our way back to the yacht.

Our two companions were sitting together in the cabin in moody silence, unwilling to cheer themselves up with the gramophone while the bodies of their two friends were being washed about on Hickling Broad.

Some years later I heard with sorrow but not surprise that Dyson had been drowned in a lake in Africa.

X

The Cricket Match against Malvern was always the high point of the summer term. Malvern were our greatest rivals, and this year, though their fast bowler and great batsman, E. R. T. Holmes, had left, they boasted two outstanding cricketers, Toppin and Welsh.

We won the toss and batted first. Valentine and I opened the innings and Valentine scored eighty. My father, who had travelled specially to Repton to see the match, was disappointed that his son did not even reach double figures. So was I.

This was my last school match. Next term I would be at Cambridge, and who knew when I would play cricket again? It would be a dream come true if in my second innings I could end my cricket career with a satisfying score.

And so it was with some dismay that I watched the last Malvern wicket fall at the end of their innings and realised that Bryan and I would have to go in again before stumps were drawn for an awkward twenty minutes.

Once more we put on our pads and walked out to the wicket. Armed with strict instructions to take no risks both Valentine and I survived. We made a total of four, a boundary by Bryan who had been unable to keep himself from taking one good hefty swipe at the ball.

Next day we resumed our innings. Bryan was early out and wickets after the first half-hour continued to fall. Word came from the pavilion for me to hold up my end at all costs.

Runs slowed but the fall of wickets was halted. We began to build back from our disastrous start. Gradually the position improved and instructions reached me to increase my pace. The score began to mount rapidly, but already the afternoon was beginning to wane. At last instructions came from the pavilion–hit out.

Now the score came at a merry pace and it was apparent that Malvern would have a hard time to pass our total now posted on the board.

I faced the bowler bowling from the pavilion end. The ball was well pitched up and to the off. Placing my foot well across I drove it with all my strength past cover to the boundary.

As the ball reached the boundary's edge a mighty cheer went up from the school sitting in a ring of deck chairs that almost surrounded the ground. I had passed my century.

The bell in the pavilion clanged, denoting our declaring, and I walked back to the pavilion, the score in my last school innings–and against Malvern–102, not out.

It was with a light heart that I watched our bowlers skittle out the Malvern side and saw our two most dreaded antagonists –Toppin and Welsh–bite the dust without scoring in either innings!

XI

In the autumn of 1925 I went up to Cambridge and in the spring of 1926 I reached the final of the Covered Court

Championships, the final of the Hard Court Championships, won all my matches in the Davis Cup trials and was selected for the great honour of representing my country in the Davis Cup competition. Unfortunately on the advice of my father and my Housemaster, Mr Carter, who had come down from Repton to see the trials, I turned it down. It was my first year at Cambridge, they argued, I was only nineteen, I had many years ahead of me in which to play.

It turned out to be a costly decision. The General Strike broke out in the summer of that year. The university was closed. I took no exercise, got thoroughly out of condition and when I was selected to play for Great Britain in an international match v. America in June I was in no fit state to play. This unfortunately I did not realise. Such things as training were unknown to me in those days. I had always got fit and remained fit in the normal course of my athletic life. The fact that several weeks' lay-off from any form of physical exercise might affect me never entered my head. I accepted the invitation, played and damaged my heart.

The heart specialist ordered me to play no games at all for four months and then only doubles for a year. All other forms of sport except some gentle golf were also forbidden.

Life at Cambridge, however, remained full. As secretary of the Cambridge University Lawn Tennis Club I was busy arranging and running tournaments and entertaining visiting teams. I studied as hard as my sporting engagements would allow and felt in better physical trim when the summer of 1927 came round.

In that year the Cambridge team was invited to visit a small industrial town in Germany called Pforzheim, a charming little place which not many years later was to take a terrible pounding at the hands of the Allied bombers. But in 1927 it was a peaceful spot. The courts where we played lay under tall pine trees beside a swiftly running river. But their surface was loose and dusty and we found it difficult to play. I survived as far as the semi-final.

Our team consisted of Jackie Baines, the treasurer of the Club; Bill Powell, the captain; Russell Young, a New Zealander; and Kenneth Horne, later to become famous on the BBC.

The night before my semi-final match a club dinner was given in our honour. But as I had to play the next day, I went to bed early. I described what happened in a book I wrote subsequently, called *Bits and Pieces.*

"I went to bed early in order to uphold to the best of my ability the honour of Cambridge while the rest of the team, free from care, were able to revel into the early hours. As the night wore on, far from forgetting me, they became anxious for my welfare and by their solicitude managed to keep me awake for the greater part of the night.

"At 11 o'clock I retired to bed. At 11.45 Jackie Baines also retired to bed, and the noise that he made would have awakened even a dormouse from its slumbers. At 12.15 Bill Powell, the captain, paid me a visit to see that all was well, and for half an hour or so we discussed, rather one-sidedly, several subjects of world-wide importance! At 1 o'clock Ken Horne came in to see if I were sleeping comfortably, and finding me awake (he had banged the door), he entertained me for a quarter of an hour with a few funny stories from his extensive stock. Russell Young appeared at 1.45 and told me that the evening was progressing well downstairs, and when he had gone, Bill Powell, hearing I was not asleep, came back to see if anything was wrong. Having solved a few of the difficulties of modern times, I was left to slumber until four o'clock, when the noise of over-turning chairs informed me that Russell Young was undressing in the dark, in order not to wake me. Shortly afterwards Horne and Powell burst in again, switched on the light, apologised for making a noise, said they would stay only a minute, and stayed half an hour. With their departure Pforzheim itself woke up and for the rest of the early morning carts rattled over the cobbled pavement beneath the window."

It was not surprising I was beaten next day!

So successful, however, was our visit in other ways that we were invited to several other German towns, including Frank-furt, Wiesbaden and Baden Baden. At Baden Baden, that paradise in the Black Forest, Kenneth Horne, Russell Young and I decided that in some way we must commemorate a memorable visit. We decided to found a Club. The question was what to call it.

We had noticed on the menus of the hotels where we had stayed that the names of the various dishes were extremely long words. But at the bottom of every menu was a small self-effacing word called 'Obst'. We had developed an affection for this word. Its modesty in the face of the bombastic words above it appealed to us. So we decided to call the club the 'OBST' Club. We further decided to limit the membership to the three of us and to call ourselves Ein, Zwei and Drei. I was Ein, Young was Zwei and Horne Drei.

We then decided on a tie. This was to be a silver bowl containing fruit embroidered on a green background. Under the bowl was the word 'OBST' and above the bowl the numbers 1, 2 and 3, a different number on each tie.

At our first meeting we decided to elect officials. As number one or Ein I proposed myself for the Presidency. But Zwei and Drei were unimpressed by my prior claim and voted against me. Then Zwei proposed himself for the Presidency. Drei and I voted against him. Then in turn Drei proposed himself. He was voted down by the same margin, 2–1.

I regret to say that though the Club is still in existence and met as recently as 1961 the election of officers has not yet been achieved!

Returning to Cambridge for my last year, the time passed swiftly and pleasantly. I was now captain of the club. I won the Varsity Tournament for the third time and retained an unbeaten record in the Inter-Varsity match against Oxford. For this I was given a cup by a great friend of mine at Cambridge, Mrs Crundall Punnett.

Mrs Punnett as a girl had been called Miss 'Batty' Bellew and before her marriage to Professor Crundall Punnett had been married to Mr Numcumquick. She had herself been a well-known player and was called the Mother of Cambridge tennis. She kept open house on Sundays where the guests included many of the Cambridge cricket team, David Burghley, the great hurdler (now the Marquess of Exeter) and several young ladies from Newnham College, one of whom was the striking daughter of the Russian Ambassador, Katja Krassin.

Professor Punnett, besides being an excellent tennis player and at that time considered the greatest expert on heredity in the world, was also a connoisseur of wines. Tennis after lunch was always of the merriest but seldom of the most accurate!

At the end of term came the final exams. They happened to follow the university match which was played that year at Oxford. The day after the university match we were entertained by Lord Birkenhead at his country place and I did not get back to Cambridge until one a.m. on the morning of the exams, when I had to climb into College. In spite of this handicap I was grateful to learn when the results came through that I had achieved an Honours Degree in History and was entitled to put B.A. after the B.A. of my name.

Some people ask me how I obtained my name of Bunny. The university magazine *The Granta* wrote that it was due to 'his quaint habit of consuming green food'. This was pure fiction though it may do as well as any other story. The truth is I cannot remember how the name came about. I only know that at Repton there came a time when my friends, tired of calling me Austin, felt some nick ame was in order. I think they hit on Bunny because my second name is Wilfred and at that time there was a comic strip in which there were three characters, Pip, Squeak and Wilfred. Wilfred was a rabbit.

At any rate, whatever the explanation, the name stuck and I have been Bunny ever since, my real names consigned to limbo where I am happy to leave them!

Soon after the Cambridge term ended I played at Wimbledon and met René Lacoste, the ultimate winner, in the last sixteen. He won the first two sets and then perhaps unconsciously easing up allowed me to win the third. In the fourth set I went mad. There was nothing I could not do. I felt as if I had the ball on the end of a string. I had Lacoste running round the court like a rabbit and won the set easily 6-1. After that I had shot my bolt and lost the last set and the match 6-2. But what stands out in my mind is not only perhaps the best set of tennis I ever played but the sportsmanship of Lacoste. Each time I passed him as we crossed over he smiled his encouragement. "Well played, Bunny," he said. It was a pleasant contrast to others whom I played who might have used gamesmanship at that point to try and throw me off my stride.

Following Wimbledon I was invited to go with a British

tennis team around the world, and another of my dreams – to travel and see the world – had come true.

My first tour abroad took me to many lands – America, Canada, New Zealand, Australia and South Africa. It was strenuous, it was exciting. I loved every minute of it. I was delighted when in the following year, 1929, I was chosen to play once more in America and was made the captain and manager of a team which consisted of John Olliff and myself.

XII

The safety valve of an engine whistled shrilly, throwing its jet of steam high towards the girdered glass roof of Waterloo Station.

Carrying a press of six racquets which I would not entrust to the porter, I pushed through the barrier and walked down the length of the Southampton boat train towards our reserved compartment near the front.

As I was about to climb in my 'team' rushed up to me in a great state of excitement, "There's an actress down the platform being photographed!"

I climbed into our compartment and hoisted my press of racquets onto the rack. "That," I replied haughtily, "does not interest me."

I climbed out of the compartment and stood chatting with the friends and officials who had come to Waterloo to see us off. I was handed a hundred pounds in crinkly five-pound notes – a princely sum to me in those days and the greatest amount I had ever carried on my person up till that time. I was given a money belt to wear around my waist. I was told that there was to my credit some five hundred more pounds in an American bank.

At last the train whistled. The guard waved his green flag. We shook hands with our friends in a flurry of final goodbyes, waving to them from the window as the boat train slowly gathered speed and rolled on its way to Southampton.

I sat back in my compartment feeling as rich as Croesus with the one hundred pounds strapped in the belt around my tummy. I contemplated the future. An actress. "H'm, very interesting," I thought to myself.

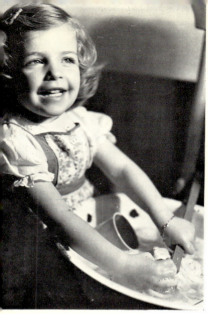

1(a). Jennifer, aged 3

1(b). John, aged 3

Family playing Canasta when
ng in Melbourne, Australia

2. Bunny

I had always had an interest in the theatre; perhaps it was inherited from my mother. She and a beloved sister of hers, my Aunt Det, had been members of a local amateur dramatic society which boasted two members later to achieve a far-reaching fame on the professional stage, Lilian Braithwaite and Mrs Patrick Campbell. One of my earliest memories is of my mother acting.

Trips to London to see a play were highlights of my young life, and at school a friend of mine and I occasionally escaped from the library and the study of history to read plays and over and over again that great and moving classic, *Cyrano de Bergerac*.

Yes, I had always been interested in the theatre, particularly in the acting side, and – it had to be admitted – in actresses. Who was this actress, I wondered, who had been photographed on the station platform?

As the train sped on its way to Southampton I wondered if we would meet.

CHAPTER TWO

Phyll

MY family came from an entirely different background from Bunny's. His parents were Celts, mine were Jewish.

I never knew my Grandfather Konstam. He lived in Germany. Father used to say that he was a remarkable and good man. Originally he intended to be a rabbi, but he could not accept all the teachings of the rabbinical college and so he left and became a schoolteacher. It had been a struggle to bring up a family on a very small pay. Father told me the greatest treat he could remember as a child was having an orange once a month which was divided between the five children.

One of my uncles, Father's eldest brother, was brilliant. He could speak Latin and Greek fluently at an early age. The school sent him home, saying they could not teach him anything more. He became an eminent doctor. People came to his sanatorium in Konigstein from all over the world. He was pioneering psychosomatic medicine fifty years before it was practised elsewhere.

Father and his second brother Rudolf came to London when Father was seventeen and eventually inherited a leather business from their cousin Hugo Konstam. Hugo's daughter whose stage name was Gertrude Kingston was a well-known actress in the first part of this century. Her home in Victoria Square was a salon for the literary and theatre world of her day. She was a close friend of Bernard Shaw who wrote *Great Catherine* for her.

Father loved England with a great passion, and he became a naturalised Englishman.

During the war my Uncle Rudolf's two eldest boys were killed fighting for Britain, and Uncle Oscar, the doctor who remained in Germany, lost his eldest son fighting for Germany.

Father, with his brother, built up a small leather business into a highly successful one. Although a clever businessman, he was at heart an artist. He loved to browse around bookshops and the studios of then unknown artists. One whom he admired greatly and whose work he bought when he was a struggling young artist was Jacob Epstein. Others were Augustus John and the young Hungarian sculptor, Gaudier-Brzeska, who was killed in the First World War.

Another was a Pole called Alfred Wolmark, and our home was full of his pictures. Wolmark never could be bothered with social graces, and he was allergic to art critics. One had only to come in sight and Wally, as we called him, would explode. He also had an odd way of treating prospective customers. "Nar, nar, nar," he would exclaim, "they don't understand my pictures. Why should I let them have them?" Or he would hang on to a picture because he liked it too much himself. Father used to say that when Wally was dead and no longer able to talk, his pictures would speak for themselves and would find their rightful place among the great artists of his day.

Father had great charm. And he loved people–old, young, rich, poor, just about anyone, except Mother's relations! He would go for long walks on Hampstead Heath, where we lived, and bring home the dirtiest little ragamuffins, much to Mother's concern for her pale fawn carpets. He would show them a book or the Christmas tree, and they would leave with sixpence or a shilling and something to eat and they felt they had found a friend, which indeed they had. Nobody who came to Father for help would go away empty-handed. He came up the hard way himself and so understood the hardships and struggles of others.

I can see him now, sitting in his armchair in the library, surrounded by books, laughing at a favourite passage. He had a great sense of humour and we children thought his jokes were terribly funny. Mother did not. The more annoyed she got with his jokes the funnier we thought they were.

Poor dear Mama, she did not have quite the same sense of humour. She had been spoiled as a child by a doting father. Grandfather Sternberg was born in Belgium and was a fine musician. He won a gold medal when he was nine years old at the Conservatoire in Brussels. He was a pupil of Wieniawski and wrote out a concerto for de Bériot when he was going blind.

The music world prophesied a great future for Grandfather, but he married young and soon a family was on its way. Having to support not only his wife and children but his mother and father as well, he decided that he could not do it as a concert violinist, so he came to England and went on the Stock Exchange just at the time of the Gold Boom. He made a fortune in no time. Mother said he was a brilliant businessman as well as a great musician. Father said he was just darned lucky. But whichever it was, it meant he lived in affluence for the rest of his life.

He was very imperious. Mother said there was a Count in the family who lived at one of the European courts and possibly there may have been a slip! It would certainly account for his courtly behaviour, and Mother, who looked rather like Queen Mary, behaved like royalty all her life.

Whenever Grandfather went abroad the stationmaster appeared to see him off and the policeman on point duty allowed his car to pass without being held up. He would take the whole floor of a hotel on his visit to Monte Carlo. And Mother was the apple of his eye. He lavished on her all his wealth and affection. He treated her like a rare hothouse plant. She never quite got over it.

She was always beautifully dressed, and with her lovely auburn hair was a very attractive young woman. As a child she had wanted to be a nurse, but her father felt she was too delicate. She was actually as strong as a horse, a point which never quite registered with her. It was a tragedy that she was prevented from following her inclination. She would have made an excellent matron of a hospital. She was a capable woman and when as children we were ill she was at her best.

Her mother was a tiny little lady, completely overpowered by her imperious husband and queenly daughter. She loved the theatre. She would think up any excuse to take me to pretty well every play in town. She used to tell me she hoped she would die in the stalls. It was from her that I got my passion for the theatre.

II

Our first home was Fifty Belsize Square, Hampstead, where I was born. It was one of those gloomy London squares with square and solid houses and steps leading up to the front doors. Although the paint was often freshened in the spring, when winter came again all its pristine glory vanished and the dirt and grime of the London fogs once again made them look dismal and dejected.

Number Fifty looked out onto an ugly church. Strangely enough I can never remember ever seeing anyone going in or anyone coming out!

Sundays have left a strong impression on my memory. I can remember the bells tolling in a very depressing sort of way. It always made me feel sad. A sense of doom and gloom descended on me. The roads were completely empty.

More often than not there seemed to be a 'drizzle', a thin fine rain. It was wet but not too wet for us to go for the dreary walks with whichever Mademoiselle or Fräulein happened to be with us at the time. It meant climbing into mackintoshes and trying to get on galoshes which always seemed far too small. After a colossal struggle we would eventually stagger out in overcoats, clutching umbrellas to which we hung on desperately in case, we were told, they turned inside out when gusty winds caught us coming round the corners. I pictured myself floating away over the rooftops, looking like today's Mary Poppins. Apart from this alarming hazard, walks round the square were heavy with boredom, grey clouds scudding overhead and the drizzle drizzling as hard as it could!

One Mademoiselle we had in those days fitted perfectly into the dismal picture. She was dressed from head to toe in black. She had a very white face, a large black hat, a long black coat, black stockings and very large black shoes. We used to struggle along in our mackintoshes and galoshes, trying to keep up with Mademoiselle while she talked to us in French about her 'rein flottant' which I discovered was a floating kidney. It perfectly matched the drizzle and the puddles of those wet Sundays. I could see in my child's mind a large pool of water and a kidney floating backwards and forwards in it.

To alleviate the boredom I used to amuse myself by trying not to walk on the lines of the pavement, but as it meant some times taking huge strides and suddenly leaping in the air, it was not considered decorum and I was made to take

Mademoiselle's hand and walk like a ramrod around the square.

Towards lunchtime my feet ached in my galoshes and I lagged behind. I just could not keep up, because she walked much too fast for my short legs. It seemed like an expedition to Mount Everest as at last we climbed those steep stone steps to the house and sank exhausted into a big chair in the hall.

There were some bright spots, however. Often at Sunday lunch Father would tell me stories. I was transported out of the dark dining room, away from the dreary square, into enchanted lands. With my mouth wide open, lost in rapture, the governess would shovel in the spinach or lumpy milk pudding without my ever knowing it had happened.

Memories of Mother are always vivid. I can see her now coming to say goodnight to us in the night nursery, her beautiful peacock blue taffeta dress, her auburn hair piled on top of her head, her lovely jewellery and the smell of perfume. She would rustle in and rustle out, while Father in a dinner jacket or tails would sit on our bed and tell us the end of one of his wonderful stories.

I would feel very secure with the light on and with Mother and Father around, but once the light was turned off, in the dark all kinds of strange fears and fancies would grip my mind. They said I was an imaginative child. I was not quite sure what that meant, but it always made me feel different from everyone else.

The night nursery and day nursery were perishingly cold in the winter. Admiral Byrd, after returning from spending six months at the South Pole, was asked what was the coldest place on earth. He replied, "A British bedroom." I am sure he was right. My sister Marjorie and I would stand shivering like frozen rabbits in our long combinations, our hands quite blue, trying to get dressed in front of a miserable little fire which was the only means of heating the room. Usually it smoked. Occasionally a tiny flame would put in a very brief appearance.

It was just after my fifth birthday that we had our first motor car. It was a snub-nosed Austin, driven by our faithful and beloved chauffeur, Smith. Smith became an institution in the family, like the Bank of England. He remained with us for fifty years.

III

Just after I was six we moved away from Belsize Square to Middleheath, West Heath Road. It was to be my home until I got married in 1931. It was a large house. At the back was a garden and in the front we looked out on a lovely part of Hampstead Heath. On a clear day we could see as far as Mill Hill, and in the spring when all the may trees were in bloom it was a marvellous sight.

The garden was Mother's pride and joy. We had a rose garden, rock garden and a tennis court. And behind the lawn there was a rose arbour and a large herbaceous border; tulips and daffodils in the spring, and in the summer tall lupins, bright blue delphiniums, London Pride, Sweet William and the heavenly wallflower.

It was at Middleheath that my sister Anna was born. I remember I was eating a poached egg on toast when my father came and told me I had a baby sister! Father took me upstairs to see her. In a pink cot lay the most beautiful little baby I had ever seen. She was quite different from my older sister and myself. Both of us had jet black hair. Anna had golden hair and large blue eyes.

Mother and Father told us they had been expecting a boy called Christopher. As Mother usually got what she wanted I could not make out how there had been a slip-up and she had got a girl instead! But they were not disappointed for long. Anna was an enchanting child, not only lovely to look at but with a very amusing and original mind.

My sister Marjorie was three years older than me. We did everything together as small children. She had a warm and generous heart. I missed her terribly when, soon after arriving at our new home, she left to go to boarding school.

IV

Some years later I was sent to boarding school myself at Bexhill-on-Sea in Sussex. The First World War was being

39

fought, and on certain days you could hear the gunfire across the Channel from France. The newspapers were full of pictures of the Kaiser, Foch, Haig, of Amiens, Arras, Ypres and stories of the terrible fighting in the trenches. News of the death of our cousins came in at regular intervals, all young men and all, we were told, fighting a war to end war.

In the holidays back at Middleheath we had parties for wounded soldiers. They wore blue hospital uniforms. Some were legless, some armless, some with faces terribly burned, some from St Dunstan's, totally blind and scarred, some who were taken ill during the party and had to be taken away in ambulances. I could hardly speak because I was afraid I would burst into tears in front of them.

I left Bexhill to go to Godstowe School in High Wycombe. It was the preparatory school for Wycombe Abbey. The school was on top of Amersham Hill, and to say it was cold in winter would be the British understatement of the year! I did not stay very long, because although it was a very nice school I did not feel that I was a public school type. I was no good at games, and gym was a nightmare. No matter how I tried I could not climb a rope, and hanging upside down on the rib-stalls was torture. I simply had to face it: I was no gymnast! I used to dread my turn to jump over the horse. When it eventually came I would shut my eyes, grit my teeth, leap onto the springboard and land plumb in the middle of the miserable thing, eventually to be dragged off by the gym mistress who would say in a very hearty, optimistic voice, "Well tried. We'll do better next time."

One morning we were all summoned into the gym to hear an important announcement. The headmistress said that the Armistice had been signed.

At first people could not believe it. Four years of war was a long time. It was normal to see men in uniform, to read of battles in the newspapers. 'Mademoiselle from Armentières' became a kind of personal friend. Then suddenly it dawned on everyone. The war was at an end! People went wild. Sedate teachers jumped into the air and cheered. Lessons were called off and we all ran through the playground leaping and shouting. But some who had lost fathers and brothers were crying.

Many of us were too young to understand what those four years had meant to our country. I did not. The very finest and best young men of a generation lay dead under the fields of Flanders. Under those rows and rows of white crosses in France lay the future leadership of Britain. Even today, fifty years later, as I write, we are still paying for it. But then we did not understand.

There were great celebrations, a big bonfire, an extra ration of sweets and no prep!

v

I was taken away from boarding school to pursue an 'artistic career'. Mother had a secret longing for another violinist in the family like my grandfather. She hoped I might be the one. So back I came to London.

I was given a small Amati violin which had belonged to Grandfather and I went to Frognal School in Hampstead. The two headmistresses wore men's felt hats!

Something happened which made those years at Frognal very memorable. There was a small drill hall close by the corner of Heath Street and High Street in Hampstead. One evening my father said that a young man called Norman Macdermott was coming to dinner to talk about his plan to convert the drill hall into a small theatre. He wanted a theatre which would appeal to all kinds of people, and he thought a good name for it would be 'The Everyman'. He wanted Father's help to get it going, which Father gladly gave. Soon the Everyman was started.

I used to pass it on the way to school and back, and it was the high point of my day. I could look at the photographs outside and sometimes even see some of the actors leaving their rehearsals. Better still, at weekends, Father took us to see the new productions.

And what productions they were and what casts they had! There was one play called *The Vortex*. The young actor who wrote it and played the leading part was at that time unknown. His name was Noel Coward. Many actors and actresses who eventually became great stars in the theatre firmament started at the Everyman.

An absorbing and fascinating new world began to open up for me: wonderful concerts at the Albert and Queen's Halls – Chaliapin, Thibaut, Cortot and Casals; evenings of enchantment at the Russian ballet; having lunch with the great Diaghilev himself at Wolmark's, and a never-to-be-forgotten matinée when I saw the legendary Eleonora Duse.

I learned to love the theatre in those early days. It was in my blood and bones and I longed to be part of it.

VI

Of all the memories of those times the most vivid is of being taken by my parents to see the reappearance in Britain of the great dancer Anna Pavlova. Wearing my best pink party frock, with my parents in full evening dress, we were driven by our friend Smith to Drury Lane.

All London was there to welcome Pavlova after a long absence. The magic of that night stays with me: the brilliant audience in evening dress, the orchestra tuning up and then suddenly, the conductor taking his place on the podium, bowing and tapping his music stand with his baton, and then the chattering ceasing, complete silence, not a sound, and the curtain going up.

The ballet was *Snowflakes* with music by Tchaikowsky. The décor was simple. The corps de ballet came whirling and twirling on, all in white. And then suddenly, in the brilliant spotlight, standing in a superb arabesque was Pavlova.

She was in a stiff white ballet dress, her dark hair drawn straight back and a sparkling coronet on her head. She took my breath away. I gasped. Never have I seen anyone dance the way she did. She was not only a great dancer; she was a superb actress.

The evening ended with the *Dying Swan*.

The great audience was spellbound. There was not a sound. Then suddenly all together they rose and cheered. They shouted 'bravo'. Flowers were thrown from the boxes and stalls and the gallery. I think everyone knew that night that they had been present at a performance which would be forever recalled in the history of the dance.

I hardly remember getting home. Such things as Ovaltine and biscuits were a horrible comedown after having been on the heights of Olympus! All the next day at school I was in a dream. I longed to be able to dance like that. Even the dark, dank cloakroom where we left wet umbrellas and misshapen felt hats could not dampen the experience of the night before.

Luckily I found a kindred spirit in Adrienne Spanier, a school friend who was the same age as I was and who had also been present at that amazing performance. Didine, as she was called, lived in Golder's Green. She told me that Pavlova lived somewhere quite close. She said she lived in a large house set in a beautiful garden near The Bull and Bush, so after school we decided we would set off and see if we could catch a glimpse of Pavlova on her way to the theatre.

We walked through Golder's Green Park, and just by the gate was Ivy House. There for several days we took up our stand. We would wait for hours but nothing would happen. Then suddenly the gates would be flung open and a large car sweep out. Huddled in the corner would be a tiny lady, Madame Pavlova. She would bow and go by so swiftly that we could hardly catch a glimpse of her. Often we would wait another two or three hours to see her come back again.

She must have been amazed to see two very small girls often standing in the rain for hours on end, and when one day we took two postcards to be autographed she took pity on us and invited us in. We nearly dropped dead from excitement. We walked through the ballroom with a long bar on one side, where Madame practised each day, into a living room where we waited with bated breath.

Then the door opened and Madame herself came in. She was much smaller than she appeared on the stage. She had on a full-skirted dress and a long black scarf round her shoulders. She sat very gracefully in a huge armchair and seemed practically to disappear into it.

Didine and I sat speechless, just staring at her. She was obviously very amused. I cannot remember what we talked about but she was very good to us. It was the first of several visits, and each one was a red-letter day.

VII

After having seen Pavlova I began to long to learn dancing, and I begged my mother and father to allow me to have lessons. At home I would put on the gramophone. It was an 'His Master's Voice' with a long green horn, and I began to improvise and make up my own dances.

At a tea party not long after first seeing Pavlova my hostess asked me to dance for a friend of hers who had just started to teach dancing. So with great feeling I did a rather ghastly little scarf dance to Mendelssohn's 'Spring Song'. The lady came forward and told me she felt I had great feeling and she would like to teach me. Her name was Marie Rambert. Now her ballet school is known all over the world and the Ballet Rambert is an institution in Britain. Madame Rambert had been with Diaghilev. I loved to sit and listen to endless stories about the days in the great Russian Ballet. I must have been one of her very first pupils.

Every day she came to my grandmother's and I would have an hour's work-out. I would learn jetés, port de bras, relevés, and all the method taught by the great old maestro Cecchetti, who had taught many of the great ballerinas including Pavlova.

Madame's enthusiasm was boundless. She would hum, bounce and dance and show me how it should be done. Even on the day that her daughter Angela was born I remember her doing a superb arabesque and entrechat quatre! It was quite an achievement.

Later I joined her classes. And one day the great Maestro himself came to see us. Cecchetti to most dancers was a legend, and to see the famous old gentleman in person was the greatest thrill.

Gradually Marie Rambert's pupils increased, and the classes were great fun. Two friends at that time were a charming American girl called Frances James, and a very amusing boy called Frederick Ashton. In the class was Diana Gould, who is now Mrs Yehudi Menuhin.

But gradually my dreams of floating around the stage as a great ballerina began to fade. I suddenly put on weight and blew up like a pneumatic tyre. Also I had rather flat feet.

Elevation was not my strong point; I could not for the life of me get off the ground.

Mother, without my knowing it, had gone to see Pavlova and asked if I might dance for her. And so one morning, very excited, I set off. In a small tunic and with some coloured leaves in my hair I arrived at Ivy House.

In Pavlova's beautiful ballroom I lumped around rather heavily but putting great feeling in all I did. She watched me with some amusement, and with great understanding she said to my mother, "This child has a very expressive face and real dramatic talent. I think she should go on the stage."

I had always known from the age of five when I was taken to my first pantomime that the theatre was meant to be my life. That day everything fell into place; I knew with great certainty that dancing was not for me but that I was meant to be an actress.

VIII

At sixteen years old I persuaded my parents to let me leave school to go to Paris and learn French and also to study for the theatre.

I was very fortunate to become a pupil of Georges Le Roi of the Comédie Française. He was not only a fine teacher but a man of integrity and character. I was also a pupil of Georges Wague of the Opera who was a well-known mime. As well as taking lessons I went regularly to see the classics presented at the Comédie Française and much theatre in Paris which was new and exciting. There were the Pitoëffs; Charles Dullin and his company at the Théâtre de l'Atelier, Louis Jouvet at the Comédie des Champs Elysées, and that great man Jacques Copeau and his famous company at the Vieux-Colombier. Copeau, the uncle of Michel St Denis, had a great vision for the theatre. He felt it should be a means of the 'renouvellement de l'homme'—the renewal of man.

I had a number of relations living in Paris. My great aunt had married the Régisseur Général of the Opera. I became friends with her daughter Sophie who had married a painter. Wearing a Greek tunic I had the audacity to give dance improvisations for her friends who effusively assured me I was a genius!

My other cousins were the André Davids. The family consisted of André, Renée and Arlette. All three were artists. André and Renée adored their only child, Arlette. The studio and apartment they lived in were very dark, but Arlette lit up the whole place. With flaming red hair, enormous vitality, a tremendous sense of humour and no inhibitions, she would arrive home and the dingy apartment would be transformed.

Arlette loved life. She enjoyed every minute of it. During the war she married and had two babies. She and her husband worked for the Resistance. He was arrested and eventually died of exhaustion in a concentration camp. Later Arlette was arrested with her two small children and taken to Germany. She was last seen getting off the train at Auschwitz. She and her children were never heard of again.

Her mother and father never believed that she would not return. They refused to leave their flat. They just sat there, waiting for her to come back. She never came. They both died, heartbroken, soon after the war was over.

IX

I returned from Paris and continued to study for the theatre. I had voice production lessons from Elsie Fogerty, at the Albert Hall. She saw through all the phoney nonsense that young actresses like myself felt we had to put on in order to make an impression. She was direct and honest, and I did not always like it. When she met my husband some years later she said to me, "You are quick and bright. He is quieter and slower in his reactions. But he has much greater depth."

She also helped me on another point. She said that being Jewish and having known centuries of persecution, we had built up over the years a tendency towards a persecution mania. She said I must always beware of looking for a snub or an insult or being on the defensive with people. I learned a lot more from her than voice production, although she was, I believe, the greatest voice teacher of her time.

While still studying I started looking for a job. I was seven-

teen and full of enthusiasm and totally absorbed in the theatre.
I ate, drank, slept and talked of nothing else. Sometimes one
was up and sometimes down, but it was all fascinating and I
loved the adventure of it.

There were discouraging visits to agents in Shaftesbury
Avenue–climbing the stairs, seeing the long queues waiting in
the dark passages when a play was being cast for the West End
or the provinces, at last getting into the holy of holies, the
agent's office, and being greeted by his forced smile: "Leave
your address. I'll keep in touch." Then long waits for the
telephone to ring and nothing happening.

But suddenly out of the blue I would be sent for by a management, and I would have the thrill of landing a job. The journey
on the tube from Hampstead to Leicester Square would go by
in a flash. I seemed to be walking on air.

There was the excitement of acting with Gertrude Elliott, the
wife of Sir Johnston Forbes-Robertson and sister of the great
Edwardian beauty Maxine Elliott, and with one of the big
matinée idols of the Twenties, Owen Nares.

One day the manager, Leon M. Lion, engaged me for a
play. He said: "I have tried putting on plays I thought the public
would want and would be box office. But they have all been
flops. This time I am going to put on a play I really like. It
will open in the hot weather, the worst time of the year, so
probably it won't run long. But I don't care. I am going to do it
anyway."

We opened in August. The play was *Escape* by John Galsworthy. It was a big success and ran for months. Nicholas
Hannen gave a fine performance as the prisoner. Also in the
cast was Ursula Jeans. It was the beginning of a life-long friendship with her and later her delightful husband, Roger Livesey.

Galsworthy himself attended the rehearsals and helped with
the direction. It was from him that I learned for the first time
that the theatre could do much more than entertain. His play
Justice led to the reform of the penal law. *Strife, Loyalties, The
Skin Game, Escape*, all had a purpose beyond mere entertainment.

I played in the revival of *Escape* and also in the film when Sir
Gerald du Maurier played the leading part. We went down to

Devon and filmed it on the bleak moors around the huge penitentiary on Dartmoor.

I also had the good fortune to be in several productions of the Repertory Players, a Sunday night play-producing society much in vogue at that time. After one play I was sent for by Nigel Playfair, who was having a great success at the Lyric Theatre, Hammersmith. His leading lady was Edith Evans, who had just been acclaimed by the critics for her brilliant performance in *The Way of the World*. I was given the part of her sister Dorinda in *The Beaux' Stratagem*. Being very young I was fearful of playing with such a great artist but she was wonderfully kind and helpful, and from her I learned a great deal.

x

In the 1920's film-making had started in a major way in Britain. Large new studios were built at Elstree and it all sounded very exciting and glamorous. I thought I would see if I could get a part there.

I had had some experience in the theatre by that time, but I realised I still knew nothing at all about filming and so thought I had better start in the crowd. I saw the casting director of British International Pictures and he told me that a large crowd was needed the next day for a film called *Champagne* starring Betty Balfour. He said if I had an evening dress then I should be at the studios by eight o'clock the next morning ready to be made up.

The next morning I found myself with about one hundred other extras in full evening dress waiting for the cameras to turn. Monty Banks, the comedian, who later married Gracie Fields, was rehearsing a scene with Betty Balfour. The crowd was the background for a gay party. I was in the back row hoping someone would spot my latent talent, when I noticed that a man by the camera was beckoning to me. I wafted towards him in the most glamorous way I could. He put me in the front row.

After the take the director himself, a very plump young man, came over to me and said, "I think I saw you in a play recently. Aren't you Phyllis Konstam?"

3(a). The team that won the Davis Cup. *Left to right:* G. P. Hughes, Fred Perry,
H. Roper Barrett (non-playing Captain), H. W. Austin and H. G. N. Lee

3(b). Victorious British Davis Cup team after retaining the Davis Cup 5–0
v. America 1935. On the right C. R. D. Tuckey

4. Original *Punch* drawing by George du Maurier given to Bunny by
Gerald du Maurier

"Yes," I replied.

"Glad to meet you," he said. "My name is Alfred Hitchcock."

Hitchy, as we always called him, gave me a small part in his next film. It was called *Blackmail*. The pictures made at that time were silent, but a new medium was beginning to revolutionise the industry. Al Jolson had just made a sensation in America in a 'talking' picture called *The Singing Fool*. 'Sonny Boy', the first song to be heard from the screen, was a smash hit all over the world.

The filming of *Blackmail* had already started when it was decided to make it into a 'talkie'. For the first time microphones appeared and a whole new technique was needed. Actors with gorgeous profiles, earning hundreds of thousands of pounds, were discovered to have squeaky voices which did not match their he-men images. They suddenly found themselves fallen idols. Hitchy's genius enabled him to use this new medium in an original way and he has become, as we all know, the great master of suspense.

XI

I was acting in a play at Wyndham's Theatre when I received a message that G. B. Stern, the authoress, wanted to see me.

She came round to my dressing room and said that her successful book *The Matriarch* had been dramatised and she would like me to see Mr and Mrs Frank Vernon, who were putting it on at the Royalty Theatre. She said I was her choice to play Val who, in real life, was herself. So I phoned for an interview, saw the Vernons and got the part.

I was tremendously interested to go to the first rehearsal, because the Vernons told me that Mrs Patrick Campbell was returning to the stage after a long absence to play the part of the Matriarch. Everybody of my generation knew about Mrs Patrick Campbell. All London had raved about her in the title role of Pinero's *The Second Mrs Tanqueray*. Later she was the original Eliza Dolittle in Bernard Shaw's *Pygmalion*, the Eliza all the world was later to love in *My Fair Lady*.

She also had the reputation of being an impossible woman in

the theatre. Her caustic but witty remarks about her fellow actors and everyone she met were as well-known as were her performances on the stage. For example, when she was playing opposite Sir George Alexander, there was tension between them and they were not on speaking terms. One night Sir George wrote a note to Mrs Campbell saying, "Would Mrs Patrick Campbell kindly not laugh at Sir George Alexander on the stage." To which she replied, "Mrs Patrick Campbell will certainly not laugh at Sir George Alexander on the stage. She will wait till she gets home."

She certainly lived up to her reputation of being difficult and different from anyone I had met. She was no longer a great beauty when I knew her, but she was still handsome with huge dark eyes and a tremendous personality. She had great power on the stage. *The Matriarch* was an immediate success.

I got to know her very well indeed. She would invite me into her dressing room and tell me about her past experiences in the theatre. "Phyll, dear," she would boom out in her very deep voice, "come in and see me and have one of these sweets I have just bought. They taste like the Walls of Nineveh." She told me about playing in *Pélleas et Mélisande* in French with Sarah Bernhardt. At one matinée Sarah put a live goldfish in her hand. Mrs Campbell said it made no difference to Sarah's performance; tears ran down her face as she played a very dramatic scene. But Mrs Campbell went through agonies trying not to laugh, with the wretched fish wriggling in her hand.

On the stage Mrs Campbell had great liberty of spirit and would often ad lib and even make remarks about the audience. At one matinée, taking a dislike to the audience, she said to me in a stage whisper which reached the back of the gallery, "Look at those women in the stalls, my dear. They look like monkeys in the zoo."

It was a warm summer during the run of *The Matriarch*, and one evening after a sweltering day the theatre was full and very hot. Shortly after my entrance Mrs Campbell called me over and said, "Phyll, dear, run down to the dressing room and fetch me my fan."

I was horrified. I was about to say my lines and I could not think what would happen if I left the stage at that point. But I could see she meant me to go and was capable of doing something far worse if I did not do as she said. In the old Royalty Theatre the dressing rooms were right under the stage. I flew down the spiral staircase and ran into her dressing room, having no idea where to find her fan. At last after ransacking around I managed to find it and raced back up the stairs, arriving panting on the stage. Mrs Campbell was sitting there as if nothing had happened, ad libbing and talking a lot of nonsense. As she was playing rather an eccentric old woman I do not think the audience noticed it; they probably thought it was part of the play!

Half way through the run of *The Matriarch* a great friend of mine got a contract to go to America. I had never been there and was very keen to go. I heard that Al Woods, a well-known American producer, was casting a play in London. Between the matinée and evening performance I went to see him at the Savoy Hotel where he was staying.

I found a big man with a wall eye, looking rather like my idea of the Ogre in *Jack and the Beanstalk*. He had a fat cigar sticking out of his mouth. He said he was going to produce *Murder on the Second Floor* by Frank Vosper. He had me round several times before he gave me the part. He talked a lot about the young actor who was to play opposite me. He said he had the greatest admiration for him and felt he might have a real future. His name, he said, was Laurence Olivier.

I was thrilled at the prospect of going to America for the first time. Terribly excited, I packed a cabin trunk and prepared to set sail on the *Berengaria*.

A few days before sailing, at breakfast, I opened the *Daily Mirror* and saw on the centre page a picture of a wedding group. I was very taken by the best man, who I noted was a young tennis player called Austin. I said to myself, "I like the look of him. He is the kind of young man I would like to marry."

CHAPTER THREE

I

Bunny

"THERE she is!"

Olliff and I were walking up the circular companion-way of the good ship *Berengaria*. Descending with a companion was the actress Olliff had seen on Waterloo platform.

Being a well-brought-up young man I could not, of course, boldly stare at her. If I looked at all I must do so discreetly out of the corner of my eye. This I did. I glimpsed black hair neatly waved, bright eyes with eyelashes heavily mascaraed, red lips.

My wife will tell you that in those days it took her an hour to make up her face. "Every eyelash," she will say, "was a masterpiece. I dared not move my head in case something fell off."

That may be a slight exaggeration, but it will give you the picture. This was the young lady who passed us on the companionway, slim and attractive and just twenty-two years old.

Of all the great games of the world, perhaps the greatest is shuffleboard! What infinite delight, when your opponent's disc is neatly sitting in plus ten, to take an almighty shove and scatter it to the four winds. What an agony of heart you suffer when your opponent does the same thing to you. For such emotional excitement there is nothing to beat shuffleboard! At least that is the way I feel.

I was enjoying this magic game which for maximum enjoyment requires a swaying deck and a good stiff ocean breeze, when Olliff and I were interrupted by a blond young man who approached me courteously. He had seen me play at Wimbledon, he said; he was an ardent tennis fan and it was a great pleasure to him to make my acquaintance. Would I like to meet a friend with whom he was travelling? And so John Olliff and I laid down our shuffleboard sticks and followed the blond young man over the decks and down the companionway to meet his friend.

My heart missed a beat! It was the actress! In a kind of a daze I stood chatting. Fortunately it was not difficult to make conversation. Miss Konstam, for that proved to be her name, was an adept at it. We no sooner got launched on one subject, than she switched to another and twenty minutes went sliding rapidly by.

Then the bell sounded. Miss Konstam excused herself to prepare for lunch. I watched her two neat legs as she walked quickly down the deck.

II

Outside the sun was sinking as the great ship slid quietly through the almost waveless waters of the Atlantic Ocean. But there were few on deck at that moment to admire the glories of the natural universe.

Down below in the dining rooms the passengers were making merry. It was the second evening out and so it was 'get-together night'. Let the passengers have a little jollity, the ship's authorities felt, a little drink, lots of paper hats, streamers, whistles and other grown-up toys and the ice of British reserve will melt and the journey will go far more smoothly, at least from the point of view of human relations. The actual smoothness of the sea, though Britain had long ruled the waves, was still beyond the power of even the Cunard company to control.

So the passengers were getting together in a big way. There was a great deal of noise and jollity and Olliff and I were thawing out with the rest at a table seating some ten people.

Suddenly behind me there appeared a glamorous figure in a low and expensive evening gown. "Good evening," she said.

My heart missed another beat. It was Miss Konstam. "Oh, hullo! May I have the pleasure of a dance?"

It was a daring gambit. One thing I disliked doing intensely, because I knew I did it badly, was to dance. I was tone deaf. I had no sense of music. I had difficulty in distinguishing between 'God Save the King' and 'Rule Britannia'. Moreover my intense shyness as a child had convinced me that no girl could by any stretch of imagination want to dance with me. I could never imagine myself interesting to any partner. So

53

I was defeated from the beginning and had never even tried to learn to dance.

But developing fame on the tennis court was like sand-paper on wood – it was rubbing away the rough corners of my shyness. I found that girls liked me and as I liked them I grew more confident.

Now I took my courage in my hands, and as Miss Konstam accepted my invitation to dance I led her to the floor.

Fortunately the floor was crowded. It was a sea of jostling humanity and any attempts to dance were out of the question. One could only hold one's partner round the waist and jostle with the crowd.

I would like to state that Miss Konstam was as light as a feather and danced like an angel. That would not be entirely true, for which I was duly glad. If she had danced like an angel, my own clumsiness would have been more apparent.

And so we jostled and talked. I cannot remember what we talked about. I can only remember that at last Olliff and I, Miss Konstam and the blond young man who had introduced us, left the dining room and went to our cabin where we played gramophone records of the latest popular songs.

Then we were wandering around the state rooms and came to the writing room. Miss Konstam found a Western Union form. She wrote on it and handed it to me. "Good night. Sleep well. Beware of B223. Remember mother's warnings. A well wisher."

III

There follows our arrival in America a kaleidoscope of memories – New York, its hectic cavern-like streets burning under the summer sun. Brief glimpses of Phyll, caught up now in her rehearsals. An evening with her at a play. Train journeys. The green of tennis courts at Southampton, Westchester, Newport. The dress rehearsal of Phyll's play, when John and I sat in the front row. Phyll's dressing room afterwards, her eyes bright in her stage make-up. The national championships at Forest Hills. Taxi rides in and out of New York to see Phyll. A long train journey to the West for the Pacific South West Championships played at the Los Angeles Tennis Club in Hollywood. Film stars studding the tennis crowds. Dinners with Ronald Colman at his home in the Hollywood Hills. Harold Lloyd, the famous comedian of silent days, and many a star now long since faded from the screen. A day at Charlie Chaplin's home. Drives from the tennis club to Malibu Beach where the great stars had homes by the sea. The journey to New York with the British Wightman Cup team. An evening watching the sun set at the Grand Canyon. A drive with Phyll to the woods of New Jersey, the trees now in the dazzling foliage of autumn. Nights backstage at Phyll's play, chatting in the wings with Laurence Olivier. Luncheons and dinners with Phyll, nonchalantly paid for from the wad of dollar bills in my pocket, each one representing a further dive into the red in my bank account at home. And at last the farewell on a New York dock, and a dreary, rough and lonely voyage home in the original and famous *Mauretania*, so long the holder of the Blue Riband of the Atlantic.

IV

Phyll

My first visit to America was a great experience. When I saw the skyline of New York for the first time I felt I had really arrived in a new world. Driving through the streets with towering buildings on either side, Central Park at night, seeing the myriads of lights in the skyscrapers, made me feel I was in a futuristic film like *Metropolis*.

My family had felt that I should not go unchaperoned to America, so I was accompanied by our great friend Nellie Davis. Nellie was the sister of a much-loved governess we had had as children, called Little Dave. When Little Dave left us I remember feeling the end of the world had come. She had been such fun, she thought of so many interesting and exciting things to do, she was so warmhearted, that I felt life without her would stretch out ahead in a grey sameness. After she left, however, her sister Nellie came to stay with us for fifteen days. She stayed for fifteen years! Nellie could do everything – sew, mend, make beautiful flower arrangements, turn anything old

55

into new. She too was great fun and has been a wonderful friend over the years. So I was delighted when I knew she would accompany me to New York.

Arrangements had been made for us to stay at the Warwick, pronounced War-wick. It was a tall apartment hotel on West 54th Street. Everything was different from life in Britain. The clerk behind the desk, instead of saying a polite 'Good morning', said, "Hi, I like your hat!" Instead of an old lift that groaned and creaked and crawled its way slowly to the third floor, there was a modern elevator, with gilt doors, which shot up to the 15th floor where we found we had a bedroom and sitting room.

Laurence Olivier lived on the floor above. Larry was engaged at the time to Jill Esmond, daughter of the playwright H. V. Esmond and his actress wife Eva Moore. Jill was also in New York acting in a play, *Bird in Hand* by John Drinkwater. We all became great friends.

It was August and terribly hot in New York City, a humid heat I had not experienced before. They said it was hot enough to fry an egg on the sidewalk. I always hoped I would see someone doing it!

My father had tried to tell me what New York would be like but it is hard to describe until you have been there—the milling crowds of people on Broadway, a polyglot of all the races, Negroes, Jews, white Americans from every background, Italians, Poles, Germans, Irish . . . New York is unique.

We were to start rehearsals for the play immediately. *Murder on the Second Floor* by Frank Vosper had had a very successful run in London. We were to open at the Eltinge Theatre on 42nd Street. In 1929 Broadway and 42nd Street were the heart of theatreland. A few doors down from the Eltinge was the Ziegfeld Theatre. A spectacular musical was playing there with the famous Ziegfeld Follies and with Eddie Cantor as the comedian. Between the Ziegfeld Theatre and the Eltinge was a Flea Circus. Larry used to drop in and see it after rehearsals and then come back to the Warwick and describe the whole thing in detail to us. He gave a brilliant comedy performance in describing the man in charge of the fleas and all the side shows.

We were also asked to appear for publicity at a women's luncheon in some big hotel. A very large lady gave a nonsensical talk on psychology. She would give some extraordinary illustration that had nothing whatsoever to do with psychology, but would sum up, "And that is what ah mean by psarchology." Then Larry and I were asked to say a few words. When we got back to the Warwick Larry put on my hat and scarf and gave a long speech on psychology. I have seen him give a good many fine performances since, but for sheer excruciating comedy I have never seen him do anything funnier.

I was also taken by the director, William Mollison, to my first baseball game. I cannot remember which team was playing but it was in a giant stadium with thousands of fans all shouting hysterically for their side, all sweating in the heat in shirt sleeves, drinking Coca-cola and eating hot dogs. One man sitting behind me got so distressed at the form of his team that much to my amazement he suddenly started saying the Lord's Prayer!

Every day when we went to the theatre to rehearse we would find the manager, Al Woods, sitting on the sidewalk in his shirt sleeves fanning himself. He was an extraordinary character, exactly like a Hollywood version of a Broadway impresario, with his hat over his eye chewing a large fat cigar. I was told a story I cannot verify, but having known him I can well believe it. At a rehearsal of one of his productions an actor spoke of Omar Khayyam. Al Woods stopped the rehearsal. "No, no, no," he said, "it ain't Omar Khayyam, it's Omar *of* Khayyam." The director assured him he was wrong. Al insisted it was Omar *of* Khayyam. The actor explained he could not possibly say Omar of Khayyam. "Aw, hell," said Al Woods, "cut it then. The play's too long anyway."

Before the play opened Bunny phoned me to say he was playing in a tournament in Westchester. He invited me out to see him play on a Saturday when I was not rehearsing. Nellie and I drove out to a beautiful country club. There for the first time I saw him play. The great heat was hard on him and he was not at his best. In the cool of the evening we sat and talked under a huge tree. The sun went down and the moon came up. It was a perfect setting. We were young and romantic. We lived in a dream world and swore eternal love. The following week I went to see him play at Forest Hills. I got my first taste of the agony of watching him play in a big championship. I found then and always that it was a refined form of torture.

After the play had opened Bunny left to take part in the Pacific South West Championship in Hollywood. He wrote me he was meeting beautiful young film stars. Gradually his letters stopped coming. I wept bitter tears and tried to console myself by going to parties which I did not enjoy at all.

In the gay bustling life of New York where everything had seemed so prosperous, things were not going too well either. Everyone was gambling on the Stock Exchange – millionaires and clerks in the offices. The maid who did my room at the Warwick Hotel told me she was having her little flutter. So was the elevator boy, so were the stage hands at the theatre. Then the crash came. People who had been very rich suddenly lost everything. There was chaos and panic. The papers were full of suicides. Wall Street tycoons jumped from skyscraper windows. All that had seemed so gay and secure became black and menacing.

The play was not a success. It soon closed. I stayed some weeks longer in New York and then returned to London.

v

Bunny
London seemed a dull place when I arrived home from America in October. I started work on the Stock Exchange, which proved to be no joy. The fog-bound city was dreary and sad in those autumn days of 1929 following the Great Crash which had destroyed the fortunes and even the lives of so many people and left millions destitute even of hope. In my relations with Phyll, too, a cooling off had come.

It was hard for me to take life seriously at that time or to settle down. Suddenly from my suburban home in South Norwood a gay world had opened up – a world of travel and excitement, the endless meeting of new people – a hello today and a goodbye tomorrow – an insubstantial life cf tennis courts and tennis parties, of soaring hopes and sobering set-backs, but with the always beckoning future of more travel, more adventure, more excitement, more gay and glamorous people to meet and more fairy tale cities to be visited.

The Stock Exchange had no great appeal for me as a business though I was to learn to enjoy the life. I got on well with the clerks with whom I did crossword puzzles and played dominoes over a morning cup of coffee or an afternoon cup of tea; and I liked the two brothers who ran the firm and who had kindly taken me under their wing. But the world of finance baffled me. Figures twisted my brain in knots. Balance sheets only succeeded in bewildering me. But it was my father's profession, the one he enjoyed and had chosen for me, envisioning me as a broker rather than a jobber, doing business for the wealthy clients I would meet in my tennis-playing life.

Through those early grey days letters of varying degrees of warmth and coolness kept coming from Phyll. When she returned to London we renewed our acquaintance over tea at the Carlton Hotel.

I worked on the Stock Exchange through December and early January, but at the end of the month obtained leave from my work to go with John Olliff to play in Scandinavia and afterwards, for the first time, in the South of France.

It is said that the course of true love never runs smooth, which goes to prove how true was the love which existed between Phyll and me! We met warmly and parted coldly. We met coldly and parted warmly. We fought, we argued, we came together again. Many a parting seemed to be the last.

But fate played a clever trick. Our two families, so very different from each other in every way, had one point of agreement. They agreed it would be unwise for their children to marry. And so when Mrs Konstam, who was planning to take her daughter to Cannes following an appendix operation, heard that I was going to play in the South of France she decided, thinking that Cannes was the tennis centre, she would take her daughter to Beaulieu instead. It happened that Beaulieu was the first tournament in which I had planned to play. Who, therefore, should be on the station platform to meet me when I arrived but Phyll!

When poor Mrs Konstam recovered from her unfortunate

mistake we had a happy time, and between glorious drives on the Moyenne and Grande Corniches, visits to the fabulous little villages which hang precariously to the mountainsides and the mountain peaks, I managed, after Beaulieu, to reach the finals of both the singles and doubles at Monte Carlo.

It was not a bad start to my tennis season. But better was to come. In the match between London and Paris in Paris the week following Monte Carlo, I became the first Englishman for many a year to beat a top world-ranking player when I overcame Jean Borotra on his own covered courts.

Phyll, who had returned to London from Monte Carlo, sent me a wire to Paris: "Please beat Borotra Bunny". When I got back to London after my success she seemed very pleased to see me. But it is time now for her once more to take up the tale.

VI

Phyll

I came back from America and started looking for a job. Once more I went out to Elstree. Hitchcock had already started work on his second talking picture, a film called *Murder*, with Herbert Marshall as the star. It was the story of a murder in a small theatre touring company. The stage manager and his wife, the comedienne of the company, were two of the leading characters.

The casting director at Elstree said the part of the wife had not yet been cast, and so I went down on the set and saw Hitchy, who told me he could not find the type he wanted. He looked at me but said, "I want a small blonde for the part." I was just prepared to leave when the cameraman came along and had a look at me and said, "Why not try her in a blonde wig?" A make-up man completely transformed my appearance and I started work that afternoon.

I thoroughly enjoyed working on that picture. There were three separate casts: French, English and German, as dubbing had not yet been perfected. I learned a great deal from Hitchy. He liked people to be real. I would have liked to have looked very glamorous but he made me play one scene with glasses on, soaking my feet in hot water.

CHAPTER THREE

Hitchy made brilliant use of sound, not just as a means of a character speaking a line but as a means of heightening the drama and the story. *Murder* was highly praised by the critics.

His next production was John Galsworthy's play *The Skin Game*. Hitchy interviewed a dozen leading ladies. I applied for the job but had little hope of getting it. Having just played a part in a light comedy I did not think I would be able to play Chloë, a tragic figure who commits suicide. But Hitchy agreed to give me a test. While I waited my turn I heard him directing a large number of actresses also being tested for the part, and as I was about the last one on the list I began to get the idea of how he wanted it played. When it came to my turn I must have played it well, for to my astonishment and joy I got the part.

I was especially glad to be working at that time because Bunny and I had become increasingly fond of each other. But both of us, and especially our families, wanted to be sure that it was not just an infatuation. My father-in-law's picture of an actress was someone in tights drinking champagne out of a slipper during an all-night orgy. I was not his idea of an ideal wife for his son. Perhaps he was a good deal more right than I realised at the time!

So it was decided that Bunny should accept an invitation to go on a three months' tennis tour in India. Much to my surprise the day he left I wept all morning. He had arranged with a florist to send me a dozen dark red carnations every Friday night with a note in his handwriting. If by Thursday I began to waver and doubt whether we were meant to marry, when the carnations arrived on Friday night I was quite sure we were!

In fact, I missed him terribly. I worked hard and made several pictures. One was called *Tilly of Bloomsbury* in which I played the main part. It was an amusing Cinderella story and very popular, and to this day people all over Britain and the Commonwealth tell me how much they loved it.

When Bunny returned from the East we talked of getting married. One evening I told a friend of mine about it. Her husband was a close friend of the editor of the *Daily Express*. Next morning to my surprise the story of our forthcoming engagement was on the front page.

Bunny

It is November 14, 1931. I wake up in the morning with a
severe headache. This is not surprising, I say to myself. All my
friends have told me that on your wedding day you are liable
to feel terrible. Well, I feel terrible. My mother puts some
brandy into my breakfast coffee. I finish dressing in my morning coat, tie my cravat with impeccable neatness and drive
off with my family to my wedding.

There is a big crowd outside the Hampstead Parish Church.
The newspapers have ballyhooed our wedding and our pictures
have recurred in the newspapers with great frequency. So tennis
fans and stage fans have lined the road on this grey November
day to witness the event.

I feel much better in the church and go round greeting our
friends as they stream in. The Davis Cup team are my ushers.
Phyll's younger sister and a cousin are bridesmaids. Phyll's
and my little nieces and the three-year-old daughter of Alfred
Hitchcock are our flower girls.

My former housemaster, Mr Carter, is one of the clergy
who is marrying us.

The ceremony is soon over and we walk down the aisle and
out into the cold November morning and the waiting crowds.
The newsreel cameras are there and cameramen in droves.
To the sound of clicking shutters we enter our car and drive
off to the reception in my in-law's home.

The reception line is a long one and after a while the room
begins to sway. I tell my wife. "Let's break away," she says.

We change and leave the reception and the memory of
it is very hazy. I do not feel well, but of course I remember all
my friends warned me I would feel terrible on my wedding
day.

I have booked a room at the Dorchester Hotel. The next day
Phyll and I decide to go to the Empire Cinema and see our
wedding pictures.

The Movietone News comes on. A voice behind us says,
"Oh, poor things, don't they look miserable." As we go out
I ask my wife, "How did I look?" "I'm afraid I was looking at

myself. How did I look?" I confessed that I too was looking at myself. We decide to go back the next day to look at each other!

The third day we go up to Hampstead to visit our new home. Though it is a cold, damp November day everything to me feels strangely hot. My neck, too, is stiff–I can hardly move it. Coming back in the underground the thought suddenly occurs to me that I may be ill.

When we get back to the hotel Phyll takes my temperature. It is 103°. It is not, after all, marriage that has been making me feel ill! I have the 'flu!

VIII

Phyll and I lean over the rail of the ship in the harbour of Barcelona. We are on the third phase of our honeymoon. The harbour is as calm as a pond and a full moon gazes down at us romantically from a cloudless sky.

"This is just like *Cavalcade*," I say.

I was referring to the scene in Noel Coward's historic play where a young couple on their honeymoon leant romantically over the rail of a ship. They talked of the future and all their plans. Suddenly there was a blackout and a spotlight picked out the lifebuoy underneath the rail where the young couple were standing. On it was painted the name of the ship, 's.s. *Titanic*'.

"I wish," said my wife, "you hadn't said that about *Cavalcade*!"

I realised it was a silly thing to have said. But the night was so fine, the harbour so calm there was obviously nothing to worry about.

As the ship got under weigh we went down to the cabin. As we headed for the open sea, suddenly there was a flash of lightning and an angry growl of thunder. The ship took an unexpected lurch.

"I wish," said my wife, "you hadn't said that about *Cavalcade*!"

In the words of Shakespeare, "the torrent roar'd; and we did buffet it," or rather it did buffet us. The ship groaned and creaked and above decks we could hear the constant clatter of running feet. In the morning even the stewardess said, "Terrible, terrible." My wife's dressing case fell to the floor and the port-hole leaked and the water that trickled through began to mix with her powder from a box that had burst open. Sleep was impossible. I watched my scarf swing to and fro on the hook on the door. There was a knot in the wood of the door. I decided that if the scarf swung past that knot the ship would overturn. Suddenly the ship rolled over, the scarf swung past the knot. For one horrible moment the ship hung poised, shuddering, and then, as if with a mighty effort, righted itself.

"I wish, I wish," said my wife, "you hadn't said that about *Cavalcade*."

Long before the end of the journey I wished I had not said it myself!

IX

The storm was over. Majorca lay clear, if steamy, in the fresh morning sun. Admiring the landscape we travelled on a horse-drawn cart across the island to the hotel.

The hotel was very romantic. It had been especially recom-mended to us. It was rather primitive, we were told, and small, but what would that matter? We only needed a bed and a roof over our head at night. The rest of the time we would be on the beach sunbathing.

As we arrived at the hotel the horizon grew suddenly dark. Out of the west began to sail huge galleons of black high-piled clouds. My wife and I tried to pretend they were not there. We went to our room and unpacked.

And then the heavens opened. It must have been like that in the days of Noah. They were eating and drinking and making merry and then the rains came.

We were hoping to make merry—on those sunny beaches we had heard so much about. True it did not rain for forty days and forty nights. At least we have no knowledge that it did. After six days of uninterrupted downpour, my wife said, "I'm going home."

And home we went. My in-laws were there to greet us at Victoria Station.

4 Whitehall Court S.W.1. 14th Jan: 1935

Don't let her vulgarity spoil her charm: that is all.

If you cannot get away with Dora I shall give you up as a hopeless duffer.

G. Bernard Shaw

Miss Phyllis Konstam
19 Well Road
The Heath
Hampstead
N.W.3

Postcard to Phyllis from Bernard Shaw referring to her role of
Darling Dora in *Fanny's First Play*

CHAPTER THREE

"Have you got all your luggage?" they asked.

Travelling for the first time as a husband responsible for his wife's belongings, I wished the question had not been asked. As we had left our hotel in Majorca in torrential rain and a gale of wind, my wife's hat box, with all her trousseau of hats, had been blown into the bay.

If our marriage could successfully survive our honeymoon, we decided, it could successfully survive anything else that lay ahead.

This proved to be true – but only just.

CHAPTER FOUR

I

Bunny

1931 had been for me a good lawn tennis year. I had played well in the French championships till I put out my sacro-iliac joint; I had been within a point of reaching the semi-final at Wimbledon and after Wimbledon, with Fred Perry now in the forefront of the lawn tennis world, we had with our teammates reached the challenge round of the Davis Cup in Paris. At the end of the year I had been ranked the number two tennis player in the world.

In the spring of 1932 I had an operation on my nose to clear away the debris caused by the fists, footballs and cricket balls which from time to time had contacted its prominence with varying degrees of violence. The operation was meant to improve my breathing and it did. It did not, however, immediately improve my game. But at Wimbledon that year, in spite of being put back somewhat in my tennis, I managed to reach the final of the singles.

In the final I had high hopes. I was the first Englishman to have reached the final at Wimbledon for many years, and I knew that all of the tennis lovers in England awaited the hour with great expectation. Moreover in the morning my mother had telephoned me with good news from the stars.

This needs some explanation. Her father, who came to London from Cornwall, had founded a wine business. He was a good businessman and he did well. He was also a keen Methodist. One Sunday, however, he went to chapel and on coming out he was handed a tract on the evils of drink. My grandfather, being a serious-minded man, took the tract home and studied it with care. He never went to chapel again!

And so my mother grew up in an agnostic family, and in later life, in search of a faith, came in contact with the ancient science of astrology. She cast my horoscope, and on the morning of the Wimbledon final against Vines she consulted my stars and found that they were all in the ascendent. She tele-

phoned me, apprised me of this fact and said I was bound
to win!

Fortified by my mother's astrological predictions, I drove into
London to see my osteopath, who had made himself in a measure, my trainer. He put me through some paces and generally
tuned me up. Afterwards I drove back to Hampstead for an
early lunch before driving out to Wimbledon.

Ellsworth Vines, my opponent in the final, was a lean and
lanky man with a huge serve, possibly as fine a serve as any
man in lawn tennis has ever possessed. He was a quiet fellow,
lacking the brash confidence so often – and often wrongly – associated with Americans. He was six foot four inches tall with
extremely long arms, so his serve was delivered from a great
height.

Vines was a better player than I. I knew this, but I was in
good condition and good form and I also knew that tennis was
a game of upsets and it was often the underdog hitting an un-
accustomed good streak who would win a match. On this
particular day I was also fortified by the secret knowledge
unknown to Vines that my stars were all in the ascendent and
I was bound to win!

When we started, however, I found I was out of touch. This
question of touch is a very important factor to a tennis player.
Tennis, as the reader well knows, is a game of great accuracy.
You can win or lose a match depending on whether your stroke
just hits or just misses a line, just skims or just fails to skim the
net. A whole match can turn on the error of a millimetre.

I started badly. So, fortunately, did Vines. The score
mounted slowly, each game in the traditional manner following
service. But in the ninth game I lost my service and finally the
first set, 6–4. But I did not worry at all. I knew my stars were
in the ascendent. I was bound to win in the end!

In the second set Vines began to play much better. He began
to get his cannonball service working and began to treat my
own service with an ever lessening respect. The score mounted
rapidly against me and I lost the set, 6–2. But still I did not
worry. My stars were in the ascendent. I knew I would win
in the end!

As the third set started it was like encountering one of those

150-mile-an-hour hurricanes you read about in the Caribbean that flatten everything before them. I was being flattened. I simply could not see Vines' services, nor could I see his returns to my services. The score mounted rapidly against me, 1–0, 2–0, 3–0, 4–0 and 5–0, and on his own service he reached 40–15, match point.

Still I did not give up hope! I knew all my stars were in the ascendent and I was bound to win in the end!

I waited for Vines to serve, watched the smooth, rhythmic and powerful swing! Boom! I did not move. I saw nothing, only a puff of dust on my service court, and then the sound of a ball hitting the stop-netting behind me. That was his service, I realised. The match was over. Vines had won! I have never been a believer in astrology since that day!

A year later, however, stars or no stars, that decision was to be exactly reversed in the Davis Cup in Paris.

II

That year I attended a variety concert given for soldiers wounded in the war. It moved me to write the following: "On November 11th fourteen years ago the Armistice which brought the great war to conclusion was signed. The guns were silent, the noise of rifles and machine guns was stilled and the edict went forth that murder was no longer legal.

"We cheered loudly and rejoiced for we had won the war. Although hundreds of thousands of human beings had been sacrificed for that end; although mothers had lost their sons, children their fathers and sisters their brothers; although budding poets, authors, scientists, industrialists and sportsmen, who carry overseas friendship and goodwill, had laid down their lives for that end we cheered loudly and rejoiced for we had won the war.

"But now we no longer rejoice for although we won the war we know that not one single belligerent country has benefited by the result and that all today are facing an economic crisis worse than any living man can remember. We know that debts have been created whose size staggers the imagination and whose weight has crushed the world into financial chaos;

and we know that the chaos has thrown into unemployment millions of those who were told that they were fighting for a better world in which to live.

"And besides all this we know that the legacy of the war is still with us and that men are still paying for it by their suffering.

"On Sunday I had the privilege of attending one of the variety entertainments that are given at regular short intervals for the benefit of these men who in their hundreds are still in hospital. All of them were crippled, many were mutilated. Those who had wives were accompanied by them and the spirit of them all surmounting their suffering was like a torch in a dark place.

"The whole of the stalls of the theatre was filled by them, some were blind, others were deaf. Some had lost one arm, others a leg. Some had lost both arms, some both legs, and one man was a limbless trunk. Another was overtaken by continuous spasms which shook his whole body. Conscious of his terrible condition he bore the look of a hunted animal and only when someone spoke to him was it replaced by one of gratitude so pathetic as to be indescribable. All through the performance stretcher cases were carried in and out, in and out; they were men who could sit only for a short while between long periods of enforced rest.

"At the end of the performance prizes were given for a lucky dip. To receive these prizes came the blind men guided by friends and the lame men on their crutches. But some were not able to come at all because even on crutches they could not walk.

"In the councils of those men who hold in their hands the future peace of the world, there should be ever present the memory of other men who with their lives, who with their bodies, who with the anguish of their souls paid for and are paying for the folly of the war.

"The lesson we have learnt is bitter; the price that we have paid for it is bitterer still and lest we forget that lesson, let the wounded who are with us still be our constant reminders and prevent us ever again from plunging into another welter of human sacrifice and carnage."

Later that year a disarmament conference met and failed.

I read the news in my Stock Exchange office in the City. Suddenly I realised that a second world war was on the way. It was as clear to me as if its announcement had been made in headline news. Deeply stirred I took a piece of paper and began to write. A few days later in the *News Chronicle* my article appeared: 'Bunny Austin looks at war'.

A flood of letters began to reach me inviting me to speak in the cause of peace. Feeling duty bound to accept these invitations, although I had no experience of public speaking, I found myself on platforms, in church halls and town halls, in lecture halls and auditoriums and finally on behalf of the League of Nations with distinguished speakers at the Albert Hall.

On one occasion I was invited to speak at Reading. I had a ten-minute speech which fitted nicely into a line-up of speakers, but I never expected to speak on my own. Therefore when I arrived at Reading, I was surprised to find a delegation waiting to greet me on the platform and even more surprised when I was driven in state to the town hall. Here I found that I was a guest of honour at a dinner given by the mayor. Uneasy feelings began to assail me, what was all this about? My feelings became even more uneasy when I was driven to the meeting and shown onto the platform where to my dismay there were three chairs, one for the chairman, one for myself and one for Phyll. I was the only speaker of the evening. Fortunately I kept my head. I spoke very slowly, spinning out my ten-minute speech into fifteen and then with a wave of inspiration I said, "I now declare the meeting open to questions." I did not know a great deal about the League of Nations, but fortunately I found that the audience knew even less. A gay time was had by all and everyone was delighted. I travelled up to London with the local MP who said I had a good voice and ought to go into parliament!

When I spoke at the Albert Hall, Lord Samuel, then Sir Herbert, came up to me and said the same thing. He said that I ought to go into politics and quite obviously I was a Liberal!

However, in spite of these flattering remarks, gradually I became disillusioned. Thousands of speeches like mine, I knew, were being made. Books were being published in the cause of peace, resolutions were being passed and pledges signed, but what were they actually accomplishing? What was being changed? Was being against war enough?

Quietly I withdrew from my speaking engagements and refused all further invitations.

III

In the spring of 1933, Phyll gave me a book. It was a large volume, beautifully bound and even more beautifully printed. She hoped it might improve my literary style. It was called *The Bible Designed to be Read as Literature.*

As literature, I began to read it. The Bible was familiar to me. I had studied it every Sunday for years at school. A credit in 'Divinity'–a study of the four gospels–had enabled me to pass my entrance examination into Cambridge University.

But now as I began to read the Gospels for the beauty of their language, the contents began to come alive for the first time. What was said was sound common sense. If men only practised what was said here we'd have a decent world. Why didn't they?

No sooner had I asked myself this question than a thought struck me: "Why don't *you*?"

It seemed a fair enough reply. If I felt that the teachings of Jesus were the way men should live it seemed fair enough that I should live that way myself. I resolved to become a Christian.

The resolve, although sincere, had no effect whatever on the way I lived. It reminded me of my confirmation. For this I had been prepared by my housemaster who was a parson and by the headmaster, who was to become Archbishop of Canterbury. When the great day arrived on which the bishop was to lay hands on my head, I imagined something would happen to me, that I would in some way be purified from sin.

The bishop laid his hands on me. Nothing happened. I was entitled now to go to Communion, but Communion did not apparently affect my nature or my desires.

In due course I went to Cambridge. Chapel, as at school, was then compulsory. But though summoned every so often by my tutor and ordered to attend chapel, I refused to do so. It bored me intensely and seemed to me to be a meaningless ritual. As far as my touch with the Christian faith was concerned I was disillusioned.

And now I was to be once more disillusioned. My resolve to be a Christian had no effect at all on my character or my actions. My desires and appetites still remained stronger than my will to control them, and the precepts of the New Testament beyond my reach to live.

And so I returned to my carefree, irresponsible ways.

IV

In June of that year Phyll and I attended the dinner of the International Lawn Tennis Club of Great Britain. The toasts had been drunk. The speeches had been made. Phyll and I were about to leave our table when a young woman approached us. Rather diffidently she asked, "Would you like to meet the Oxford Group?"

I looked at her with interest. I remembered reading about an Oxford Group meeting held in the Caxton Hall. It had struck me as I had read the account that they were a group of young men and women with considerable conviction and a great deal of courage. I was interested to meet any body of people who claimed to have an answer for the world's needs.

However, I hesitated a moment before answering. Yes, I would very much like to meet the Oxford Group, but when? This was the Saturday night before Wimbledon. Ahead lay the championships and after that Paris, the inter-zone final of the Davis Cup against America and, I hoped very much, the challenge round against France.

"When do you suggest?" I asked.

A day was arranged when we could meet the Oxford Group after the Davis Cup.

V

It was a long drive out from the hotel where we stayed in the Place de la Concorde. At least on this day in July 1933 it seemed a long way. As always before a big game, my stomach felt tight; and today it was hot, the thermometer registered

96 degrees in the shade, and the Parisian streets were shimmering in the heat.

Dan Maskell, the professional coach, was with me in the taxi. We had been through such times together before—the Interzone Final and Challenge Round in 1931 and many another Davis Cup encounter in many another part of the world, in Spain, Holland, Belgium, Germany, Poland, Hungary, Czechoslovakia, as well as Britain and now again in France. Dan was a faithful friend, tireless in his zeal, indefatigable in the giving of himself at all times, whether as our opponent in practice or in simple friendship off the courts.

The taxi drove down the Rue Henri Martin and at last we were passing through the gates of Auteuil, and very soon the great stand of the Stade Roland-Garros loomed up. We drove up to the entrance and climbed from the taxi amid the crowd of milling people.

How I loved to play in Paris! The atmosphere was like champagne bubbling with the excitement of the people. Taxi drivers would insist on our autographs; men and women would stop us in the street. In the hotel we were treated like royalty. And the crowds themselves! They were the greatest joy of all, roaring their disapproval of the linesmen's decisions, shouting at the umpire if he made a mistake, and clamouring from time to time for him to be removed. Every now and then fights would break out on the stands, and the game would be held up until quiet and order were restored.

The umpire would stand up in his chair, a large jovial and imposing figure wearing a huge sombrero. With a voice that scarcely needed a loudspeaker to magnify it, he would shout in stentorian tones, "Messieurs et Mesdames, un peu de silence, s'il vous plaît." The crowd would shout back at him good-humouredly, and at last quiet would be restored. I remember once seeing two Frenchmen in a stand who were having a violent argument with each other, gesticulating in apparent fury. I asked a friend what was the matter. He shrugged his shoulders, "They are discussing Borotra's backhand drive." Such was the enthusiasm of France during the time they held the Davis Cup. Tennis had become their national game and aroused the excitement and interest of the whole country.

How could we wrest the Davis Cup from France? It was one thing to play against another Frenchman; it was another to take on the 14,000 spectators as well, all of whom were vociferous in expressing their desire to see you beaten.

But I must not get ahead of myself. We were not yet in the Challenge Round, and as far as we, the British team, were concerned, today was our stiffest hurdle. We were playing against America, and I was pitted against Ellsworth Vines in the first match.

On paper our chances seemed slim. Ellie was the greatest player in the world, better at that time even than Fred Perry. He had crushed me at Wimbledon the year before and there seemed no reason why he should not beat me again. They had, too, the finest doubles combination in the world, Lott and Van Ryn. Their second singles player was Allison. If we were to win this round, both Fred and I had to beat Allison and one of us had to beat the great Vines.

In the dressing room I began to change. Dressing for a match with me was a kind of ritual, two pairs of socks, one wool, one silk to prevent blisters, then the left shoe first; it was necessary to placate the gods of the tennis world and get them fighting on your side.

Today, because it was so hot, I put a wet handkerchief round my neck, and a jockey cap on my head to shade my eyes. Then I selected the best four of my six racquets, and was ready for the game.

It was always an exciting moment, but a moment in which nerves were most tense, when you stepped from the shadow of the stand into the glare of the bright sun and the thousands of watching eyes. This day the heat hit you like the heat from an oven door, as the sun beat down on the concrete stands, on the rubble court, and the spectators, the men in shirt sleeves and the women in their lightest cotton clothes.

As always there was a battery of cameramen to greet us. Then there was a moment of pausing by the net, side by side with your opponent, for further pictures and to give the newsreels their chance. Side by side I stood with slim Ellie Vines, six foot four to my five foot eight. We tossed for sides. He won and chose service.

Now for me was the anxious time as we rallied in the warm up; this was the time when I felt at my worst—my legs felt like jelly, and it required an effort of will to control the movements of my arms, and I would wonder to myself, if I felt like this now would I be able to stand on my feet when the actual play began?

"Play!"

There was a sudden hush as the umpire called players and spectators to order and the game began.

I wondered, as I watched Ellie take his position on the far side of the net, how I would handle his cannonball service, which had been so devastating when I had played him in the final at Wimbledon the previous year. I watched Ellie prepare to serve, the long graceful and devastating swing, and watched the ball coming to me at the speed of a bullet. The ball struck the rubble surface of the court, its speed imperceptibly halted. I swung my racquet aiming at a cross-court drive. The ball, perfectly struck, went swiftly for a winner.

Perhaps it was this early treatment of Ellie's first service that unsettled him. Never in the first two sets did he really find his touch. Drives would strike the top of the net, or miss the lines by inches. I returned the ball to him relentlessly and accurately. I was informed after the match that in the first two sets I made only two errors. The score mounted in my favour until the first two sets were mine, 6-1, 6-1.

Now was the dangerous time. I must neither get over-confident nor over-anxious. Having taken the first two sets so decisively from the champion of the world, the next set would be the test. I must at all costs win it. I must strain to maintain my level of play and not allow Ellie to work into his best form.

The game was resumed. Ellie began to lift his level of play. He began to hit the sidelines more reliably. His flat drives began to lift the extra inch that made all the difference above the level of the net.

Here was the time, if any, when nerves might have failed me, but I remained calm. I just had to keep ahead. I just had to prevent Ellie succeeding in doing what he was striving to do, to get on top.

The score mounted to 5-4 in my favour. The game score:

40–30, match point. Now I must do it. Now I must clinch this all-important game. Win this match and the chance of winning the rubber was ours. I drove to Ellie's backhand and advanced to the net. He returned down my forehand line. I plunged to my right, racquet outstretched. I caught the ball at the very top of my racquet. The ball, feebly leaving it, just skimmed the net and dropped dead for a winner on the other side. It was a lucky shot–but the point and the match were mine.

A wave of relief washed over me, and a wave of excitement, as suddenly the truth dawned. I had beaten Ellie Vines! Thousands of Frenchmen roared their applause. A ball boy lifted my arm in a gesture of victory, as if I were a prize fighter in the ring. Ellie and I walked quietly from the court.

Great Britain led America by one match to love.

VI

The lights lowered in the cinema and the Movietone News flashed on the screen. There was a montage of the world's activities–sport, politics, war.

The montage ended and lettering came on the screen, "Austin and Perry bring lawn tennis glory to Britain". There was a shot of Vines and myself before our match–the long and short of it, like Mutt and Jeff. There were flashes of the play, the final concluding game of the Challenge Round, and at last the presentation of the Davis Cup.

As I sat in the theatre I remembered the agonising moments we had passed through before that Cup was finally won. In the final match of all, Perry had played Merlin, the young French-man appearing in his first Davis Cup encounter. It was the deciding match, the score standing at two matches all. Merlin had won the first set and was leading in the second. The crowd were delirious with excitement.

I delighted to watch Fred Perry play–a magnificent figure of an athlete who moved with all the grace and power of a panther. But this afternoon was an exception. The whole fate of the Davis Cup hung in the balance, and Perry who should so easily have beaten Merlin was struggling for his life.

It was not easy for Fred, as I knew only too well. I had played

Merlin in the first match. I had won the first set easily, 6–2. But then Merlin had begun to play above himself, a youngster in his first Davis Cup match with everything to win and nothing to lose. The crowd had begun to sense victory in Merlin's improved play. Every winning stroke he made was applauded vociferously. A groan went up if a winning stroke should come my way.

I began to realise it was far more than the skill of one Frenchman I was playing against. I was pitted against the wills of 14,000 Frenchmen. It was as if I were playing against an invisible and intangible wall–an unseen force which was a very present reality, against which I had to battle with every bit as much energy as against the meteoric strokes of my opponent. I was in a very critical situation. Let Merlin win that second set and the whole power of those Frenchmen's wills for victory would be fighting against me. And I would have no moral support other than from the handful of my teammates in the stand and my wife sitting amongst them.

It was essential at that moment that I hold the line against that youngster on the far side of the court, bobbing about opposite me like an inspired cork and making all sorts of impossible returns. The score had mounted slowly, 1–1, 2–2, 3–3, 4–4. And then the break had come. I had won my opponent's service for the set. I was two sets up and the match was as good as in my pocket.

And that is what the French audience sensed. The moment for possible triumph for their hero had passed. And suddenly that invisible wall of French wills, urging their hero to victory, had disappeared. The court had returned to normal. The match had become once again a simple struggle between Austin and Merlin. And I won the third set 6–0.

So I sympathised with Fred Perry on the court below. His was an even worse predicament than mine had been. I had been threatened with Merlin taking the lead. In Perry's case, Merlin was already ahead. The crowd which had resigned themselves to defeat because Fred was far the superior player had suddenly realised that victory was once more a possibility. The crowds were on the edge of their seats and the atmosphere was electric with their excitement. I knew that Fred was up against that invisible wall and if in those days I had known how to pray, I would have been praying then.

Phyll and I were sitting in the front row of the stand. I was chain-smoking cigarettes though I normally smoked only three a day. Phyll, normally a non-smoker, was smoking two at once because she felt it was luckier!

If ever Fred in his long and brilliant career on the courts had a testing moment, it was now. Merlin was performing feats of prodigious skill far beyond his normal form. He was, as the books say, playing far above himself, inspired by the occasion and the cheers of the highly partisan audience. The score in the second set mounted against Fred and Merlin moved to set point. The crisis had been reached.

We in the stands lived through an agony of suspense. The crowds were hushed, tense. To and fro flew that little white ball on whose trajectory at that moment it seemed that the world depended. To and fro it flew. Merlin advanced to the net. Fred, with perfect control moved to the ball and steered it past Merlin down the sidelines. It was in! The set was saved.

That was the crisis. Fred went on to win the set. The crowd sensed the peak had been passed. The inspiration ebbed from Merlin's racquet. Fred Perry had no difficulty in winning the remaining two sets for the match, the Championship and the Cup.

We had long dreamed of winning that Cup, the emblem of national lawn tennis supremacy. And now it stood on its stand on the court, flag-draped, and it was ours.

We stood by it at attention as the national anthems of the two countries were played and received the Cup from the hands of Monsieur Lebrun, President of France.

That night we took the Cup round the night clubs of Paris and the following day we returned to England across the English Channel in a gale of wind that turned us green. Friends were there to meet us at Dover. And there was handed to us on the dock a message of congratulations from His Majesty the King.

At Victoria Station thousands of people had turned out to greet us and the mounted police had to clear a way for us through the crowds.

So we had come back triumphant to England and one of my dreams ever since I had begun to knock the ball against the nursery wall had been fulfilled.

VII

The shouting and the tumult had died, the captains and kings of the tennis court had departed. The Davis Cup was safely on display in London. Now the day had arrived when Phyll and I had arranged to meet the Oxford Group.

We went to Brown's Hotel, where the Group had a one-room office and a sitting room, into which we were ushered. About a dozen people were standing round having tea. Who they were I do not today remember, but I do remember one man who particularly struck me. He was a young American journalist named John Roots.

Roots had been born and brought up in China, where his father was the Episcopal Primate, and had returned there after studying at Harvard University to write articles for the *New York Times* and other American papers. There he met Borodin, the Chicago dentist who pioneered the Chinese Communist revolution. Roots' profiles of him and the other Communist leaders—Mao, Ho Chi Minh, Chou En-lai and the rest—were among the first to reach the West.

Roots had been immensely struck by Borodin's complete dedication to the Communisation of China. On his suggestion, he had travelled to Russia where he saw a lot of Karl Radek, later on the editorial board of *Izvestia*. Radek took him to meet a roomful of young Chinese he was training in Moscow. "You may not think much of these young men now, Mr Roots," he said, "but in thirty years they will be the rulers of China." In Radek, as in Borodin, Roots discerned a dedication and breadth of vision which set him furiously thinking.

He instinctively distrusted the ruthlessness of Communism, but where, in the democracies, had he seen men of equal conviction? He could only think of one man, Frank Buchman, whom Sun Yat-sen described as "a Christian revolutionary—the only man who tells me the truth about myself". When Roots returned to America, he sought Buchman out. He had been working with him ever since to bring a Christian answer to the needs of individuals and nations.

I, in my turn, was captivated, that day in Brown's, by the passion and purpose of Roots and his friends. Their argument was the strongest in the world, for it was not so much what they said that convinced, but what they obviously were. It seemed to me that I had suddenly seen the ideas I had read about in *The Bible Designed to be Read as Literature* walking about on two legs.

I was fascinated, too, by the stories these people told of the modern miracles in the lives of men and women who were not only prepared to pray to God but also to listen to the answer.

It would be a poor sort of God, they pointed out, who had no plan for the world He created. It would be a poor sort of God, they added, who, having a plan, could not convey it to men. If the world was in a mess it was not God's fault. It was the fault of men who denied Him, or, admitting His existence, were keener to tell Him what they wanted Him to do than to find out from Him what He wanted them to do.

Here I began to see the hope for the re-ordering of the world – a universal plan to which all men could adhere, with benefit and advantage to all; a common plan for every race and class and nation, a plan in which there existed no discrimination between any types of people. As it was, the world was torn apart by men's wills – the fanatical ambitions of a Hitler just then risen to power; the imperial dreams of a Mussolini, and the economic imperialism of a Stalin. And all the lesser wills of smaller men with smaller schemes but all of them determined on their own ways.

Before the long tea party was over – we stayed to dinner and talked till eleven o'clock – I realised that my life had been in thought and experience leading naturally up to this meeting with the Oxford Group. I felt like a traveller who had reached a destination. But it was not, in fact, the end of a journey. It was the beginning.

VIII

Phyll
My reactions to our first meeting with the Oxford Group were entirely different from Bunny's.

5(a). *Left to right:* Ronald Colman, Edna Best, Phyllis and Manoel Alonso at Colman's home in Hollywood

5(b). *Left to right:* Phyllis Konstam as Chloe in film version of Galsworthy's *The Skin Game*; Alfred Hitchcock, the Director; Ursula Jeans and Edmund Gwenn

5(c). Phyllis with Gladys Cooper at Wimbledon

6(a). Phyllis as Emily Ross in Barrie's *The Will*, Westminster Theatre, 1939

6(b). Phyllis as Lil Wiggins, a part she created for a war-time revue

I remember a room full of people who in one way seemed very ordinary, but in another had a quality which I find hard to describe. I think I would call it openness. I remember one woman and her daughter talking about the difference it had made to them when they measured their lives not against their neighbours' standards, but against the standards of Christ which they defined as absolute honesty, purity, unselfishness and love. The resulting change had united them and enabled them to break out of their self-preoccupation.

Their talk of absolute standards was a shock, but I quickly thought of a great friend of mine, an actress who had just lost her young husband. She was inconsolable. I thought these people could help her. So I went to the phone and she joined us after dinner. On the way home she was doubtful, and I found myself arguing hotly on the Group's side against her. Her arguments seemed stupid and shallow, for if you were honest you could not deny that honesty, purity, unselfishness and love were right—or were they? Well, of course they were right for her. Yet, later, as I spent a restless night, I was not so sure they were right for me.

What happened to me was a little like an inoculation. At first you do not feel anything; then suddenly your arm becomes inflamed and it hurts like the dickens, then your temperature goes up. For many years I had been able to rationalise my conscience out of existence. If I wanted to do something which I knew was wrong, I was able to silence that inner voice completely. But after talking with these people I began to get uncomfortable prickles of conscience. Everything they said began to irritate me. I felt as if I had been stirred up with a teaspoon. Things I had quite forgotten suddenly came back into my mind and popped out at me like bogies.

At breakfast next morning instead of saying, "Of course those people are right. If you really want a new kind of society it has to start rather closer to home than I had hoped," what I actually said was, "I don't like those people. I don't like the look on their faces. The more I think of them, the more I feel they are dangerous. Don't let's have anything more to do with them."

IX

Bunny

Six months after meeting the Oxford Group, I was in the South of France for the tournaments at Beaulieu and Monte Carlo. It was marvellous to see again the yellow mimosa against the blue of Mediterranean sea and sky, and to feel the southern sun penetrating through the chill January air. And this year there was an added interest, for Frank Buchman was staying at Beaulieu.

I was staying at a small pension in Cimiez in the hills above Nice, with an Irishman called George Caulfeild who was the first tennis coach I had ever had. He was a cousin of William Orpen, the painter, and had a remarkable knowledge of many things, from painting and flower-growing to the ballet and the technique of tennis. His knowledge of the French language, however, left something to be desired. "Which way to Beaulieu?" he would ask a passing pedestrian. "Tout droit," would come the reply. George would happily turn to the right and wonder why the French never seemed to know their way anywhere. He was an interesting companion. Penniless as always, although innumerable cousins had left him innumerable fortunes, he was at that time looking after a dipsomaniac friend.

Caulfeild drove me into Beaulieu each day, and I had my meals, as in previous years, at the hotel where Buchman turned out to be staying. With him were four others, including John Roots.

I was interested to see John again, and was more than interested to see Buchman. I had only met him once before, on the stairs at some function in Knightsbridge. Typically he had said little, introducing me to his companion, Jim Newton who plays a decisive part later in this story. At Beaulieu, where I saw much of Buchman in the ample leisure between matches, my first impression was confirmed. He said little, preferring, it seemed, to let the others do the talking; but what he did say had a curious way of sticking in my mind.

My main impression, in those days, was the atmosphere Buchman created around him. There was, among his friends, none of the competition or downright antagonism to which I was accustomed in the worlds of tennis and the theatre. As I left them and mingled with my other friends, I became sharply aware of the rub of personality on personality. I could almost see the sparks fly. Buchman and his friends, I reflected, were not concerned to put themselves across. They had a larger purpose.

I felt that some of their serenity rubbed off on to me. I began to play tennis with extraordinary freedom and skill. Fear of defeat left me. Joyous and confident, I swept through the two tournaments without the loss of a set though the opposition consisted of all the finest players in Europe.

One morning, while the tournament was in progress, John Roots asked me if I would like to make the experiment of listening to God. I agreed. We went to a quiet corner of the club and sat down on a vacant seat. Below us the white-flan-nelled figures pursued the elusive ball over the red-coloured courts. Beyond them the Mediterranean lay 'lulled by the coil of his crystalline streams,' brilliantly blue under the sunlight.

John told me he generally noted down any thoughts that came to him. He handed me a piece of paper and a pencil and we sat quietly. Two thoughts came into my mind. "This life is right," I wrote down and then I added a but . . . "I would like to be the champion of the world first." After all, I thought to myself (but I did not write it down), I'm beating everyone hollow. Perhaps I could win Wimbledon.

I told John my first thought, but not the thoughts about Wimbledon. Nor did I express the deeper knowledge which had come to me as I listened. Though I wrote down little I knew that in that moment of quiet I had been in contact with a power I had not known before, a power which could control and redirect my life, if I would allow it. I decided that I would do as John suggested, and begin to listen first thing every day.

I left the South of France clear that I wanted to take part in the work of the Oxford Group. I now felt ready to do so, even if it interfered with my tennis career, which after my victories seemed to have almost limitless possibilities. When I arrived home I found Phyll in bed, resting after strenuous rehearsals for her leading role of Rose in C. B. Cochran's pro-duction of Louis Golding's *Magnolia Street*, directed by the great

83

Russian director Theodore Komisarjevski. She said she was
tired. She also admitted that for some weeks she had been
suffering from nerves.

Very concerned, I thought of how I had lost my own nervous-
ness in my tennis matches in the South of France and how a
new confidence had come to me as I started to experiment with
times of quiet.

"Darling," I said, "I have the very thing you're looking for."

Phyll showed not the slightest interest, turned over and went
to sleep.

x

It was seven-thirty in the morning, a couple of weeks after my
return from France. Phyll was still asleep. I got out of bed
quietly, shaved and went to my study which looked out over
the famous Jack Straw's Castle. I sat at my desk, took a sheet
of foolscap, and, in the quiet of the morning, began first to
pray, then to write. I put down the thoughts that came into
my mind in quick succession. I did not flatter myself that all
of them came from God; but by the time when, half an hour
later, I went into the dining room in my City clothes, I felt
well prepared for the day.

Our cheerful and incomparable housekeeper Mary was there
to give me breakfast. After breakfast I went back to the bedroom
to kiss my sleeping wife goodbye. Then putting on my bowler
hat and taking my umbrella from the stand I left for the City.

At the Hampstead underground station I bought *The Times*.
In the crowded train I unfolded it and scanned the headlines
for the major news. I turned to the sportspages – always of great
interest to me, especially if my own name were mentioned – and
then dutifully to the financial news. Getting off at the Bank I
joined the jostling City throng, bowler-hatted, stiff-collared like
myself, and made my way to our office near the Stock Exchange.

Just before I joined the Stock Exchange in 1929 the whole
thing had collapsed. The great boom had burst, and tragedy
came to millions both rich and poor. In our office there was no
tragedy, only an almost total cessation of work. The clerks who

had earlier been so busy that they had been sleeping on the premises, now only had a little routine work. There was almost nothing for me to do. By 1934, however, business was improving. I had been made a Bluebutton and so was allowed on the floor of the House. My job each morning was to collect the prices, a job which I enjoyed. I had no sense that I was cut out to be a stockbroker, but I liked the cheerful contact with the friends I made on the House floor.

Since my return from France I had formed the habit, after the day's work was done, of walking across London to the West End to see John Roots and every evening Phyll would drive down to Brown's Hotel to pick me up.

Except for a brief skirmish about the Oxford Group on my first day home all had been quiet in my relations with Phyll. There had been little chance to talk before her first night, and after it, as she continued to show a complete disinterest in my new-found convictions, the subject had not come up. But on this particular evening when Phyll came to fetch me and as I climbed into the car and took over the wheel she asked me what I had been doing.

I had had what I felt was an interesting and illuminating time with John. We had been talking about the divisions in the world and the underlying causes of war. He had told me that you could not hope to heal division if you were in any way divided in your life from anybody else, and had asked me if there were any divisions in my own heart. On replying I had no idea, he had suggested a time of quiet. Quite unexpectedly the thought had come into my mind that I bitterly resented a fellow tennis player whose gamesmanship had fooled me out of an important championship. Telling this to John he had asked me what I felt I should do about it. Again I had replied I had no idea. Again John had suggested a quiet time. Again a thought had come clearly that I should write and apologise for my resentment.

To my intense amazement and surprise when I got to this point in the story Phyll flared out angrily. "You write that over my dead body," she burst out. "You were absolutely right."

I tried to reason with her, but the more I reasoned the more furious she became. We argued all the way home and all the way through dinner and when she got to the theatre that night she rang me up and continued to argue with me over the phone.

This went on for days. Phyll called in her friends to argue with me and I called in mine to reason with her. The original cause of the argument was long since forgotten in the flood of Phyll's full fury about the Oxford Group, Frank Buchman and everyone connected with it. For six weeks the battle raged and for six weeks I held out, but in the end she got the better of me.

"The thing that gets me about you," she said one day, "is your sickly sweet voice. I wish you'd shake me or something."

My sickly sweet voice indeed! I felt my manhood had been challenged. I had wanted to shake her for days. I shook her.

Phyll burst into tears. That shook me! And as, day by day, she wept more and more, I felt that although I was sure deep inside me that what I had been learning was right, I just could not go on with the Group if it made my wife so unhappy.

I decided to have nothing more to do with them. My first loyalty, I reasoned, was to Phyll.

I visited John Roots once more. As we sat with pencil and paper, a thought came into my mind and I wrote it down.

"Morally and spiritually you will die."

"What came to you?" asked John.

"Nothing," I replied, and, crumpling the paper, threw it into the fire.

It was some years before I saw Roots or Buchman again.

XI

Phyll

Realising that Bunny's interest in the Oxford Group was serious, I became very concerned. As the days went by, my feeling against his new friends grew and grew. I hated them. I was overjoyed to pick up all kinds of unpleasant gossip which I passed on with relish to my husband and friends without ever checking the sources from which they came or knowing whether they were true or not.

The fact was, I was afraid of being shown up. I led a selfish and indulgent life smeared over with a thin layer of idealism and occasional good works. I felt I either had to admit that Bunny's friends were right and do something about it, which I had no intention of doing, or I had to prove that they were wrong to everyone I met, but most especially to myself.

When Bunny's interest increased every day, it made me very angry indeed. "For heaven's sake," I said, "I don't want to be married to a bloody saint."

When we were first married we would not fight openly. I had an explosive temper and Bunny followed a policy of appeasement–anything for a quiet life. To our friends we seemed a very happy couple. At parties I could turn on gobs of charm, but once the guests had gone and as soon as the front door was closed, oh brother!

I had things very much as I wanted them. Now that I found my chosen way of life threatened, I fought like a demon. I did not give a damn about the kind of world we lived in. That thousands of men were unemployed, that millions were hungry, that whole families lived in one room, even in our own country, did not really bother me. "Why don't you leave me alone," I said to Bunny. "I am perfectly happy as I am."

"Yes, I know," he replied, "but you are the only one who is!"

Finally I used a woman's best weapon, tears! Bunny, being tender-hearted, could not bear to see me sobbing. So once more I got my own way.

It was very nearly the end of our marriage.

CHAPTER FIVE

I

Bunny

WHEN I turned away from the Oxford Group, I remained loyal to them in my heart, but I had little contact with them. I once wrote an article about them for the *Daily Mail*. Once, too, John Roots came to see me and we went for a walk on Hampstead Heath. And in July 1937 I went on the invitation of a cousin of Phyll's to a Foyle's Literary Luncheon at which some Oxford Group people were to speak.

To my mind the luncheon was a quiet and decorous affair. Godfrey Winn was in the chair. Dr Buchman, if I remember rightly, was beside him, and lower down the table on Winn's right was Margaret Rawlings, the actress. Next to her was Tom Driberg, at that time writing the William Hickey column in the *Daily Express*. Loudon Hamilton, Buchman's earliest Oxford colleague, had been placed in that seat. He had received a message which turned out to be a false alarm, that he was wanted on the phone, and when he returned, found Mr Driberg in his place.

Sixteen or seventeen people spoke, among them a bishop, a general who trained race horses and a leader of the East London unemployed. The only name that registered with me was that of Austin Reed, the founder of the famous clothing store, perhaps because he bore my name! It was all in the best of taste. I remember a lanky Canadian singing a cowboy song. I was enjoying it very much, as were the hundreds of others who had paid to be present.

Then came the bombshell. Miss Rawlings arose to address the luncheon. It seemed to be a prepared speech, for she read it or at least constantly referred to notes. Whether someone had told her that there would be lurid public confessions, a rumour which had been current for some time, I do not know. All I do know is that Miss Rawlings said she was shocked by the Group's 'immodesty'. Exposure of the soul was, to her way of thinking, as indecent as undressing in Piccadilly. She spoke about the Japanese who built high walls round their homes so that they could enjoy the utmost privacy. I remember thinking at the time that the Japanese, who were then murdering and raping the Chinese in Manchuria, were odd exemplars for her to choose.

Imagine yourself at a quiet Kensington tea party when a little girl gets up, insults everybody and then sits down again. This was the effect of Miss Rawlings' speech. I was astonished. If the chairman had caught my eye at that moment I would have told the luncheon that if anybody had bared her soul it was Miss Rawlings. I might even have asked Miss Rawlings why if she felt it indecent to undress in Piccadilly, she so charmingly exposed so much of herself every night in her current play in a theatre not far from Piccadilly.

In the somewhat stunned atmosphere which followed this attack by Miss Rawlings, who was the Guest of Honour at the luncheon, Godfrey Winn, the Chairman, rose to draw the proceedings to a close. He was certainly placed in an embarrassing position, from which I felt he extricated himself with considerable *sang froid*. With the tact of a highly skilled diplomat he made a few well-chosen remarks and the luncheon was over. I went across to greet Dr Buchman as he made his way from the room. I greatly admired him at that moment. He gave no outward evidence, as he cheerfully returned my greeting, that he was a man who had just been hit violently below the belt.

That evening I left for Eastbourne where I was playing with the Davis Cup team against America in a friendly practice match to keep us in tune for the Davis Cup challenge round the following week. As I travelled down there in the train, I wondered if I should write to the press in answer to Miss Rawlings' attack. But I asked myself whether anyone, except the evening papers, would take an attack from her seriously.

Next morning it was clear that I was wrong. The press gave Miss Rawlings tremendous publicity, and few other speakers were even reported. Tom Driberg, who devoted his whole column to the occasion, modestly stated that he gave her "moral support". Miss Rawlings, perhaps fearing slander proceedings, wrote to the *Daily Sketch* some days later, saying she had not criticised anything said at the lunch or "even referred to the other speakers",* but this disclaimer never caught up with the initial sensation.

I wondered again whether I should write to the press, but decided I did not want to get involved. I did not realise then how closely mud will stick no matter by whom it is thrown. It was a lesson I was to learn at some cost in the years ahead.

II

It was 1938. Great Britain had for three years successfully defended the Davis Cup. I had reached the finals at Wimbledon again that year and was at that time ranked the number one player in the world.

And to Phyll and me a baby had been born.

It was during the first week of the championships at Wimbledon. Phyll had moved to the nursing home on the Wednesday night when her labour pains had started.

I had had a sleepless night. Phyll was in difficult labour.

I went to Wimbledon next day anxiously and hurried home after the day's play was over. The baby had not yet arrived.

The nurse called me up from the nursing home on Thursday night. The labour pains had stopped, she said. There was no need to worry. The baby could not arrive that night. Grateful for the information I slept soundly.

Again the next day I was at Wimbledon. Once more I called the nursing home on my return. Phyll was in labour again. They would let me know.

I waited anxiously. Phyll had been in the nursing home now for forty-eight hours. I did not know then what I learned later, that she had been in labour all that time. Something had gone wrong and there had been great anxiety. Phyll had told them to call me on Thursday night to say all was well so as to reassure me and make certain for the sake of my tennis that I had a good night's rest.

* Miss Foyle also issued a statement that "Miss Rawlings' remarks bore no relation to what was said at the luncheon, which was a reasonable and objective presentation of the case for moral and spiritual renewal at a time of world crisis." This was not reported in any of the papers which had printed the original report.

Now, not realising all Phyll had gone through, I sat waiting for the news of the baby's arrival. I sat by our window overlooking Hampstead Heath. To my right I could see London. There was St Paul's Cathedral, rising like a mother hen proudly watching over its innumerable progeny of chicks. It was one of those perfect English summer evenings. The sun was low in the sky, barred from view by a few high-flying cirrus clouds. Through the clouds came one golden shaft of the sun, pointing directly on London's West End.

The telephone rang with a message from the nursing home. The baby had arrived. It was a girl.

Putting down the telephone, I raced down to the nursing home by car. I crept into Phyll's room and found her lying half-asleep.

And then Jennifer was brought in. She had the largest blue eyes I had ever seen in any child. I looked at her in wonder.

I suppose most fathers have the same experience when they see their first child. I was awed at the majesty, the perfection and the sheer miracle of such a creation. From a tiny seed this little creature had been born with eyes that could see and a mind that could think – an intricate maze of nerves and blood vessels, veins and arteries, of hairs that miraculously grew in their predestined places, of teeth not yet grown but which in due course and in their appointed season would appear; a heart set in motion at birth and that, barring accidents, would continue faithfully to beat for perhaps the next eighty years; lungs also set in motion that also for eighty years would breathe in and expel the air that gave life to the body; a stomach, a labyrinth of intricate intestines which would dissolve the food brought to it by the mouth and play its appointed role as a sustainer of life.

I was too excited to sleep that night, and when the next afternoon I went down to Wimbledon to play on the centre court, I was weary as well as excited. My great hope was that the match might be short and that I might win in three sets. But I knew this was unlikely, and my hope was denied me. My opponent was Gene Mako, at that time one of the finest doubles players in the world and no slouch in a single. He won one of the first three sets, by which time I had little energy left. The only thing to do was to take a rest. I let the fourth set go and lost it to love.

In the fifth set I rallied my forces. I broke through his service and reached 5–3. Here I again rested, making no effort to win his service game and banking everything on holding my own service for the match. No one could have accused me of having a great service – I relied on my ground shots not only to break through my opponent's service but to hold my own – but on this occasion my gamble paid. I won the final set 6–4 and found myself for the ninth time in Wimbledon's last eight.

I cannot remember whom I played in the next round, but in the semi-final I played Henkel, who had beaten me 6–2, 6–2, 6–2 in the final of the French Championships. Now I beat him 6–2, 6–4, 6–0. In the final I met Don Budge, then at the height of his game.

As I left Wimbledon on the night before the final, I met a woman player who told me I could sleep well that night and enjoy the game the next day, as, of course, I had no hope of winning. I did not agree with this. On paper Budge was a much better player than I. But so was Vines when I played him in the Davis Cup in 1933 and beat him so easily. To accept defeat before a match started was, to my mind, a poor approach to the game, and my hope was that if I played above myself, I might win.

When the match started the next day, I felt happy. I knew in the warm-up that I was playing well, and I held my first service game to make the score 1–1. I had played Budge four times before and each time we had had a close and keenly fought match. This, I said to myself optimistically, was going to be another. But suddenly I found the man on the other side of the net was possessed. There was nothing he could do wrong. His service was fast and accurate. His ground shots, taken almost on the half volley, were clipping the side lines. He covered the net as if his arms were telescopes, and his smashing was devastating. I continued to play well, but he scored winners off my best shots, and often he had passed me almost before I had started for the net. There was nothing to do but wonder and smile.

I did not feel embarrassed for myself because you cannot do more than play as well as you can. But I was embarrassed for the crowd, many of whom I knew had been queuing all night to see us. They had come to see a match, and here was a massacre instead.

III

From 1–1 in the first set I did not win a game until Budge led 3–0 in the third. Then the storm seemed to be abating and a hope flickered in my heart. I knew it was impossible for any man to play indefinitely as brilliantly as Don had played. A memory came back to me – of big Bill Tilden playing little Henri Cochet on the centre court in 1927. Big Bill, striding the court like a colossus, was making Cochet look like a beginner from the parks. Devastating serves shook Cochet's racquet almost out of his hand. Returns of Cochet's service left him shaking his head in wonder. Big Bill led 6–2, 6–1, 5–1 with his own serve to follow. One waited for the 'coup de grace'. It never came. Cochet miraculously won the next sixteen points to reach 5-all and went on to win in the fifth set. Bill was like a wounded lion, shorn of his power.

Could I, I wondered, produce the same miracle? Would Budge become human? Could I possibly wrest the third set from him and win the last two?

If there had been any hope of such a thing happening, it quickly faded. It rained. I went into the dressing rooms, ultimately coming out to a slippery court for an anticlimax that gave Don the third set 6–3.

I have a photograph of Don shaking hands with me at the end of the match. His expression is not that of a triumphant player who has just won his second Wimbledon. He looks worried. "Gee, Bunny," he is saying, "what was wrong with your game? You were way off your form." The remark was typical of Don's good heart. But he was wrong, I had been playing my best. But my best had not been good enough. Nor, I believe, on that day, would the best of anyone, past, present or to come, have been good enough. Don Budge is, to my mind, the greatest of them all; and if it was a poor match, as a match, the crowd were privileged to watch one of the greatest exhibitions of lawn tennis skill ever seen.

IV

All players will agree there is no tournament experience to equal the championships at Wimbledon. The vast attendance, the excitement of the crowd, the perfection of the conditions, the efficiency of the management, all combine to lift it above any other tournament or championship in the world.

For me it held a magic which was almost too nerve-racking. As a child, Wimbledon seemed a dream far beyond any ability of mine to reach.

When at last I did come to play there myself, it was always a time of high excitement when the first day of Wimbledon dawned and when each day I drove–or was driven by Phyll–from our Hampstead home, trying to arrive at Wimbledon as nearly as possible at the moment when I would need to change and be ready for my match. This was never easy and often there were the difficult minutes or hours of waiting. Fortunately I was, in those days, a member, and could relax in the members' lounge. But if I wanted a cup of tea I had to leave the centre-court building and go over to the competitors' lounge. Immediately I ran into the hazard of the autograph hunters who would appear from nowhere and buzz around like a swarm of bees, asking for autographs on backs of envelopes, bus tickets, or any bits of paper that happened to be handy.

Then at last came the moment when I had to change for my match. When I was due to play on the centre court, I could hear the applause in the dressing rooms and could sometimes gather from its rise and fall the situation of the match in progress. Overhead there was often a sound of tapping as someone in the committee box above registered his applause by tapping his walking stick or umbrella on the committee-box floor.

People talk of centre-court nerves. They did not affect me. I was no more nervous playing on the centre court than on any other. Rather the reverse. On the centre court you felt you had arrived, you were there. There was no greater court on

94

which to play a match. You were, for that moment, the focus of the world's tennis attention. I found this not frightening, but exhilarating.

But nerves were there all the same. There must be some form of tension if you are going to play your best. It was not the moments before a match I found most difficult, even though tension at that time was at its height. It was the mornings and evenings before and after matches. How to occupy myself without getting tired? This question of tiredness was always a preoccupation—how to preserve my limited and somewhat uncertain energies, how to keep my mind off the game when not actually playing? Sometimes physically I seemed to go into a trough and be deprived of all energy. I did not discover until a few years later when I was in the Army that I suffer from periodic bouts of jaundice brought on by a congenital defect of my liver. Perhaps it was as well I did not know this in my playing days. Would I have felt justified in representing my country in the Davis Cup? However, it turned out that although I suffered bouts of weakness both at Wimbledon and in the French championships, I recollect no period when I suffered from this in my Davis Cup matches.

v

I have written of Wimbledon. What of the other great lawn-tennis championships of the world?

After I got married I travelled very little, and, with rare exceptions, played only in the summer months. I once played in Australia. The championships were in Adelaide and the day I was beaten it was very hot. It was 105° in the shade. I played a man from Brisbane. I won the first two sets. Then my opponent took his sweater off!

I played in the American championships three times, but never very much enjoyed them. This was no fault of America or of American hospitality. Forest Hills, for me, was too hot and humid. The temperature was often in the nineties and the courts, during the years I played there, had been damaged by leather-jackets and consisted more of plantains than grass. Big serves were at a premium; ground strokes at a discount. I

only played there once after my marriage in 1931. It was there
that I first wore shorts.

The day was extremely hot, 92° in the shade with high
humidity.

I had often debated in my mind the question of shorts for
tennis. The idea first came to me when I was playing in Boston
in 1928. There too the heat and humidity were intense. Trousers
got soaked through and it seemed to me weighed a ton. Why,
I asked myself, carry all that additional weight flapping round
your legs? Wasn't it ridiculous to play a strenuous, fast-moving
game in trousers? I tried to visualise rugger, soccer and hockey
being played in trousers. The thought was ridiculous. It seemed
to me equally ridiculous to play tennis in trousers. It was simply
an old tradition harking back to the less strenuous days when
tennis was mainly a garden-party game.

Over the following years the thought of wearing shorts
rummaged around in my mind. I talked it over with my friends.
Many thought it was a good idea. I realised it just needed
someone to take the first step, wear shorts, and see what
happened.

At Forest Hills in 1932 I bought a pair of shorts and put them
on. There was quite a sensation. The press naturally made the
most of it. What the so-and-so, they wrote, does Austin think
he's doing? But the heavens did not fall, the stands did not
collapse, nor was there any official remonstration. I decided
to keep on wearing them.

"Aha," said some people, "you are prepared to wear shorts
in America, but you won't have the guts to wear them in
Europe."

I did not play in Europe until the following winter when
I went down to the South of France and played at Beaulieu
and Monte Carlo. I had some special shorts made by my
tailor, modelled on what was then worn on the rugby field. I
put them on. Again the heavens remained stable and players
and public seemed to accept them without undue astonishment.

However, it had its humorous side. As I was leaving my
hotel one morning to play my match, wearing an overcoat with
my bare legs protruding beneath, a young hotel porter came

7(a). Austin and Borotra

7(b). Perry and Austin

8(a). Budge and
Austin

8(b). Austin *v.*
Budge, Final,
Wimbledon 1938

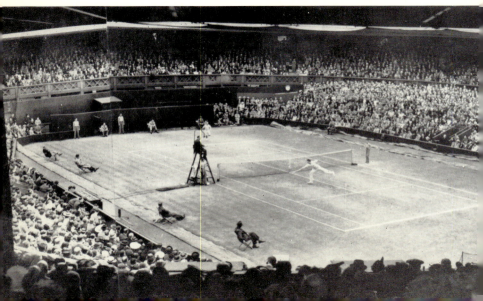

up to me anxiously. "Excuse me, Mr Austin," he said, "I think you've forgotten your trousers."

So far, so good, but "Aha" said some people again, "you are prepared to wear shorts in the South of France, but you won't have the guts to wear them at Wimbledon." That of course was the test. Wimbledon had always been, and still is, strict about players' clothes. For one thing they have to be white. An American who had once appeared in striped trousers had been politely requested not to appear again in the offending things.

However, fashions had been changing over the years. Women's dresses had vastly abbreviated in length and even stockings had been dispensed with. I hoped that I might appear at Wimbledon in shorts without too much fuss.

And so it happened. I appeared in shorts, joined now by three others who had followed my example. No explosion took place. The decorous stands at Wimbledon remained unshaken. No complaints were received from the committee. Shorts, as far as I was concerned, had come to stay.

After that, more and more players began to wear them, though many an old die-hard stuck to long trousers and even today at Wimbledon the more ancient veterans stick to the more ancient garb. But apart from these, shorts are today universally worn for tennis and the days of long trousers for men are almost as archaic as the days when women played in long dresses with long sleeves and starched collars and cuffs.

I played in the French championships many times and they were always most enjoyable. Paris is at its best in May when the championships are played. The chestnut trees are in blossom and dinners in the cool of the evening at the restaurants in the Bois de Boulogne are memories never to be forgotten.

It was often as hot in Paris as in Forest Hills, but it did not affect me in the same way. It was 95° when, in the last eight in 1935, I played Roderick Menzel, the champion of Czechoslovakia. The first three sets were a titanic struggle and lasted for two hours. We were both tired when we went in for the ten-minute rest after the third set–those ten minutes when you dash off the court, take off your wet clothes, dash under a shower, put on dry clothes, and dash back onto court again, slightly more exhausted than you were before! And because of our exhaustion and the heat, Menzel and I thought it a good idea to take a little stimulant on the court with us. Menzel took on some brandy and I took on some gin.

When the match re-started Menzel jumped into a lead of 4–1, and as he was also leading by two sets to one, he felt that that was the psychological moment to drink his brandy; it would give him the extra zip he needed to carry him through to victory. And so he went up to the umpire's chair and drank his brandy; and then, feeling rather thirsty, he thought he would have a sip of water. But unfortunately what he thought was water was my gin. And my gin got together with his brandy – and I won the match!

Next day Menzel was in bed with two doctors in attendance. I was on court in the semi-final against Gottfried von Cramm who beat me in another five-set match.

During my match against Menzel, Phyll sat watching in the stands with a young Czech diplomat whom I had met some years before in Prague. None of us could have guessed on that cloudless summer's day in Paris that this gay light-hearted son of the great founder of his country was later as its Foreign Minister to meet such a tragic end. His name was Jan Masaryk.

VI

Out of the clear blue sky after that successful Wimbledon came the world-shaking Munich crisis. Trenches were being dug in the London parks, the few available anti-aircraft guns were taking up their positions and confused ARP wardens were issuing gas masks.

The full impact of the crisis came home to me when, on the morning of September 11, 1938, a warden called with gas masks for us. He said our baby would have to have a gas proof tent. Suddenly I realised that my forebodings of six years earlier had come true. And what had I done about it? I had been brought in touch with an answer – and had turned away, betraying the best in myself, betraying my wife and betraying my fellow men. For I believe that if the countless Englishmen like myself who had met the Group in the early 'thirties, had wholeheartedly accepted its challenge, there could have been such a stiffening of morale that Hitler would never have doubted our willingness to fight. As it was, we in Britain had drifted towards war unwilling to face what Germany was doing, although it was spelt out for us in *Mein Kampf*.

When I turned away from the Group, I turned away from reality. I put my head in the sand and said, "It isn't going to happen." And not only in public affairs. For when Phyll had said to me, "I don't want to live with a bloody saint," I thought to myself that I could oblige her in that, at least. And before long, I was behaving in a way which, but for the grace of God, would have wrecked our marriage. By this Munich time, Phyll had lived to regret her words; but it was only now that I saw the full cost of my wrong decision.

On that September day when the warden spoke of Jennifer's gas-proof tent, the two words 'Oxford Group' lit up in my mind like neon lights. I scarcely hesitated. I rang up their head-quarters and found that John Roots was in London. I went down that evening finally to throw in my fortune with him and his friends.

As we sat listening together, the thought came: "You shall have life . . ." I remembered with a jolt the words which had come to me last time we had listened together: "Morally and spiritually you will die." I had thrown the paper in the fire, but the words had come true.

In the uneasy years that had followed my decision to turn away from the Group, Phyll had often said that if I ever wanted to 'join' the Group, she would not stop me again. But when she found I had done so, the old fury against the Group returned. And once again I found myself violently attacked.

But this time I had learnt my lesson. I believed that if I stood firm, I would not only find a new life for myself, but for my wife, and that the day would not be far off when my wife would be standing by my side. This was an act of faith. There was no indication that such an outcome was likely. Phyll remained obdurate in her antagonism. And if anyone connected with the Group called at our home, it was not long before they were out on their ear.

VII

My identification with the Group meant for me a simple but radical change. I began to take Christ's absolute standards of honesty, purity, unselfishness and love seriously.

Some people think it arrogant to aim at the absolute. But Professor William Hocking, the distinguished American philosopher, writes: "It is a mark of the shallowness of Western life that it should be thought a conceit to recognise an absolute and a humility to consider all standards relative, when it is precisely the opposite. It is only the absolute that rebukes our pride."

I decided that I would turn to God for direction in everything—not just in emergencies or on special occasions, but every day and many times a day. I did not think—nor do I think now—that every thought which comes in a time of listening is from God; but I know that I am more likely to receive the guidance which Jesus promised to us if I give time every day to listen for it, than if I do not. St Francis of Sales said that half an hour's listening each day is a basic minimum, except when you are exceptionally busy, when a full hour is necessary. The saintly Père Gratry added: "God does not stop talking to us any more than the sun stops shining. When shall we listen to Him? In the morning before the distractions and activity of a busy day. How? You write it down. Write it down so that you may preserve the Spirit in you and keep His words." This is the practice which I adopted.

I did not accept thoughts without question. I learnt to check them against my knowledge of God's will as revealed in the New Testament—admittedly at that time a slender knowledge. I also checked them against the four absolute moral standards—and against the wisdom of friends whom I trusted.

VIII

My identification with the Group also meant that I took a different attitude to the crisis. Up to this time my thought had been "How does the crisis affect me?" Now it became "How can I affect the crisis?" Or, more realistically, "How can the force of Moral Re-Armament affect the crisis?"

With the wisdom of hindsight, one can see that that effect was drastically insufficient, though I still believe, as I have said, that an even greater response, especially in Britain, might have turned the tide. As it was, the monstrous Nazi machine ground on and ultimately the world was engulfed in the horror of increasing Jewish persecutions, the rape of Poland, the conquest of France, the bombing of Britain, the invasion of Russia.

But, in 1938, while there was life, there was hope. I found that Buchman had, in the years since I had last seen him, built up a formidable force. His successful intervention in Scandinavia where, according to Oslo's heroic Bishop Berggrav, he had initiated "the greatest spiritual movement since the Reformation", had set on foot a powerful movement towards unity among the smaller nations of Europe.

Party leaders in Norway, among them J. L. Mowinckel, the former Prime Minister and originator of the Organisation of Oslo States, and C. J. Hambro,* had been reconciled, and tensions had been eased between Norway and Denmark.

The Spectator also noted the co-operation between Hambro and Foreign Minister Holsti of Finland, as due to Buchman's work, and described both as "transparently honest men".

Queen Wilhelmina of the Netherlands, in initiating Moral Re-Armament in Holland, described it as "a campaign against defeatism".

The Dutch Foreign Minister, Dr Patijn, settled a long-standing dispute with Belgium on the basis of Group principles.

The *Daily Telegraph* reported that General Ludendorff's paper was alarmed at the "Group's sweet poison seeping across the frontier" and Group literature was banned in Germany. It was an alarm shared by the Gestapo for in 1939 its head office was preparing its 126-page report entitled *Die Oxfordgruppenbewegung*, which described Moral Re-Armament as opposing "the Cross of the Swastika with the Cross of Christ" and "uncompromisingly taking a frontal position against National Socialism."

On the day before I saw Roots, a letter appeared in *The Times* headed, "Moral Re-Armament–The Need of the Day". It was

* President of the League of Nations Assembly and for many years President of the Norwegian Parliament.

signed by sixteen of the most distinguished men in Britain, including leaders of all three Services, as well as scientists, lawyers, educationalists and a former Prime Minister. Twenty top leaders of the Labour movement wrote a letter of support, and the Earl of Athlone, in a further letter, stated that "the choice is between Moral Re-Armament and national decay".

Almost exactly a year later a staff writer of *The Saturday Evening Post* would write, "It is probably true that as much as any agency, Moral Re-Armament has advanced the programme of England's military preparedness on the non-military side. To it is due an important part of the credit for the fact that, since Munich, British morale has improved at least as fast as Britain's fighting machine."

Dr Buchman himself was, at the time I re-visited Roots in London, leading the first international assembly of Moral Re-Armament at Interlaken. A few days later he addressed League of Nations delegates from 53 nations in Geneva, and Jean Martin, the editor of the *Journal de Genève*, sent a special MRA supplement of his paper to the principal editors of Europe. He wrote, "Whatever happens in Europe, Moral Re-Armament remains the only answer to recurrent crisis and the one foundation for reconciliation and permanent peace."

IX

My immediate part in this campaign was to mobilise the backing of the world of sport. Thirty-five of Britain's best-known sportsmen joined with me in a call for Moral Re-Armament through sport. We followed up this appeal by speaking to large sporting crowds.

One day, for example, I went to see my old friend, George Allison, the great manager of the Arsenal Football Club. George had taken me under his wing in the early 'thirties and I had gone out to the Arsenal ground for training. Tom Whittaker was the trainer at that time and later took up duties with the Davis Cup team. Tom was a remarkable man. "I have 33 men to look after at the Arsenal," he once told me, "and I have to treat them 33 different ways." Tom was both tough and extremely sensitive with a deep understanding of men. But he found tennis too exciting for him. I discovered him once in the dressing room when Fred Perry was playing a Davis Cup match on the centre court. "Tom, why aren't you out there rooting for Fred?" I asked him. He shook his head. "You know," he replied, "I have never left the field when Arsenal were playing – not in a League match, not in a Cup final. But," and he shook his head again, "I can't watch this game. It's too exciting for me!"

My object in seeing George Allison was to ask him if he would like to put something about MRA in one of his football programmes. While George was pondering this, the thought came into my head to ask him if one Saturday I could speak to the crowds. Instantly he responded. "We're away next Saturday," he said, "but I can certainly arrange it for Saturday week."

On Saturday week I appeared at the Arsenal football stadium with George Eyston, the racing motorist who at that time held the land speed record. A microphone was set up on the field and George Allison introduced us. Fifty-eight thousand people, there to watch Arsenal play Chelsea, listened quiet as mice. Pictures of this event appeared widely not only in Britain but across the world.

Then the thought occurred to me that I should write a book. I talked it over with Frank Buchman. He felt the most valuable thing I could do would be to collect the recent statements about Moral Re-Armament and publish them as a 'white paper'. With the help of friends the statements were collected, I wrote a forward and the book was published. The book was conceived on December 1; it was printed and on the book stalls on December 14. I was used to moving with speed on a tennis court; I was not used to moving with this speed off it! The book sold rapidly. It was advertised on ten thousand posters up and down the country, generously given by the advertising agencies. The first edition of 250,000 soon sold out. The second quarter of a million copies were printed.

The tempo of my life was completely changed. I had been used to an early bed and to get up about 7.45, have an 8.30 breakfast and go off to the City – or in recent years to the room where I was writing a novel.

Now I found myself getting up at 6. At 6 in winter I found it was dark. It seemed to me like getting up in the middle of the night. During these days there was a running MRA conference at Eastbourne and I spent a lot of time there. The first meeting of the day was at 7.30. It seemed an impossibly early hour to me, especially as I did not often get to bed before midnight. One morning I tottered into the room where the 7.30 meeting was being held. Frank Buchman looked at me with a twinkle. "I'm not going to feel sorry for you!" he said.

I certainly felt sorry for myself! And I acquired a heightened respect for the men and women with whom I was working. They worked these long hours and they worked without pay. If you had asked them how much money they had, many of them would have replied with a sum varying between nothing and a pound. They seldom had more than just enough to cover their immediate needs. They gave without thought of reward – and have continued to do so for the rest of their lives. Yet they were people who could have commanded large salaries in any business or profession.

I was brought up against a tremendous challenge. My life up till now had been comfortably soft and easy. Certainly tennis had made great demands. It meant strict training. It meant disciplined hours. I drank very little and smoked only three cigarettes a day, but this was only for a limited period of time. The tension eased for me very often. But this new life I had adopted was nonstop. Sometimes it meant working round the clock. It meant a willingness to be on the give all day and night. I learned that day and night were of little difference to Frank Buchman. He was available at all hours to meet any need that might arise.

Phyll could not understand all this. It did not at all meet with her approval and she did everything in her power to prevent me from continuing my work.

x

Phyll
Bunny has written about my fury. To use an old cliché, it knew no bounds. One morning Bunny told me he was going to Eastbourne for the weekend to attend a big conference. I was furious with him. Nevertheless, he went. I decided to go down and get him back.

CHAPTER FIVE

On the Saturday I took the train to Eastbourne. I walked into the hotel where I knew he was staying. I looked in the lounge but he was not there. A little grey-haired woman of perhaps sixty got up from a group of people sitting by a window. She came towards me and said, "Are you looking for someone?"

"Indeed I am," I replied. "I am looking for my husband, Bunny Austin."

She held out her hand. "My name is Annie Jaeger," she said. "Why don't we sit down together and wait till he comes in."

I had intended to be as rude as I possibly could to anyone I met in MRA. But there was something in this woman's face which was so warm and welcoming and genuine that, in spite of myself, I sat down with her. She was quite different from all my glamorous theatre friends. She had on a simple blue suit, no make-up and she talked with a strong North-country accent. Later I learned that she was a widow who had kept a little hat shop in the poor part of Stockport. She had sold everything for £40 and gone 'on the road' with the Group.

Mrs Jaeger asked me if she could help me. I said she most certainly could and I poured out my story. I told her how angry I was that Bunny had gone away for the weekend. She said, "Well, I quite understand. Homes are so important. No nation can survive if the home life breaks up."

"Exactly," I agreed. "That is why I am so determined that Bunny should not go travelling around. He should stay at home with me."

She looked at me with much amusement and said, "Of course, the trouble in the homes, my dear, is so often the women. They are so selfish."

I wanted to be angry but somehow I could not be. I felt that she was my friend, that she really cared. I had many friends but with some of them I was never quite sure how genuine their friendship was. They probably felt the same about me. In my world there was a lot of kissing and 'darlings', but plenty of back-biting and jealousy, too, and some friendships depended on whether one was successful or not. I felt instinctively that Mrs Jaeger could know all the worst about me and it would make no difference to our friendship.

I do not pretend that I was different from then on. I was not.

105

But that meeting affected me profoundly. Mrs Jaeger had a radiance that did not come out of a paint box. I found myself wanting more than almost anything the quality and peace that I had seen in her face.

XI

Bunny

One thing that Phyll had always said in her arguments against MRA, was that they would want me to go to America. This I had pooh-poohed. "Nonsense," I would say, "they do not want to divide husband and wife. They want to unite them."

In March of 1939 I went down one morning to the headquarters of MRA and Phyll came with me. It was a Thursday. As we were talking to one of my friends, he said, "I hoped we would see you today. We wondered if you would feel it right to come to America with us on Saturday?"

Phyll's reaction can be imagined. Wasn't this exactly what she had always said? Hadn't she told me?

We had an uncomfortable drive home that morning.

It was a shock to me. I did not know at all what to do or what to say. But I did not intend to be guided by Phyll's anger. On the other hand I did not want to ignore it.

I spent a sleepless night, tossing and turning, trying to figure out what I should do. Somewhat haggard I tottered out of bed in the early dawn and tried to get guidance. Nothing happened. I rang up a friend and told him my dilemma. "Have you prayed?" he asked. I had not. "Well, pray," he said. I did so.

With clear illumination I had the thought that it was right to go to America, not on that Saturday but three weeks later, and that I should devote those three weeks to Phyll.

I sprang upstairs and bounced into our bedroom. "I know what's right," I announced.

"I can see you do," said Phyll. "You look quite different. What is it?"

Phyll was quite satisfied. We had many happy days together and when the time came for me to leave for America, she sent me on my way with a cheerful goodbye.

CHAPTER SIX

I

Bunny

IT was a busy time in America. We were interviewed by the press. I spoke over the radio many times, once coast-to-coast with Mrs James Roosevelt, the President's gracious mother. We spoke at luncheons and formal and informal gatherings. I travelled to Canada, speaking at a luncheon in Montreal and later over a national radio hook-up. I was one of many speakers at a meeting in Madison Square Gardens, New York. In June I was in Washington to speak with Frank Buchman at the National Press Club and later to a packed audience in Constitution Hall.

Before this last occasion I was invited with a friend to speak to the Sixth Form and the masters of Groton School, sometimes called the Eton of America.

Afterwards the headmaster, Mr Endicott Peabody, told us that he wanted to inform a former pupil of his of "the great healing that Moral Re-Armament was bringing to the nations". He wrote the letter, placed it in an envelope and handed it to us. It was addressed to Franklin Delano Roosevelt, President of the United States.

That night my friend and I travelled down to Washington. On the train we met John Roosevelt, the President's youngest son. He very kindly promised to deliver the letter to his father, with whom, he told us, he would be having breakfast the following morning.

We went to the Mayflower Hotel to await word from the President. We waited all through the day and through the following morning. In the afternoon I went to the telephone and called the White House. I asked to speak to the President.

A feminine voice came over the phone. It was Missy Le-Hand, the President's secretary. She asked me to hold the line. A moment later she was back again. The President would be pleased to see us. Would we go round immediately to the

White House? We jumped into a taxi and were soon being ushered into the famous oval room.

All the world knows that Mr Roosevelt was smitten in young manhood by polio. His legs were paralysed, and he could only stand with help. But as we entered the room and he reached out his hand to shake ours, he gave every impression that he was rising from his chair. "Why," he said to me, "I would have recognised you anywhere from your photographs." Here was the famous Roosevelt charm in action.

I introduced my friend as a man who played a game called cricket.

"Cricket!" exclaimed the President, "I used to play a lot of country house cricket in England. I know the game well. Sit down."

The preliminaries over, an atmosphere of total cordiality reigned.

Soon we were launched on the subject we had come to talk about. "I want you to know," said the President, "that though some at one time may have laughed at MRA, today it commands great respect." He asked us about its reception in different parts of the world and then enquired what he could do for us.

We told him about the successful meeting we had just held in Madison Square Gardens in New York. Many people felt, I told him, that the only thing missing was a message from the President. We were about to hold a meeting in Constitution Hall, Washington. Would he send a message to that?

The President instantly agreed. "Fine," he said. "I'll have my secretary get a message ready for you right away." He pressed his bell. Then, stretching out his hand to say good-bye, he once more gave the impression of rising from his seat.

"The underlying strength of the world," ran the President's message, "must consist in the moral fibre of her citizens. A programme of moral re-armament for the world cannot fail, therefore, to lessen the danger of armed conflict. Such moral re-armament to be most highly effective must receive support on a world-wide basis."

The message was read out to a packed audience in the

Constitution Hall in the flat Mid-Western voice of a Senator from Missouri. His name was Harry S. Truman.

II

Phyll

For a week or two after Bunny's return from America things went quite smoothly. Then one day when he was out, the phone rang and a woman's voice said, "Your husband has written to me saying that he is going back to America shortly and therefore cannot speak at the World Youth Congress to which I had invited him. Could you please tell me when . . ." I slammed down the receiver.

Bunny had never mentioned going back to America to me – it couldn't be true! I was beside myself with rage. I waited for him to return.

Our house in Downshire Hill was old and a little rickety. Everything shook that night as I rampaged around. He let me finish my tirade and then said, "Yes, it is true. I am going back. There will be a meeting in the Hollywood Bowl. Why don't you come with me?" He did not in any way insist. He simply left me to decide for myself. I was very much torn. The idea of going back to Hollywood appealed to me very much. But I did not want to do anything that would please anyone in Moral Re-Armament.

After many sleepless nights and plenty of fireworks I decided to phone a friend of mine, an eminent doctor to whom I had poured out my woes and whose opinion I respected. I thought he would say "Don't you budge." What he actually said was, "Yes, if your husband is going I think you should go too. Your place is by his side."

So having refused to meet or talk with any of the people Bunny was working with, I found myself on a boat going to America with half a dozen of them. At home I could always throw them out of the house. I could not very well throw them over the side of the boat. So I decided to be frigidly polite and keep myself to myself as much as possible. But we had meals together and very reluctantly I realised that I rather liked them. One was a minister of a church, another an M.P. There

109

was a socialist and an industrialist. They were genuine and sincere. They reminded me very much of my meeting with Annie Jaeger. I found myself beginning to relax and enjoy myself.

In New York we took a train to Los Angeles. A few days later I found myself sitting on the platform of the Hollywood Bowl.

It was an amazing sight. All the twenty thousand seats were taken. Another ten thousand were jammed into the standing room at the back. The newspapers reported the next day that there were another fifteen thousand who could not get in. The *Los Angeles Times* wrote, "They came in limousines, they came in jalopies that barely chugged along the traffic-laden roads. They came on foot, in wheelchairs, buses, taxi-cabs. One and all they came marvelling."

I was one of those who marvelled. It was quite different from anything I had expected. It seemed to me that every country was represented on the platform. And as I listened I found myself fascinated by what I was hearing. When Bunny had talked about changing the world I thought he was crazy. What could he do, or anyone, for that matter? I thought of Moral Re-Armament as a small movement. I had listened to people calling them cranks and crooks because I had wanted to think that that was what they were. That night in the Bowl I knew that they were none of those things. I had to admit that, uncomfortable as it might be, they spoke the truth. Of course you could not create a new society unless you could create new men and women. You could never make a good omelette with bad eggs.

I began to realise that I was the bad egg in the omelette. I had talked very big but lived so very small. I was appalled at many things which were taking place in the world, especially at what was happening to the Jews in Germany. I discussed the problems of the world but I was far too lazy and selfish to do anything about them. I wanted peace but I lived war with my husband and my mother and with anyone who crossed my will.

I left that meeting very thoughtful indeed.

III

Phyll
Up to the time of that meeting in the Hollywood Bowl I was
an atheist. Any mention of God or religion gave me the willies.
I thought it was a prop for the weak. I hated piosity and still do.
My family were not Orthodox Jews and so I grew up without
a faith, though Father's hero, he always said, was Jesus Christ.
I went to Church when I was at boarding school but it had no
effect on me. And although I was baptised in order to be able
to get married in church, I became a Christian in name only.

During the days in California we were staying with friends
and after the Hollywood Bowl meeting I sat on the porch and
talked far into the night. Bunny had gone to bed but Jim
Newton, the friend he had met with Frank Buchman in
London, stayed up and talked to me.

Jim had been a brilliant young business executive, the right-
hand man of Harvey Firestone, and a close friend of Thomas
Edison.

No longer belligerent, I found myself asking him questions.
I could not deny that what I had heard that night was true.
But this business of listening to God – I could not possibly
accept that. I did not believe there was a God, so how on earth
could I listen to someone or something which did not exist?

Jim spoke of Thomas Edison and his great discovery of
electric light. If people had been told beforehand that there
was a power that could make this light they would not have
believed it. But Edison made an experiment. It worked. Now
we had electric light in almost every home. "Maybe," said Jim,
"there is a power, the Supreme Good or God, to which you
could tune in and listen and which could illuminate your heart
and mind. There is," he went on, "a built-in mechanism in
every man and woman, a small voice which tells us the difference between right and wrong, good and evil, if we will listen.
We try to silence it. Many of us succeed in doing so. But it is
there just the same."

"I can talk to you for hours," he added, "but I can't prove
it to you. Like Thomas Edison, you must make your own
experiment and find out for yourself if it is true."

III

"No," I replied adamantly, "I can't do that."

"Why not?"

"Because it's dangerous."

"Then may I ask you a question?"

"Certainly."

"What are you guided by?"

I thought for some time and then said, "Ambition, I suppose, and fear a good deal of the time."

"Aren't those things more dangerous than being guided by God?"

"I suppose so," I admitted. "But surely you might do crazy things and say it was God who told you to do them. Many people have."

"Yes, of course they have," he replied. "But that doesn't mean the real thing doesn't exist. You can check the thoughts which come to you by four absolute moral standards. If they are absolutely honest, pure, unselfish and loving then it is safe to carry them out. But if there is any doubt it may be wise to talk them over with friends whose judgment you respect."

I had many arguments. "What is right for one civilisation or one country might not be right for another," I said.

"A yard remains a yard in Britain or Timbuctoo," he answered. "I have talked with men and women from many countries and backgrounds. It is astonishing to find that eternal values are the same in every language."

This business of listening, he said, is the factor missing in our modern society. Some of us talk to God. We ask Him to give us this and that, but we never listen or meditate on what He wants us to do.

He quoted Abraham Lincoln, "I have so many evidences of God's direction that I am satisfied that when the Almighty wants me to do or not to do any particular thing, he finds a way of letting me know it." He spoke of Moses, who argued and made all manner of excuses why he should not do what God was asking of him. But when he listened and obeyed he led the children of Israel out of captivity and away from the tyranny of Pharoah's Egypt.

I was very thoughtful. I thought of my own people, my own relations fleeing from Hitler's Germany. If only, I thought,

THAT ESKIMO'S SNOW-SHOE WHICH MR AUSTIN IS USING AS A RACKET

— HAS BEEN STANDING ON ONE LEG IN THE FROZEN NORTH EVER SINCE LAST MONDAY WEEK WAITING FOR AUSTIN TO BE BEATEN —

MR AUSTIN HAS GOT THE LIMIT — AND —

— SOMEWHERE IN THE FROZEN NORTH A LAPLANDER IS WALKING ABOUT WITH ONE SNOW-SHOE BECAUSE MR AUSTIN IS PLAYING AT WIMBLEDON WITH THE OTHER.

Cartoon by Tom Webster

there were a way to stop this insane cruelty. If only our daughter, still a small baby at that time, could grow up in a world where horrors of that kind would no longer exist.

"Why not try to make that experiment," I heard Jim saying. "Tell Bunny tomorrow morning that you would just like to try. You can't lose. If it works, fine. If it doesn't, you can always go on as you are.

"Good night," he said, and left me.

The next morning I made the experiment with Bunny. Clear thoughts came into my mind. "You have lied your way out of all the wrong things you have done. You have hated your mother. You have been a rotten daughter and you need to apologise for it. It is no good your screaming against injustice and cruelty. If you want to put right what is wrong in the world the best place to start is with yourself."

"Well," Bunny said, "did you get anything?"

"Of course not," I replied. "It's a lot of nonsense. It doesn't work."

IV

Although I tried to forget those thoughts I could not get them out of my mind. I knew perfectly well that they were not nonsense. I knew they were uncomfortably true.

I began to do a lot of thinking. Of course I wanted peace in the world. Every sane person does. But most of us, I realised, simply wanted peace in order to continue our own private wars or private ways. I thought of the big speeches made about brotherhood and humanity; of the phoney idealism of myself and so many of my friends. There was no relation between the way we talked and the way we lived.

An actor I knew would practically weep at any kind of social injustice but was the most cruel father and husband it was possible to meet. A statesman who was trying to make peace between nations had not spoken to his own brother for two years. It did not make sense.

I realised that if I meant what I said, if I really wanted to find the way to unite class and class, race and race, nation and nation, it was hypocritical unless I was willing to be united with my own mother. I had made an experiment. I knew I should follow it through.

For several weeks I refused to do this. But one morning soon after I returned to England I finally decided to go and have an honest talk with my mother. I found her in her room, sitting as she always did, bolt upright in her chair. My heart quailed. But I plucked up my courage. I told her what a liar I had been and how sorry I was that I had been such a rotten daughter, often blaming her when I had been so wrong myself.

The wall that had always been between us disappeared. For the first time I could talk to her without fear. A large block of ice melted in my heart and I was able to love and understand her as I had always wanted to do.

It was a first step in a new adventure of faith.

v

Mary was our cook-housekeeper, a gallery first-nighter, a great theatre fan. When she read in the newspapers about our getting married she wrote and asked if she could come and look after us as a cook-housekeeper. We interviewed her and felt she was just the person we needed. She turned out to be the proverbial treasure. She came from Yorkshire, and she had the wonderful down-to-earth, rugged qualities of that part of Britain. She became our devoted friend. Goodness knows what we should have done without her.

Often she would leave home about 5.30 a.m. to put down her stool in a queue outside a theatre before a first night and would return in time to cook us our breakfast. She would bring us back all the gossip. "*They* say it will be a flop" or "*They* say we will give her an ovation. She deserves a success." When we used to ask who '*they*' were it was just '*them*', and '*they*' knew.

We would find her in the kitchen with her feet up, reading Shaw and Shakespeare. On the walls of her bedroom were signed photos of all the stars. And she loved meeting all the theatre friends who came to our flat.

After coming to be with us she also became a tennis fan, and during Wimbledon and the Davis Cup she would do everything for Bunny except hit the ball over the net.

When Bunny went to play the Davis Cup matches in Paris we invited Mary to come with us. She was very hesitant at first to leave England. She had never been abroad. However, we finally persuaded her and she not only saw the tennis, but more museums, art galleries and historical monuments in three days than I am sure most Parisians have seen in a lifetime. After seeing Napoleon's Tomb in Les Invalides she said, "I stood there looking at it and thought, 'Good 'eavens, all that on top of that little man!'" She also said, "I walked down the Champs Aleeses in me black satin dress, but I felt very lonely without King George." She enjoyed her trip, but she was greatly relieved when she eventually set foot again on British soil at Dover.

Mary had been one of fourteen servants in a large country house in Yorkshire and had also been in service in many big homes in London. She lost most of her friends in service when she came to us because, as she put it, "Now I am only a single."

Our first dinner party just after we were married consisted of G. B. Stern, the authoress, John Drinkwater, the poet, and Eddie Marsh, who had been Private Secretary to Winston Churchill. We wanted to make a good impression. The table looked lovely and all was well with the soup. We waited for the next course but nothing happened. It seemed hours to me. Finally Mary arrived with a very wild look in her eye and a very strange concoction on the dish. Afterwards she told us that in bringing it in on a three-tiered tray the whole thing had tipped up and her beautifully arranged platter had spilled onto the floor. She had had to scrape it all up and put it back on the dish as best she could.

Mary loved us dearly but with her North-country shrewdness she saw through all the glamorous nonsense which surrounded us. When we first met the Oxford Group Mary saw at once that it was just exactly what we needed. It also made sense to her strong love of country. Her husband had given his life in the First World War but for what, she often asked herself? Not just so that people could go on living selfishly. God, King and

Country meant everything to Mary. "They made you want to live your best," she used to tell us.

She could not bear to see the character of Britain being whittled away through soft and selfish living. She loved us but she hated the selfish way we lived. "I don't envy you," she said to me one day. "You 'ave everything but you 'ave nothing." When Bunny knew that we needed a complete change of motive in our lives and I fought like a steer to defend our comfortable way of life, Mary was a true friend. She stood with Bunny and incurred my wrath.

When our daughter Jennifer was born Mary loved her like her own. "You must try to be different for 'er sake," she used to say to me. "Think what kind of a world you've brought 'er into. Listen to these people. They can teach you a lot. They talk much more sense than you do."

CHAPTER SEVEN

Bunny

ONE day early in the December of 1939, I was sitting in my office when a cable was handed to me. It was from Frank Buchman asking me to join him in America where vital work connected with the war was being done. It would mean being away from Britain about eight months,

The cable brought a shock of surprise. Nothing was further from my mind than the thought of leaving Britain now she was at war. I had, amongst other things, just arranged to help Daphne du Maurier with a book of stories of how British people were facing the war–a book which I would have to leave to others and which, published under the title *Come Wind, Come Weather*, was to sell 800,000 copies in Britain alone. It took me a long time before I was willing to open my mind to the possibility that to accept Buchman's invitation might conceivably be right.

There was obviously so much involved in this invitation that I went to see two of my most trusted friends to talk it over with them. The important question was of course a very simple one: was it right or not? The only way to be sure was to put the question in God's hands and find out what He wanted.

I sat in quiet with my two friends and clear as light came the thought, "It is right to go." I asked my friends what they thought. They were equally convinced of the rightness of my going. But before the final decision could be made there were two other necessary steps to take, the first to talk it over with Phyll, the second to consult with the various government departments concerned. A man of military age could not, of course, leave the country without full government backing. I went to carry out the first step and telephone to Phyll.

This was not a job I relished. Phyll, following her experience at the Hollywood Bowl, had been totally different in her attitude to the work I had undertaken. But the decision we had to face together was a difficult one for any couple to make.

For the past three months I had been staying with some friends in a house at Hampstead. Phyll had been evacuated to the country with our daughter Jennifer and was staying with friends in a house at Much Hadham where I visited them on Sundays.

I rang through to Phyll, and told her of the cable and that my thought was to accept.

It was as I had feared. Phyll was seized by all the fury with which she had originally opposed me, and the wires crackled with the violence of her assault.

I told her we could not argue over the 'phone. I would go out and see her.

It was dark when I took the train from London, and when I stepped out on to the blacked-out station of Much Hadham, I could see nothing.

Suddenly in the darkness I felt someone approach. I felt two arms around my neck and a kiss on my cheek. It was Phyll, all warmth and tenderness.

"Darling," she said, "I feel it is absolutely right for you to go."

Astonished, I asked her what had happened.

II

Phyll
It was perhaps the hardest decision we ever had to make. After the decision was made I wept most of the night. He did not want to go. I did not want him to go either. I remember vividly the pain of those days.

We had been a popular couple. A near neighbour recently told me, "I saw your husband this morning. He looks much the same as he did in the 'thirties. He used to be my 'Beatle'." Many, many women all over the world have told me that he was their pin-up boy in the 'thirties. And when I was acting in a play up in Aberdeen a foreman in a fish factory said to me, "Let me shake your hand. Millions of us ordinary people loved Bunny. We were proud of him."

It was fun to be popular. I think I enjoyed it even more than Bunny. Of course it flattered my vanity and it was very childish. But when you have had a reputation of that kind it is hard to give it up. I longed for him to continue to be a hero in the eyes of the British public. And so when I heard he had been invited to go to America to do a special job, but one which could easily be misunderstood, I wished that it had not been so.

That night when I received his phone call I was weak and wobbly and fearful and angry. "Why must this happen to us? No, no, no," I kept saying as I walked up and down my room. "Anything, oh Lord, but that." Then suddenly the experiment I had made at the Hollywood Bowl came back to me. Listen to the deepest thing in your heart. And so I sat down· and prayed with all my heart for God to show me what was right.

A slow, sure certainty took possession of me. It would not be understood, it would not be popular, but in the perspective of history what he and his friends were out to do was right. I could see to the end of my nose, but God could see into all eternity. "He must go" came with increasing force.

And so when I met Bunny at the station, instead of a vitriolic attack of pride and prejudice I could say with all my heart, "You must go. I know now it is right."

III

Bunny

With a lighter heart, I now got in touch with the Foreign Office and with the Ministries of Labour and Information, and told them about Buchman's invitation. All three agreed and gave me permits to go, only stipulating that I should return within a year if requested. This proviso was never invoked, for the British Embassy in Washington made it clear when the time came that they thought my colleagues and I could best serve our country in America.

I said goodbye to Phyll at Waterloo Station and boarded ship, the s.s. *Volendam*, of the Dutch–American Line where it lay at anchor outside Southampton. It was blacked out. Not a light glimmered anywhere. At early dawn we got under weigh in a dead calm, foggy sea. Our lifeboats were hanging over the ship's side ready for instant lowering. There was danger of magnetic mines.

It was dead calm for two days. I rested, glad of the change after months of hard work. I lay in a deck chair and read.

And then the storm got up. On Christmas Day we were hove to, headed into a gale. Gigantic waves thundered by, shaking the ship. A full moon was shining and the sea lashed into a foam by the gale, shone like a brilliant, moving, mountainous field of snow.

The rough voyage ended at last. We rode into a New York harbour white with a thin fall of snow. I had never before seen New York in winter. On my previous visits it had always been hot—stiflingly hot. Now it was equally cold, only a few degrees above zero with an icy wind blowing up the avenues and coming at you round the corners.

I found Americans for the most part little interested in anything but their own immediate doings. They seemed strangely unconcerned and little shaken by the war in Europe. It was especially striking to me after living in blacked-out cities, waiting for the wail of sirens and seeing the preparations and first actions of a nation at war. I was afraid for America, that she was so little in touch with the reality of the world situation.

Almost immediately on arrival I made a broadcast into which I put much of what I was feeling. People congratulated me and were sympathetic about my concern. They understood perfectly that I should feel concerned. After all I was British. My country was at war. But America was not at war. She was safe and secure, three thousand miles away from the scene of all the trouble. Why should they worry?

Frank Buchman was in New York when I arrived. I went with him to many engagements. Many times I heard him say, "There may be a war in Europe but America has her war too. America's war is for industrial cooperation and national unity."

Men smiled and nodded their heads and congratulated Buchman as they had congratulated me. It would be splendid of course if America had industrial cooperation and national unity. But they did not see with Buchman that these things were not mere luxuries they could do without but urgent necessities.

Soon I travelled to the West Coast. It is a coast of sunshine, of mountains and Pacific seas. But it is also one of the most highly industrialised areas of America and in 1940 was fast becoming the aircraft arsenal of America – and of Britain. It was also in 1940 the hot-bed of labour disputes and there was a determined attempt to disrupt the aircraft factories.

The Russians were still allied to Adolf Hitler. The war in their eyes was still an imperialist war and their effort was geared to undermining the Allied war effort. Their agents were at work, particularly in the great aircraft factories of Boeing and Lockheed which were turning out the planes which later were so essential to Britain's war effort.

Here where the fight was thickest the work of MRA was centred. There were workers in Seattle, Portland, San Francisco and Los Angeles. Their aim? To create a dynamic spirit of unity and the atmosphere in which the problems of labour and management could be solved. Meetings were held which had the power to bring together men who would have met under no other auspices.

On December 29, 1939, the *Seattle Star* in a full-page editorial invited Buchman to hold a round table conference of all the elements in their city.

I reached the West Coast myself in time to be present at this. It was held against the background of the fall of France. The giant headlines of the papers in the hotel lobby were screaming the first news of the German breakthrough at Sedan. The German panzer divisions were heading for the Channel ports. We watched on maps their ominous progress and the encirclement of the British and Belgian Armies. Soon Belgium was to capitulate. Soon the British were to retreat from Dunkirk. Soon France was to be under the heel of the conqueror.

Frenchmen were to tell one later that France failed in the factory before she failed at the Front. That her leaders could not get together. That industrialists refused to sacrifice. That workers refused to work. That in her hour of trial, desperation was no substitute for preparation. France was lost.

Was there in the crumbling of France a warning for America? In calling for industrial cooperation and national unity long before the nation realised its danger, or was awakened to its need, Frank Buchman had struck a prophetic note.

To that round table came men and women of all shades of

opinion. They reached the full circle from extreme right to extreme left. They met in an atmosphere that created mutual trust and confidence. They began by agreeing to disagree without being disagreeable. Many ended by finding in Moral Re-Armament a basis for a common action.

Deeply impressed was a young, lean-faced labour leader from a great aircraft factory, Garry Cotton. He had been in touch with MRA. When standing for election as head of his union his photo had appeared in *The Aero-Mechanic* along with those of other candidates. Under them were printed their election slogans. He had called for 'Moral Re-Armament'. Elements in the factory ganged up against him and he was defeated, they themselves gaining control. From the time of the round table conference he set out to reverse this. A year later when the elements who had opposed him were expelled in a body from the union for activities inimical to the corporation and the country, the International President of the same union—the head of over 400,000 men—looking for a man he could trust, picked this fellow as candidate for union head. The men elected him unanimously. (The union in 1943 numbered 20,000 men.) He was in one of the key positions in the defence industries.

The International President, Harvey Brown, later gave his opinion of the work of Moral Re-Armament. "For years," he said, "American industry has been seeking some common programme to resolve conflicting interests of men and management and unite the strength of each in battle against those forces which endeavour to divide and destroy. Here at last is the programme. May we all be given courage and strength and wisdom to carry it through."

Other labour leaders valued our work no less highly. Mr Dalrymple, organiser of the heavy industry trade unions in Oregon, said, "Since these men have been up and down the West Coast helping to solve labour and industrial problems . . . the assistance they have extended has been almost unbelievable."

Mr Frank Morrison, Secretary and Treasurer of the American Federation of Labour for forty-three years wrote, "One of the greatest forces binding our country with yours in this grave hour is the devoted work of British Moral Re-Armament workers in America who have won the confidence and affection of responsible leaders of all our labour unions. We feel confident Britain will gladly allow us to retain the patriotic services of these gallant fighters for freedom."

A member of Congress wrote, "Representing as I do the State of Washington I have had exceptional opportunity to observe the work of the British MRA workers at first-hand. Leaders of labour and industry up and down the West Coast are emphatic in praise of their achievements. These people have won a coveted position for themselves and their country in the hearts of Americans from coast to coast."

IV

During the days when the most important results were being achieved in the aircraft factories, the London *Sunday Pictorial* got into the act. It launched an attack. This newspaper, which had often carried my picture in the past, carried it once again. This time it was right in the middle of the centre page spread. Beneath it were the names of many of those with whom I was working in America. Across the top of the page ran a large, black headline: "These Men Are Making Fools of Themselves – And Britain."

This was followed by an attack in the *Sunday Despatch*. It set out to present 'two sides of a controversial question'. The first side, the attack, consisted of eleven lines of headlines and about twelve inches of type. The second side, the defence, consisted of a pathetic four inches of type. But those pathetic four inches carried a punch! They were so phrased that they were more damning than the attack itself!

It was not an altogether pleasant experience to be attacked in this way. Yet I was not surprised. Phyll's onslaught perhaps had prepared me. I had learned to expect opposition. I had learned that whereas, when I had lived entirely for myself, I was elevated almost to the position of a hero, when I decided to try and live unselfishly there were many who were only too ready to condemn me.

And it interested me too that whereas to my knowledge there

were six other British tennis players in America at that time, I alone was singled out for attack.

In the face of these attacks – work in the aircraft factories of the West Coast having proved successful – Frank Buchman took his force to a camp at Tahoe, near the borders of Nevada to train for the battles ahead and to think through future strategy.

This training period lasted several weeks and out of it there emerged not only a closely united dedicated force but a force armed with vital weapons. The first of these was a booklet on the foundations of national strength entitled, *You Can Defend America*. A foreword was written to it by General of the Armies John J. Pershing and it was supported by commendations from the War Department and Educational Authorities. It was to sell 2,000,000 copies. At the same time a musical revue with the same name and with the same theme was produced and it was with these weapons that we once more launched forth into the nation.

v

Throughout these months Phyll and I had been in the closest correspondence and in the summer of 1940, along with hundreds of other mothers and children, Phyll was evacuated with our daughter Jennifer to Canada. She landed in New York and before leaving for Canada was able to visit me for a short while at Tahoe and to play a part in the production of the revue. With the launching of it into the country, however, the time came for her to rejoin Jennifer and she left again for New York.

I drove with her to Reno, where she was to catch her train. It was midnight when we arrived at our hotel in this 'the biggest little city in the world'. The train was due to leave at five o'clock in the morning. We would have to be up at four. There was little time to sleep.

Reno was still wide awake. The slot machines were clicking, the little balls swishing in the roulette wheels, the dice tumbling. In the bingo houses the gamblers were still sitting in their rows.

Neon signs flashed their brilliant lights into our room, off and on, off and on. The room was almost bright as day. We sat talking in the unfamiliar atmosphere, so very different from the stillness and simplicity of the camp at Tahoe.

There was much to talk about. We had heard so much about Reno. We had friends who had been there – to be relieved of marriage bonds that were no longer congenial. We had come close to being separated ourselves – and here we were in Reno!

But we did not talk of divorce, rather of re-marriage, of bonds made new and stronger. For something was happening in our married life. Two people who had so often sat together and tried to reach each other over miles and miles of a desolate separation of spirit, had found over miles and miles of desolate separation of space – the answer. Going together towards the same goal we found ourselves, in spite of a long separation, closer to each other than perhaps we had ever been before.

And so Reno can at least boast this: that one married couple in the heart of the city found not the end of an old married life but the beginnings of a new.

We woke at four and dressed and packed and walked through the still-lighted city to the station. A few tired wheels still turned, a few tired dice still tumbled. An occasional slot machine swallowed with noisy gulp yet another silver coin. But Reno, for a few brief hours at least, seemed temporarily played out.

We stood on the lighted platform. It was chilly in the early morning air. Distantly the clanging of a bell rang through the darkness, drew nearer, more loud. A bright light flooded its ray along the track. A great engine hove in sight, groaned by drawing its load of heavy cars, slowed then staggered to a stop.

A few car doors opened. The passengers climbed in. There was a few moments' pause. Then the drawling ominous sound floated down the platform, "All aboard".

The engine hissed. The train shuddered, heaved, then slowly began to slide from the lighted platform into the darkness and mystery of the night.

Phyll was gone.

VI

The *You Can Defend America* handbook and revue achieved a wide success on the West Coast and were later launched on the

East Coast with the help of the Governor of Maine and the Commanding General of the First Corp Area, General Wilby. From the Bath Ironworks, where destroyers were being built for Britain, and the Bridgeport Brass Company, where the 25 millionth shell had just been manufactured, the programme moved to Frank Buchman's home ground of Philadelphia. After a performance of the play in the Philadelphia Academy of Music, sponsored by the City Fathers and the Civilian Defence Authorities, the Hon. J. B. Kelly* remarked, "I thought I had all the patriotism I needed but as I watched the play I felt here was a group of people who almost looked over my shoulder and read my mind and produced the answer I have been feeling America needs."

Early next morning the Japanese attacked Pearl Harbour. America was at war. Her defence was no longer a slogan or a patriotic theme. It was a military necessity. Very soon both the revue and handbook were receiving national acclaim. Enthusiastic audiences greeted us as we travelled the length of America's eastern seaboard from Maine in the New England states, south through New York, New Jersey and Virginia, through the mountain country of North Carolina, through South Carolina and Georgia, down to the steamy heat of semi-tropical Florida and then northward to the great Middle-Western industrial cities and finally to the heart of American industry, Detroit.

A distinguished group of national leaders summarised the impact of this programme: "It is stimulating the personal self-sacrifice, industrial cooperation and national unity vital to our Allied cause. It is staffed by a most self-effacing and self-sacrificing volunteer personnel. They are directing their efforts with unerring accuracy at the most strategic centres in the country and are achieving results out of all proportion to their numbers and their means.

"The enthusiastic response of Governors, State Defence Councils, labour, industry, agriculture, the press, the Armed Forces, is convincing evidence that here at last is a force which can rouse and unite the most diverse elements among our people for a programme of total victory."

* Father of Princess Grace of Monaco.

In spite of this wide support, news of attacks continued to reach us from England and began to be echoed in America. Wherever we travelled rumours pursued us like an evil-smelling gas. "Look out. Beware. These men are pacifists, appeasers, fascists."

The rumours, though ludicrous and directly in opposition to the evidence of the revue and its massive backing, yet often touched a chord of fear in people's hearts. Panic gripped them and reason was unseated. Even the most ridiculous rumours were sometimes believed. "Haven't you heard?" went one of these, while we were still at work in a city in the Mid-West. "These people are dangerous. They have just been sent in a sealed train to the Coast."

Before long it became apparent that a serious attempt was being made to destroy the work of Moral Re-Armament, both in Britain and America, and that the elements behind this attack on both sides of the Atlantic were in collusion. The great mass of MRA men and women of military age were already in the army. They had enlisted early in the war and many of them were to be decorated for gallantry or to give their lives before the war was done. A small number of whole-time workers had remained to maintain the work, and the focus of the attack was to break up the MRA force by drafting these irreplaceable men into the armed forces.

In Britain, this campaign had succeeded, the last eleven men had been called up, and now the same attempt was in process in America. It was spearheaded in the more sensational papers of the city of New York, where decisions about the draft status of the British workers, like myself, had to be made, since that had been our port of entry to America. The local New York draft board took decisions on these men, one by one, and, from the first, its decisions became available to newspaper men even before they had been officially taken. On January 14, 1943, the *Daily Mirror* in London published in the morning the decisions of a meeting which was only held in New York on the evening of the same day. And every piece of adverse publicity in America was swiftly reproduced in Britain and vice versa.

Some of the most influential men in America intervened to try and retain us in the work to which we had been called. In

April 1942, Senator Truman and Congressman Wadsworth who drafted the bill setting up the Selective Service Administration, together with the Presidents of the two national labour organisations, William Green of the A.F. of L. and Philip Murray of the CIO, wrote to President Roosevelt:

"We feel it would be nothing short of calamitous and a contradiction of the spirit of the Selective Service Act, should these trained morale-builders be assigned to any other type of war service than that in which heretofore they have been so usefully engaged. We, therefore, ask that the accredited status due to them be given these men who are intelligently and successfully fighting this battle.

"We believe, Mr President, that this programme, by virtue of its positive philosophy and its proved powers of capturing the public imagination, deserves your most careful consideration. . . ."

President Roosevelt's official response was to acknowledge the letter and pass it on to the Selective Service Directors for consideration. His personal conviction was reflected in a letter written a few days previously to his old headmaster, Dr Endicott Peabody, in whose school at Groton I had spoken, and who had been most impressed by *You Can Defend America*, play and book. The President wrote, "We need more things like this to maintain and strengthen the national morale. From all accounts they are making a splendid contribution to patriotism and I hope a large number of communities will have the benefit of witnessing a performance."

But personal conviction and political pressures do not always coincide. Moreover, the Selective Service—national call-up system—had no power to create a status conferring group deferment, and the issue was as hot for the legislators in Washington as it had been in Westminster. The massive press campaign won its way and one by one we were called up.

Quite apart from everything else, I happened to be entitled to deferment as a 'pre-Pearl Harbour father'. But when I wrote to the New York Board informing them of this fact, I received the reply that the Board had no proof that I had a bona fide relationship with my wife!

9(a). Bunny and his squad on basic training Atlantic City

9(b). Bunny and MRA members of Armed Forces, Mackinac Island, Michigan. In background the old Fort once occupied by the British

10. Dedication of the Westminster Theatre in memory of MRA service men and women who gave their lives in the war. Miss Agnes Leakey reads last letter from her brother, Nigel Leakey, V.C., who was killed in Africa

Much of the press campaign at this time focused on myself, and I was widely misrepresented in my own country. It is only for this reason that I quote from a speech made in the United States House of Representatives in 1946 by the representative from Michigan, the Hon. Harold F. Youngblood.*

"Many of you know H. W. Austin as a Davis Cup tennis star. You may not know that he served for three years during the recent war in the American Army. As a civilian he has worked for this country without salary for the better part of eight years in the programme of Moral Re-Armament. Thousands of Americans from coast to coast have come to know and love this great ambassador of Britain who has so loyally and sincerely served the best and common ideals of our two nations and has been the means of inspiring thousands more to fight for the democratic ideal that alone can bring the nations into harmony and peace."

Colonel John Langston, the Chairman of the Presidential Appeals Board, in preparing an Intelligence analysis for the Selective Service Administration, took a more general view. Noting that Moral Re-Armament drew the fire equally of Nazis and Communists, of aggressive atheists and narrow ecclesiastics, and that it had been charged "by radicals with being militaristic and by war-mongers with being pacifistic", he added that in Britain MRA was accused by some of being a brilliantly clever front for Fascism; in Germany and Japan of being a super-intelligent arm of the British and American Secret Service. One day a section of the press would announce that MRA was defunct: and the next that it numbered nearly the entire membership of the British Cabinet at the time of Munich, and was responsible for engineering Hitler's attack on Russia.

"Nothing, but a potentially vast moral and spiritual reformation of global proportions," concluded this analysis, "could possibly be honoured by antagonisms so venomous and contradictory in character and so world-wide in scope."

* Congressional Record.

CHAPTER EIGHT

I

Bunny

"EVERYBODY out!"

The voice of the sergeant echoed down the passages and rumbled into the rooms of the hotel, stripped bare, for the purposes of war, of all their peace-time furnishings.

The sleepy GIs tumbled out of bed, cursing the sergeant, cursing the war, cursing everything to do with it.

Five minutes later, coughing the cough that was the trade mark of the GI performing his basic training in Atlantic City, they fell out by companies to answer roll call, an unhappy and ragged looking group, forming long lines down the passages.

All present and correct, the companies were marched away to breakfast.

The doors through which they filed to the mess hall bore in gold letters the painted slogan: "Through these halls pass the best damn soldiers in the world."

The exploits of the American Army on far-flung battlefields were proof indeed that the Americans were the equal of any other fighting man, but the observer at that moment watching the group of newly enlisted GIs pass through those halls, might have been forgiven for having some doubt. But one thing he would not have doubted, and that was that the American Army was the best fed in the world. And if it was true, as Napoleon said, that an army marches on its stomach, then the American Army was likely to outmarch any other army in the world.

Breakfast finished, the companies returned to their bedrooms and there began the cleaning of floors, baths and basins, the polishing of shoes and buttons and insignia that were necessary to pass inspection. One speck in the basin, one shoe not shining like a mirror, one bed not made exactly according to instructions and there would be no passes out the following weekend.

"*Everybody out!*"

Once more the sergeant's voice echoed down the passages.

Once more the GIs tumbled out of their rooms and stood in ragged rows in the corridor outside.

Once more they were called to attention and a moment later were clattering along the stone passages of the hotel, out on the famous Atlantic City Boardwalk, scene in peacetime of the display of so much fashion. But now the Boardwalk was deserted except for the soldiers, and the fresh sea breezes that in peacetime brought back vigour to the tired businessman or jaded socialite were now pouring their health-giving ozone into the latest recruits of the Army of the United States, Private Austin, HW, 39292943 among them.

II

"Squad . . . halt!!!"

The squad came to a straggling halt. The dust from the cinder surface of the parade ground, burned dry by the wind and sun, arose around us, blackening shoes and fatigue uniforms, and penetrating even below our uniforms to blacken our socks and vests as well.

"Stand at ease! Easy!"

The squad relaxed, not a very impressive sight. It seemed impossible for men of the Air Force whose theme song was, 'Off We Go Into The Wild Blue Yonder' to take very seriously the business of drilling on the earth below.

"Private Austin fall out."

Surprised at this unexpected command, Private Austin fell out. I saluted the lieutenant smartly and stood at attention before him.

"How would you like to apply for Officer Candidate School?"

This was unexpected, but not unwelcome. "Very much, sir," I answered.

"Report to me in the morning. I'll have the papers ready for you."

"Thank you, sir." I saluted again and returned to the ranks.

Next morning I reported to the lieutenant. I saluted smartly. "Private Austin reporting, sir."

The lieutenant returned my salute. "Oh. I'm sorry, Austin," he replied, "I'm afraid you've been put on a shipping list, and

it's not much good applying for OCS here. But of course you'll
be able to do this at your next base."

Disappointed, I saluted again and retired.

I was 'shipped' to Buckley Field a camp near Denver,
Colorado, the 'mile-high city', three days and three nights
distant by train from Atlantic City. The camp was situated in
glorious countryside, and in the distance towered the snow-
covered peaks of the Rocky Mountains. I was placed in a
'clerical pool'.

The morning after my arrival I reported to my commanding
officer. I saluted smartly. "Sir, I would like to apply for OCS."

The officer returned my salute, receiving my request sympathetically. "Sorry, Austin, but to apply from here would only
hold you up. You'll be shipped from here to Army School. If
you do well you will automatically be recommended for OCS.
Good luck."

"Thank you, sir." I saluted and retired.

I was duly shipped to Army School in Fargo, North Dakota,
where the Red River runs that flows down from the Canadian
north. The farmlands are flat. The corn was ripening in the
late summer sun. The mosquitoes from the Red River came and
bit us happily while we mustered on parade. The food was unbelievably good. We had a busy but merry time. I came out
second in my company and was duly awarded with the promised letter of recommendation for OCS.

My next stop was at Salt Lake City, that fabulous metropolis
built by the Mormon, Brigham Young, in the heart of a track-
less and seemingly waterless desert. I was once more placed in
a 'clerical pool'.

Once more I went to see my CO. Once more I saluted
smartly. "Private Austin reporting, sir. I would like to apply
for OCS."

Once more the officer regarded me sympathetically. But
once more I was disappointed. "Sorry, Austin, you can only
apply for OCS if you are assigned to the base."

"Sir, will you kindly assign me to the base?"

The officer did as I requested. I was assigned to the base.
I went to see my new CO.

"Private Austin reporting, sir. I would like to apply for OCS."

Again the officer looked at me sympathetically. "Sorry, Austin, you've just been transferred to the Twentieth Bomber Command in El Paso, Texas."

I went by train to El Paso, calling on the way to see friends in Los Angeles. I arrived in El Paso late at night.

In the morning I awoke to another desert landscape, a base training the crews of Flying Fortresses and Liberators.

I went to see my new Commanding Officer. I saluted smartly. "Private Austin reporting, sir. I would like to apply for OCS."

This time the officer looked at me searchingly and pondered for a few moments. "I don't like to recommend men for OCS until I have known them for at least two weeks," he replied. "However, in your case I'll make an exception." He fumbled in his desk. "Fill out this form. Here are the papers."

I filled out the forms and returned to report. I saluted smartly. "Private Austin reporting, sir."

"Sorry, Austin," said the officer, "there has been a special request for you over at the 310th Air Base Squadron. I am afraid you can't apply for OCS from here. But take your papers along and apply again there."

Once more I packed my kit bags and trundled them over to my new quarters. The next morning I went to see my new Commanding Officer. Once more I saluted smartly. "Private Austin reporting, sir. I would like to apply for OCS."

Again the officer looked at me searchingly. "I don't like to recommend men for OCS. until I have known them for at least a fortnight," he replied, echoing my previous CO's words. "But in your case I am happy to make an exception." He handed me more papers and once more I went away and filled them in.

Although the job I was assigned to, Special Services, had nothing to do with all the training the Army up till that time had been to such pains to give me, it seemed that at last I had reached the point at least of temporary stability. It was with some hope that I handed in my papers to the CO, together with a letter of recommendation from the famous explorer Rear Admiral Richard E. Byrd.

The next day as a matter of routine on arriving at a new base I was sent for a physical check-up. Clad in my birthday suit the medical officer looked at me critically. "Are you always that colour?"

"What colour, sir?"

"Jaundiced."

I recalled that all through my life my family had talked about my 'yellow days'. I told this to the MO.

A needle was jabbed in my arm, blood was taken and I was ordered to report back next day. I had jaundice. I was transferred from barracks to a hospital ward.

There I stayed for four months while all the genius of American medicine attempted to discover what on earth caused my recurrent attacks of jaundice from which apparently I had suffered all my life and which had often caused the up-till-then inexplicable periods of weakness that had sometimes led to my downfall on the tennis courts.

I never got to Officer Candidate School after all!

III

It was 4.30 a.m. I climbed down from the top of my double-decker bunk and roused the fellow in the bed below me.

It seemed that Providence had thrown us two together. I had met him first at our induction centre at San Pedro, California, where he had occupied the next bunk to mine. We were among the twenty-two out of four hundred who had been selected for the Air Forces and had been shipped together to Atlantic City. Now we occupied the upper and lower beds of the same double bunk.

He had become interested in MRA and we had begun to keep morning quiet times together. The fellow in the next bunk to us had also become interested and each morning we got up at 4.30, when the three of us would spend a time of quiet together.

This morning the door of our room opened and a young Jewish fellow came in. He took a startled look at us.

"Jesus Christ! Are you crazy? What the so-and-so do you think you are doing?"

"We're listening to God," I said.

The Jewish boy took this on the chin and sat down. He looked at me in even greater astonishment.

"You're a Jew," I said, "you probably know about the great men of your race, Moses, Jeremiah, Isaiah. They listened to God. Take Moses, for example. He listened to God and led your people out of captivity in Egypt. He listened to God and gave your people and posterity the ten commandments. He listened to God and gave your people all the Law. Joshua succeeded him. He listened to God too and led your people triumphant into the promised land. In fact," I said, "almost the whole of the Old Testament is the story of men and women who listened to God—or failed to listen to God. And the great lesson your people have to give to the world is that when in those days they listened to God they prospered and when they did not disaster fell upon them. Perhaps," I added, "it is the destiny of your people to give this answer to the world."

The young fellow remained in silence. "Do you still think we're crazy?" I asked.

"No-no-no," he stammered in reply, "not at all."

He left the room and we continued to do as the great Jewish prophets had done, as those great Jews had done who gave Christianity to the world, as indeed so many had done whose lives were effective in bringing back moral and spiritual principles to the world. "Be still," God had said to man long centuries ago, "Be still and know that I am God." "For the sons of God," St Paul had written to the Romans, "are those who are guided by the Spirit of God." Joan of Arc listened to her voices and in a year had accomplished what for ninety-seven years her leaders had sought to accomplish and had failed. In the modern idiom Frank Buchman had said, "When man listens, God speaks. When man obeys, God acts. When men change, nations change."

IV

I knocked and went into the office of the Commanding Officer of Special Service on my Air Force base. I saluted.

"Private Austin reporting, Sir. I would like to know what I am supposed to do."

The lieutenant returned my salute. "I don't know, Austin. The captain's away on leave. You'd better see the sergeant."

I went to see the sergeant. He recommended that I go and

see the lieutenant. When I told him I had just seen the lieutenant, "Well," he said, "I don't know what you're supposed to do. You'd better just sit around."

The captain would not be back for another three weeks. I prepared for those three weeks to 'sit around'. However, my first experiences of this new occupation were soon interrupted.

"Can you write?"

I looked up. A young corporal was looking at me with an enquiring face.

"Yes," I answered boldly.

"Fine," he said, "you're the man I'm looking for. I'm the editor of the camp newspaper. I've got to have an article on war bonds. No one in the office can write it. Do you think you can do it?"

"Sure," I replied.

I wrote an article on war bonds. The editor was delighted. My next assignment was an article on the 'March of Dimes'.

"Look here," said the editor, "what are you doing in the office?"

"Sitting around," I replied.

"Well that's fine. Tell you what. You work with me. I'm the only fellow assigned to the paper. The sergeant helps occasionally and Micky"–he indicated a civilian employee. "You're exactly the fellow I want. When the captain gets back we'll tell him you're working on the camp newspaper. He won't mind."

I was destined to work on the camp newspaper for the next nine months during which I wrote articles and feature interviews and every week an editorial.

v

"I've come to warn you. As a friend of yours I want you to know that some of us on this base don't like what you're doing. It would be better for you if you were to stop."

The speaker was a soldier called Joe. I had first met him when I was in the Base hospital. He was a fellow dark of hair and dark of countenance, with a long, rather sharp nose. He held a great dislike of the British whom he called the 'Brutish'.

When I had first met Joe something had warned me to be careful in my relationship with him. It had been impossible, however, to avoid him altogether. We ate together in a small special-diet dining room in the hospital. There were only five of us in all who ate there. The other three had not much to say for themselves and in due course Joe and I had got into conversation.

I told him about MRA and he took an instant interest. We talked of quiet times and how by the power of God human nature could be changed.

When both of us in due course left the hospital, I continued to run into Joe and he continued to express an interest in MRA. Then one day I found his attitude to me had completely changed. He had been in touch with some friends of his in Detroit, he told me, and he had learned from them that MRA was a very dangerous thing. As a friend he would like to advise me to stay clear of it. He did not doubt for a moment my sincerity. Obviously I was a good fellow. But he warned me I was being fooled. He could only repeat that MRA was a very dangerous thing.

Joe hastened to reassure me that he was not a Communist, although I had never suggested that he was. But although he told me he was not a Communist he took pains to explain to me the Communist ideology. He explained to me the thesis of capitalism, and the antithesis of Communism and the great synthesis that would come when at last capitalism and Communism would clash in a great world war and the classless society would be born. "But mind you," he would always add at the end of these explanations, "I am not a Communist."

Now Joe, 'my friend' as he styled himself, had come to warn me against what I was doing on the base.

I was not surprised. Every week I was writing editorials. The captain was delighted with these. When he returned from leave he had called the editor and myself into the office. "I don't know who is writing these editorials," he had said, "but I like them. Keep them up. I have already received many congratulations on them." The Base Chaplain was also pleased with them and once paid a special visit to our office to thank me for one I had written. And the Roman Catholic Chaplain preached a Sunday sermon on one of the editorials I wrote on the war of ideas.

I had also been asked to speak. One day as I was talking to the captain about the war of ideas, the Air Inspector of the Base walked in and joined in the conversation. At the end he said, "I am very interested in our talk. This may be what I am looking for." A couple of days later when I saw him again, he asked me what I was doing on the base. I told him I was writing editorials. He thought for a moment. "Tell you what," he said, "you must speak to the Officers' Club, to the Combat Crews and to the Chamber of Commerce in El Paso. In fact," he added, "you had better make me your campaign manager."

And so the following Sunday in off duty hours I prepared the outline of a speech and went over it next day with the Air Inspector. We then sent a copy to the colonel of the camp for checking.

Next a copy went to the Director of Training. He returned it with a note: "I highly approve of this speech. When will Austin give it?"

Apparently the Director of Training could not give the authority to me to make the speech, so the Air Inspector advised that I should see the Commandant of Combat Crews.

Meanwhile the young WAC officer in charge of the WAC detachment was having trouble with her girls. She called up the editor of my paper to ask his advice. "Better get Private Austin along to speak to them," advised the editor.

Then the CO of the Medical detachment asked me to speak to his men during their morning and evening orientation hours. At the end of the morning session a tall sour-looking corporal stood up at the back of the room. "Is this Moral Re-Armament?" he asked. I answered that it was. The corporal left the room.

A few minutes later the Medical CO came up to me in a high state of excitement. Objections he told me had been raised to my speech. He was obviously extremely worried. "I'll come back this afternoon to hear what you say."

I had myself no fear of what I was saying. My speech had been checked and passed by the colonel in command of the camp. The Director of Training had 'highly approved' of it.

The CO of the WAC detachment had been 'deeply impressed', chiefly because her fifty-two undoubtedly hard-boiled young women had listened intently in spite of the fact that it was off-duty hours. (As I had arrived to speak one young woman had looked at me ominously, "It's off-duty hours; you'd better be good".)

I was not concerned about the corporal's attack. But it made me wonder about his ideology. I took care to remember what he had looked like.

The Medical CO was present at the evening session when I spoke. It was the same talk as I had given in the morning. I spoke of the three ideologies fighting for control of the world: the idea of Fascism – the Master Race; the idea of Communism, the Master Class, and finally the great idea of inspired Democracy, a society based on absolute moral standards and directed by the Spirit of God. I told stories of the change in the lives of men who had met this idea and how these related to the world we live in and the future we were fighting for. I spoke at the end of the need for God not just as a life-buoy to be used in time of danger or difficulty, but as a permanent directing force in our lives.

The Medical Officer came up to me afterwards. "I don't see anything at all wrong with what you have said. In fact it is the war of ideas. It is exactly what Washington has been telling us to give."

"Perhaps, sir," I said, "you are in the middle of the war of ideas yourself."

The corporal's attack was not the only one levelled against me on the base. Through my editor I heard of a staff sergeant who did not like my editorials. "They are too long," had been his first complaint, and when I shortened them at the editor's request, "They are confused."

I took me a little time to grasp what was happening. I had no exalted opinion of myself as a writer and was prepared to believe that my editorials needed clarification. But then the truth dawned. The reason this fellow did not like my editorials was not because they were confused. It was because they were not confused. Like the corporal in the medical detachment he stood for a different ideology.

I got to know this staff sergeant by sight and would surprise him round corners in conference with the corporal. I began to realise there was a cell on the base. There was a WAC for example who was part of it. There were repeated attempts to get her made librarian–an excellent position for purposes of propaganda. There was a captain in charge of a department. I found out about him because he showed a friend of mine a letter warning the captain of that 'dangerous Fascist' H. W. Austin who was stationed on the base. In all I got to know some twenty-two of these people who were operating this cell.

And so when Joe came into my office that hot summer evening on the base and said, "Some of us don't like what you are doing," I knew exactly to what he was referring.

I personally had no intention of stopping what I was doing but my editor was getting worried. One day he refused to put in one of my editorials. "It's all very well for you," he complained, "you may not mind. But I don't want to get strung up to a lamp post."

Joe and his friends had really scared my editor.

And then I went away on furlough. When I returned I found that the officer personnel of the base had been thrown into a panic.

During my absence a four-page sheet called *In Fact*, edited by a man called George Seldes, which followed every twist of the party line, had issued an attack on me. My 'friend' Joe had, the sheet stated, supplied the information. It quoted, out of context, one of my editorials–the editorial on the war of ideas on which the Roman Catholic chaplain had preached a sermon. It spoke at some length of the activities on the base of 'that dangerous Fascist, H. W. Austin'. It mentioned the name of the Special Service officer under whom I worked and the name of the editor. Their names were ringed around in red and a complimentary copy was sent to them both.

When *In Fact* arrived neither of them quite knew what had hit them. My CO consulted with other senior officers on the base. There was only one thing to be done: to send for the Federal Bureau of Investigation.

An FBI man arrived on base and I was investigated in absentia. My papers were looked into; my friends were enquired about and my habits were also investigated. My editorials—all twenty-five of them—were duplicated and were studied with care by the intelligence officer and other high-ranking officers on the base.

"I like these editorials," commented the FBI man.

My name was cleared. Joe was transferred off the base.

But though Joe was banished and I was complimented by the man from the FBI, life for me on the base altered completely. I was no longer able to write editorials, or talk to the men. I was told it was against army regulations to propagate a movement. I pointed out I had propagated no movement. Quite apart from the fact that MRA was not a movement, I had never mentioned it at all. All I had been writing and talking about were the fundamental principles of democracy for which we were fighting a global war, and for which up till that time I had received only praise. But the top brass of the base had received a rude shock and were fearful of taking a stand that might jeopardise their future rank, so in spite of my total clearance by the FBI, I was silenced.

VI

In May 1944 I received a letter from Phyll telling me *The Forgotten Factor*, in which she was playing, was being performed at the National Theatre in Washington D.C. the following Sunday. It was being sponsored by Senator Harry S. Truman and Congressman J. W. Wadsworth who were sending invitations to all the members of Congress and all the top military, naval and air force brass of the various countries stationed in Washington at that time. She told me she had had guidance to post the invitation to me. I was grateful to receive it but had no expectation of going to Washington. I was in hospital at the time with a recurrence of my liver trouble and Washington was 2,000 miles away.

I was released from the hospital the following Saturday and went at once to my office, where I spent the morning. The camp newspaper had been put to bed the night before and as usual on a Saturday there was little to do. After lunch I decided I would go to the barracks and rest.

Better have guidance first, I said to myself. I did so, and almost as if it had been spoken by a friend at my elbow, the thought came to take the invitation and show it to the major who had made himself my 'Campaign Manager'. Although the major did not work there at that time my thought was to go to the headquarters.

There I found the major. I saluted. "I thought you might be interested to see this, sir," I said and handed him the invitation.

He looked at it closely.

"Bet you'd like to go?"

"I certainly would, sir."

"Wait a minute."

He got up and disappeared into the colonel's office.

"The colonel's out for a moment," he said, re-emerging. "Go back to your office and I'll call you in ten minutes."

Ten minutes later the major was on the phone, "The colonel will put you on special orders to go–if you can get there. Sorry to say the last plane for Washington left here at 2.30. There are no more from this base today."

My mind moved rapidly. "I'll call you back, sir," I said.

There were two alternative ways of going. One was to hitch a ride on an army plane passing through the airport in El Paso, the other to fly by commercial airline. The first was extremely uncertain, but so was the second. The commercial routes to Washington were crowded with high-ranking military personnel flying to the capital. Without a high priority one was unlikely to get on a flight and getting on, even more unlikely to stay on. What hope had Private Austin?

The other disadvantage was that the flight to Washington cost 220 dollars, of which I had only the remains of my previous week's pay, which was about seven dollars.

I told two civilian employees in the office what had happened. Both became extremely excited and eager to help me in any way they could. "Have you any money?" asked the one called Micky. I told her my situation. "I'll lend you some." She looked at her watch. "I've just time to get to the bank before it closes," she said, and rushed off.

I phoned the major and told him of my decision to go

by commercial airline. "Come back to headquarters," he said.

I found the major in the adjutant's office. The adjutant was dictating my special orders to the sergeant-major. The major was on the telephone to the airlines. "Take a seat," said the major.

There I sat while the headquarters office did the work for me. "I can only book you as far as Big Springs," said the major, "and we can only give you a fourth class priority. Good luck. Pick up your ticket at the airport."

I saluted, thanked the major, the adjutant and the sergeant-major and went back to my office. There I was handed the money by Micky who was as excited as if she were going herself. I packed my kitbag, called up the motor pool for transport and drove off to the airport.

At 6.30 I caught the plane to Washington. I spoke to the airline's hostess. "I'm only booked to Big Springs 500 miles away. Don't let them put me off!" I pleaded. She smiled, "I'll hold thumbs for you."

I made myself as small as possible, hoping to escape from the ominous words, "Will Private Austin kindly give up his seat."

Our plane touched down at Big Springs and I held my breath waiting. Nothing was said. At last the plane took off and I sighed with relief. But I was by no means in the clear. There were other stops and each one might be my last. Hour after hour the plane flew through the night, touching down at the great cities of the Southern States. But the ominous words were never spoken. I kept my seat. I arrived at Washington at 10 o'clock the following morning.

It was a gala occasion. The National Theatre was packed with Congressmen and Washington's top brass. Generals and admirals swarmed around me. I was introduced to Field-Marshal Sir John Dill, and spoke at a reception after the play. In all that glittering array of stars, batons and eagles, my private's uniform for once seemed to hold a certain distinction!

Next day a friend came up to me and said, "I don't know how you paid for your flight, but my guidance is to give you nine dollars." I thanked him warmly. Then another friend, saying the same thing, gave me eleven dollars. A third friend gave me all of his previous month's pay as a captain. It was 200 dollars. I had 220 dollars, exactly the cost of my flight.

The colonel in El Paso had put me on special orders for five days. My guidance was to return after three. This was just as well. On my flight back to El Paso I was put off the plane five times and it took me two days.

VII

Late in 1944 I was transferred off the base in El Paso to a place called Dalhart in the Panhandle of Texas. Here I was assigned to a Bomb Group awaiting the arrival of the great new planes, the B29s, before being sent overseas. I was given the job of assistant to the file clerk.

However as my liver complaint disqualified me from overseas service, I was eventually transferred to the camp newspaper and resumed my journalistic efforts under the maternal eye of a young WAC who was the newspaper editor.

Dalhart is a small town consisting of one street, set in a barren and treeless waste. There was very little for the men to do on the base and nothing off it, and morale was low. I was made a member of an enlisted men's committee to devise schemes for its improvement. However wild our schemes sounded the colonel in charge of the base grasped them eagerly. One scheme was to run excursion buses to the White Sands in New Mexico, 300 miles away. Even this met with the colonel's hearty approval.

The only natural relief was the vagaries of the weather. If anyone feels inclined to criticise the uncertainties of our weather in Britain, let them visit Dalhart. One day it will be snowing, another raining, a third burning hot under a cloudless sky. Often I would leave for work bundled up against the freezing cold, to return in 80° heat. One afternoon it was 75°. An hour later it was 5°.

In spite of the dreary and forbidding nature of the base, I enjoyed my few months at Dalhart, but was not sorry to be transferred to a base in Kansas where the grass was green, the birds sang and the weather was sunny and pleasant. Here I was assigned to the office of Director of Flying Training, an

11. Hollywood Bowl Meeting, California, July 1939

12. A view of Mountain House, Caux, called by Arthur Baker, when chief of *The Times* parliamentary staff, 'The headquarters of the hope of the world'

office staffed with men who had served their turn as fighter
pilots overseas.

By this time I had risen to be a corporal. The office should
theoretically have been run by a technical sergeant, a corporal
and a WAC. However there was no WAC, no technical
sergeant and Corporal Austin was in charge.

This for me was an entirely new job about which I knew
nothing and for which I had no training. Every morning I had
to ring up to find out which fighters were in service and what
was wrong with those out of service. At first the various complaints from which the planes suffered were so much double-
Dutch to me, but gradually I began to master them, not that
anybody seemed to mind unduly. The American fighter pilot
was a delightful and wholly unpredictable personality. Suddenly the captain would announce, "Come on boys, we're off to
Wichita" and like magic the pilots would fade away and
Corporal Austin would be in sole charge.

Communications were through a loudspeaker or 'squawk
box' in the office. Suddenly a garbled voice would crackle
through which I was totally unable to understand. "Yes sir"
or "No sir," I would answer, according to how the inspiration
hit me and on most occasions this seemed quite satisfactory.

My job started at 8 in the morning. After supper I had to
type out all the flying times of all the planes on the base. This
needed to be impeccably done and absolutely accurate as the
information next day would appear on the desk of the Commanding General of the United States Army Air Forces. Unfortunately I was no typist and had never before typed figures.
I was seldom through this job until 11 o'clock at night and
sometimes later when I put the carbon paper in the machine
the wrong way round.

Every now and then a pilot would take pity on me and off
we would go 'into the wild blue yonder' for a trip in a training
plane, not always the best experience for my liver. One day
the pilot said that we would do some 'lazy eights'. We twisted
and turned this way that way up and down until I was an unpleasant colour of green and then the pilot, recognising I had
had enough, we started for home. Unfortunately en route we
encountered a couple of B39s which made passes at us. The

pilot like an old war-horse reacted instinctively, and started taking 'evasive action'. I was totally forgotten. I was not sorry when at last I reached the ground.

It was while I was in Kansas that the war came to an end. Soon I was transferred from Kansas to Colorado where I was assigned to the office dealing with flying accidents.

At last I was transferred to my checking-out base and flown by an English Group Captain, assigned to the American forces, to our MRA Assembly Centre at Mackinac Island. Here I was once more free to take up without restriction the purposes to which I had given my life.

CHAPTER NINE

I

Phyll

DURING these years Jennifer and I were centred in Ottawa. Our host and hostess Helen and Warren Oliver lived in a small semi-detached house on the outskirts of the town. Another mother and daughter, evacuees from Scotland, were already staying with them when we arrived.

It was an entirely new experience for me to live amongst people who knew little or nothing about the theatre world. I was an intellectual snob and felt myself superior to women who only looked after their homes and children. I had never been domesticated and I felt cooking and housework were both boring and beneath me. Because my family were well off and my husband made good money writing and on the Stock Exchange, and because I earned an excellent salary in the theatre, we had been well able to afford help in our home and a nurse for our daughter.

It was very difficult for me to learn rather late in life what I should have learned as a much younger woman. To cook, to keep house, to look after my own children, were not easy at first, but this was the best thing that could have happened to me. It knocked off the artificial, unreal, actressy approach to life.

I had very little money. When Bunny was in the Army I had a small family allowance. I still had a small income in England but during the war no money was allowed out of the country. Our daughter hardly ever had a dress of her own until she was fourteen, and of course there was no help in the house.

As we were three mothers in one home we each took it in turns to cook for the family. My first efforts were disastrous. Everything I touched was burnt to a cinder. I used to stand over the pots and pans with tears streaming down my face–and not only from the onions!

One day when I was in the kitchen standing over a frying pan with everything going up in smoke, the door opened and a

147

friend who had worked in our home in England walked in. She had been our housemaid. She had married before the war and had settled with her husband in Canada. Her eyes popped out of her head and her mouth opened wide when she saw me in the kitchen. "Good heavens," she said, "what on earth has happened to you?"

She stayed and helped me, and after lunch we sat in the kitchen and talked for a long time. I told her how lazy and selfish I had been, expecting everyone to serve me instead of my serving them. I said, "The way I lived must have made you very bitter."

"Bitter," she said. "You don't know the half of it."

I told her that I was sorry and that it was women like me who made class war inevitable. We had a frank and honest talk together. She told me that she was distressed because her boy was fed up and leaving home that night. She said, "You have just apologised to me. Now I realise I need to apologise to him, because I have been a dictator in my home. I am going home to put things right with him." She phoned the next morning to tell me that her son had decided not to leave.

I learned many things in that home in Ottawa. Helen Oliver was Canadian, Virginia Hutchison was Scottish and I was English, and we came from entirely different backgrounds. After many heaves and hos and nearly scratching each other's eyes out in the process we learned the secret of how to get on together.

Helen Oliver was a very practical, down-to-earth housewife. She had the utmost contempt for me because I was not. On the other hand, I had the greatest contempt for her because she knew nothing about art or the theatre. Virginia was Scottish and was quite convinced that if only we could do things the way she had always done them, everything would be perfectly all right. The fact that we ended up firm friends and willing to learn from one another was, to put it mildly, a modern miracle.

II

We made many friends in Canada, amongst them the Reynolds family. Norah and Howard Reynolds and their four sons have

148

been some of our closest friends ever since. Howard is not only a fine actor, but a gifted director. We have worked closely together for many years.

Soon after Jennifer and I went to stay with them, their second son, Michael, went down with chicken-pox and scarlet fever and so all the household were in strict quarantine for twenty-eight days. During those days of enforced isolation, we started to dramatise in revue form the ideas we felt were most needed in the country at that time. In between washing and ironing and looking after the children, we wrote songs and sketches, which eventually became a war-time revue called *Pull Together, Canada.*

We first gave the revue in a small hall in Toronto. Mr Elliott Little, the Canadian Director of Selective Service was in the audience. "As I saw it," he said, "it seemed to me we were seriously missing something in this country. Something was stirred up in me tonight. I felt, why do we sit around and waste so much time? You are doing the real job. I am not sure whether Selective Service should take you over, or you should take over Selective Service. I am serious about this remark. You are doing a great job. For God's sake, keep on."

After a performance in Ottawa, attended by members of the government, we were invited by both labour and management of the Dominion Coal and Steel Company to take the revue to the coal and steel area of Cape Breton in Nova Scotia. Coal and steel were essential to the war effort and repeated stoppages were seriously affecting output.

We opened with the revue in Glace Bay in Cape Breton, on the easternmost tip of Canada. With snow and ice and bitter winds blowing from the Atlantic, with grey piles of slag and coal dust from the mines, Glace Bay is as bleak a spot as you can find.

One of the friends we made there was a miner called Mac-Donald the father of nineteen children, and his wonderfully humorous and warmhearted wife. What teas we had in their kitchen! The table laden with hot scones and ham and sausage rolls, we would sit round it talking with them and their friends far into the night.

One of the neighbours was a gay very little lady who had

recently become a widow. When I commented on her courage she said, "I have no regrets. I treated my husband well. I decided he would never haunt me and he never has!"

In another mining town close by we got to know the leader of the union, Bob, and his wife. Night after night they came to see the revue. They had fifteen children. One night, he told us, his wife was out and he had to put the younger children to bed. "How did you get on?" she asked him when she returned. "Not too good," he said. "The little lad with red hair screamed the place down. I had a real tussle to get him in". "Good heavens," she replied. "He's not ours – he's the neighbours'!"

Two of the cast stayed in Bob's home. He was a real leader and the men followed him. During our time there he and his wife found a new unity. His wife had nagged him because she wanted new linoleum for the kitchen floor. Bob spent too much of his pay packet on drink. When they learned how to settle their differences Bob went off to his work in the morning in a different spirit.

One day he had a talk with the mine manager, whom he had hated. He said, "I have had a chip on my shoulder at home. Every morning I have come to work in a bad temper and taken it out on you. I fought you on everything, right or wrong, and I am sorry. Let's settle things from now on on a basis not of who's right but of what's right."

Bob never ceased to be a fighter but he became a conciliator as well. He told us, "I used to fight for the right things in the wrong way."

In another town there was trouble in the steel mills. This time it was the manager, whose wife refused to get up and give him breakfast before he left for the office. He too left home angry and frustrated and took it out on the men. A young woman, a member of the cast, helped his wife to understand the importance of sending her husband out of the house in the mornings in a good spirit. After she decided to get up and cook him his breakfast he changed so much that the men said they could not believe he was the same man.

We had been set the task, before we went to Nova Scotia, of raising production 5 per cent which would be, we were told, the equivalent nationally of adding 50,000 men to the war effort. That target was exceeded, and the Minister of Labour, Mr Humphrey Mitchell, seemed to think it had something to do with us. In May 1944, he cabled Congressman Wadsworth: "We need a new spirit of teamwork between labour and management if industry is to weather the difficult days ahead. My department has received considerable evidence of the valuable contribution the forces of Moral Re-Armament are making to produce this essential factor."

III

It was in 1942 that I first began to understand the war of ideas. I had heard of contending ideologies, but I had hated the word ideology. One morning in my quiet time I asked for illumination, and suddenly I began to understand. Ideas were competing for the minds of men and women all over the world. The ideas which won would decide the future of our children and our grandchildren. I might hate the word ideology, but I had to recognise, whether I liked it or not, that we had moved into an ideological age. Not to recognise that fact would be blind and foolish. Ideas had become a modern means of warfare. They knew no boundaries. With the mass media of the press, radio and television (the last still in its infancy), theatre, literature and art of every kind, millions were being indoctrinated. Men were trained to use guns, ships and planes. They were now also trained to capture the thinking of whole nations.

Around that time I read a book on the Russian theatre which described how theatre companies went into farming areas, into small villages and large cities, indoctrinating people with the ideas of Communism.

I began to think back to the early days when Bunny first met MRA. He had said that we needed a theatre which could bring renaissance–rebirth–to men, a theatre which would give faith and hope to mankind. I had told him I thought he was crazy and had dismissed it as utopian nonsense. Now I realised that far from being crazy, it was commonsense. If a theatre was being created to banish the myth of God from the mind of men, why should there not be a theatre which could create faith and

151

not destroy it, and which could unite people, instead of dividing them?

When the summer of 1942 came, I went with the cast of *Pull Together, Canada* to Mackinac Island, Michigan. Buchman had felt the need for some conference centre where those who had responded to the challenge of the two revues both in America and Canada could come for training. For this purpose he had been lent, for a dollar a year, an old hotel on Mackinac Island called the Island House. The hotel, when we arrived there, was in a bad state of repair. Plaster and paint were peeling off and there were cracks in the walls. Luckily one member of the cast from Canada had been a plasterer, another was a builder, and with them we all set to work to scrub and clean and repair the whole building. By the time the first visitors arrived for the first conference the hotel was unrecognisable.

At the back of the main building was an old wooden barn. Here a small stage was built. It was in this barn, in the autumn of 1942, that the vision that Bunny had had three years before began to come to fruition.

Mackinac Island is a small island situated in the Straits of Mackinac where the Great Lakes of Michigan and Huron meet. The summers are warm and sunny but there is always a cool breeze, and it is never as hot as on the mainland. But in the autumn, when the leaves turn, it begins to get cold. There is much rain and chill winds blow across the Great Lakes. Finally the lakes freeze over and the island is held in a grip of snow and ice.

When a few of us first started meeting in the barn it was bitterly cold. There was no heat. We used to light oil stoves and sit wrapped up in overcoats. We were a company from many different backgrounds. There was Marion Clayton and her husband, Robert Anderson. Marion was a brilliant actress. She was trained at drama school in Seattle, Washington, and became well-known on the stage in Los Angeles. After playing the title role of *Peter Pan* she went into movies: *Mutiny on the Bounty*, *The Barretts of Wimpole Street* and many others. She was put under personal contract by Sidney Franklin, a leading director of Metro-Goldwyn-Mayer.

Robert Anderson met her at drama school. They were an

attractive couple and Bob was a talented actor. Marion had also developed a gift for direction.

There was Cecil Broadhurst, a relative of George Broadhurst, the well-known theatre manager who owned the Broadhurst Theatre on 44th Street in New York. Cece was Canadian and had had a varied career. He had piloted small planes across the wilds of northern Canada, and had been a cowboy on the prairies. He also had a gift for writing songs, which he sang with his guitar. He eventually became a radio personality in Winnipeg. On Sundays he was the Voice of the Westminster Choir and on Tuesdays and Thursdays he was Barney Roy the Minstrel Boy! He was a born comic and acting came as natural to him as breathing.

There was Howard Reynolds, the friend whose family I had stayed with in Canada and with whom I and others had helped to create *Pull Together, Canada*. He had known the depression after the war and had been a shoe salesman. His father was a businessman and also a gifted artist whose pictures captured the strange beauty of the snow-bound Canadian winters. Howard inherited his father's love of art and the theatre, and had, we discovered, a real flair for acting and direction.

There was Dorothea Hagedorn, the daughter of Hermann Hagedorn, the poet and biographer of Theodore Roosevelt. She later married another of the company, Eric Parfit, an artist, a skilled film technician and director of documentaries.

There was George Fraser, a gay and enchanting writer of lyrical music, "One of the six best in the world" as he was later described by a Hollywood musician. His songs through a series of musical plays or simply written for individual people or individual towns or industries or states or countries were destined to reach the hearts of millions around the world.

Two other musicians were Frances and Richard Hadden, pianists and composers. Frances had studied to be a concert pianist and was the sister of our friend John Roots.

Others included our friend the plasterer, Richard Stollery; Harriet Taylor, a Broadway stage director, and last, but most important, Alan Thornhill, a former Oxford Don, and a gifted author and dramatist.

We discovered an interesting fact. At first several of those who had had no experience of acting were self-conscious and could not act at all. But as we sat together before the rehearsals discussing the plays, and as expressing the meaning of the play became more important to them than personal success, self-consciousness fell away. There was a complete freedom from theatricality, from stilted, unreal and artificial mannerisms. Gradually people who at first could not act at all became good actors. Interestingly enough, without knowing it, these untrained actors began to achieve through simple honesty, the reality which the drama students who study the 'method' try to reach by great effort.

'The method' is based on the teaching of the great Russian actor-director, Konstantin Stanislavsky. At the turn of the century Stanislavsky, with a group of amateurs, started a new experiment in theatre in a large drawing room in his home near Moscow. Determined to rid the theatre of its artificiality, he brought a new depth, honesty and purity of purpose to the theatre. "Act with truthfulness and integrity of purpose," he told his students. Another time he asked, "Did you come here to serve art and to make sacrifices for its sake? Or to exploit it for your own personal ends?" He built up one of the finest companies of this century, at the Moscow Art Theatre.

"Do you realise why a real artist must live a full, interesting, varied, exacting and inspiring life?" he once asked. "He should know not only what is going on in the big cities but in the provincial towns, far away villages, factories and big cultural centres of the world as well. He should study the life and psychology of the people who surround him, or various other parts of the population both at home and abroad. We need a broad point of view. We are asked to interpret the life of human souls from all over the world. The actor creates not only the life of his time but that of the past and the future as well."

As we began to experiment in the Barn Theatre, we came upon these truths from another angle. If one was honest in one's own life it brought a new clarity about oneself and a new insight into other people. It gave one a deeper understanding of human nature. No drama class could teach one the functioning of the human heart, but the searchlight of honesty into one's own motives reveals a storehouse of every emotion—love, hate, jealousy, greed, lust, pride. Everyone experiences these emotions and they are all there for the actor to draw on for his interpretation of a character which he is called upon to play.

I realised how superficial my life had often been. I had not cared enough to find out what went on in other people. Far from knowing people in towns, villages and factories and men and women of other races and nations, I had spent my life in a small theatrical circle, who largely ate in the same places, met the same people and talked theatrical shop. There was a restaurant where many of us used to go day after day if we wanted to be seen by agents and producers. A dramatist who had written several West End successes used to sit at the same table at lunchtime every day. I once went to New York in a play for six months, and when I returned there she was sitting at the same table talking to the same people just as if she had never moved.

Although we were at the very beginning of our experiment, the plays we did in that Barn Theatre had an extraordinary power. "The play's the thing wherein I'll catch the conscience of the King," said Hamlet. Many people came to see us after the plays and told us, "I saw myself on that stage tonight." Or, "That was my mother, my sister . . .". It became increasingly clear that here was a theatre that gave insight, faith and purpose to its audiences.

In the years since then, those of us who started in the little Barn Theatre at Mackinac have worked together in the closest collaboration over many years and have taken this new theatre to the majority of the countries of the world.

IV

The Forgotten Factor by Alan Thornhill was our first major production. It had been another product of the time at the training camp at Tahoe in 1940.

It was while Alan was rooming with Bunny after my departure for Canada that the idea for a play came to him and he asked Bunny if he felt that I could write it. Bunny said, "Send her the synopsis," which Alan did. But after sending it, he said to Bunny that he thought he would have a go at writing it himself.

Bunny had been at school with Alan and received his idea of writing a play with some scepticism. He knew him later as an Oxford Don, a lecturer on the New Testament, an intellectual, yes, a man of wit and keen understanding certainly, but a playwright? However, not wishing to discourage him he said, "Why not go ahead?"

That night Alan had returned to their room saying he had written two acts and would like to read them. Bunny, tired and still sceptical, had groaned inwardly—he had had plays read to him before and knew it could be a tedious experience. But as Alan began to read he found himself thoroughly alert. He realised that the play was inspired. Knowing the third act was often the most difficult to write he asked Alan if he knew how he would finish the play.

"I have got it in my head," said Alan.

"Better write it down now before you forget it," urged Bunny.

"Oh no," Alan had replied, rather casually Bunny thought, "I'll go to bed and write it in the morning."

Alan went to bed and to sleep. Bunny stayed awake worrying about the third act!

In the morning Alan got up, had his quiet time and returned later in the day with the third act written and as inspired as the other two.

It was a play that was to launch Alan on a career of playwriting. None of his plays was to come as swiftly as that first one. Some were to be written only after months of hard study. It was, Alan said, as if that first play had been dictated. He had found it difficult to write fast enough to keep up with the thoughts as they came.

The Forgotten Factor was translated into sixteen languages and played to a million and a quarter people in all parts of the world. It was the play which radically changed the lives of a labour leader and his wife, John and Rose Riffe. John was to become Vice-President of the five million men of the CIO.

After a performance of *The Forgotten Factor*, Rose was reunited with her husband John, and step by step they were led to unravelling one of the most bitter and bloody strikes in the steel industry in America.

After the first production in the Barn Theatre I toured with *The Forgotten Factor* in many of the major cities of the North American continent. At the beginning of the tour we wondered if the play would have the same impact on the general public as it had had in Mackinac. There was no need to fear. Vast audiences crowded the theatres wherever we played and were gripped by the play from the moment the curtain rose to the time it fell.

In Philadelphia the first performance was attended by Congressman Wadsworth and Senator Harry S. Truman. After seeing the play Senator Truman said, "I wish *The Forgotten Factor* could be seen by workers and executives alike in every plant in the country. There is not a single industrial bottleneck I can think of which could not be broken in a matter of weeks if this crowd were given the green light to go full steam ahead. We need this spirit in industry. We need it in the nation."

Later he was to say that *The Forgotten Factor* was the most important play to come out of the war years. No one could then know that on the death of President Roosevelt, Senator Truman would have to take on the gigantic task of President of the United States.

v

I was delighted at the end of a long tour that we were scheduled to open in Los Angeles. I remembered my first visit with Bunny, the year after we were married, when he had played in the Pacific South West championships and had been so royally entertained by Clive Brook, Ronald Colman and other stars. I looked forward to meeting many old friends again.

In the early days of our marriage we had been very close friends of Jill and Laurence Olivier. I was delighted to find on my arrival in Los Angeles that Jill was living in Beverly Hills with her son Tarquin. I phoned her immediately and went to spend a weekend with her. I had not seen Tarquin since he

157

was a baby. He had grown into a delightful small boy – warm-hearted, outgoing and very musical.

I learned from Jill that Gladys Cooper lived close by in Pacific Palisades. Gladys, who was a tennis fan and keen player herself was another great friend. From the balcony of our flat in Hampstead we could look across the Heath and see her home in The Grove, Highgate. It was there, with her neighbours the John Drinkwaters and J. B. Priestleys, we would have many a game of tennis which though not up to Wimbledon standard made up in enthusiasm what was lacking in skill!

When our daughter Jennifer was born Gladys became her godmother. She was not only a famous beauty but she was a woman of rare character and courage. I was delighted at the thought of seeing her again and drove out the following week. She looked tanned and well. She has unbounded energy. She gardens, swims, plays tennis, walks, drives for miles, runs her home, looks after her children, and now her grandchildren, acts on the stage and screen, goes to parties and leads the life of ten women rolled into one.

One of her neighbours, Helen Wills Roark, wanted to see me again. Helen was the famous Wimbledon champion who had retired from first-class tennis and was now married to Aden Roark, the polo player. When Helen saw me she said, "Good heavens, what on earth has happened to you? You used to be the smartest woman in London." I think she voiced what others were thinking. I said I had not the money to buy expensive clothes and was wearing a suit that had been given to a friend who had given it to me.

Having in the past spent a great deal of time and money on my appearance, I had now made the mistake of going to the opposite extreme. I had always worried about what people thought of me. Now I was much more interested in what I could do for people. But in looking frumpy and untidy I realised I had given the wrong impression. I told Helen I would try to do better next time.

When I got back to where I was staying, I looked at myself in the mirror, and had a good laugh. I really did look a sight and needed some new clothes badly, but I had no money. That night I got down on my knees and said to God, "Lord,

I don't give a darn about being the best-dressed woman in town, but I do need to look a bit better than I look now."

The next day someone came up to me and said, "You can't go visiting your friends looking like that." She handed me an envelope. In it was enough for a new dress and a new suit. I went shopping that afternoon and said to the salesgirl, "Please find me the prettiest dress in the shop. I want to try and look as gay as I feel!"

CHAPTER TEN

I

Bunny

IN the autumn of 1945 I had been demobilised from the Air
Force and in the summer of 1946 a Canadian friend put at
our disposal a house in the Ontario countryside where Phyll,
Jennifer and I were able to enjoy our first holiday together
after the long separation of the war years.

By now we had a son called John. He had been born in a
hospital in Ottawa. Again it had not been an easy time for
Phyll, nor was it an easy time for John. He arrived looking like
a squashed orange. However, this did not diminish my love for
him. I had been delighted that our first child was a girl and
was now equally delighted that our second was a boy. Like
many fathers, I believe, I longed to have a son and my belief
that the baby would be a boy was so strong that before his
arrival I wrote out all the telegrams I wanted to send, naming
him as John and only leaving a blank for his weight.

It was a very happy period for both Phyll and me. Two nights
before John's coming we had been able to talk over together
something I had done wrong which was a deep pain in Phyll's
life. It was a shadow between us. We had never before been
able to talk about it as it roused Phyll's jealousy and so her
anger. But that night she had had the thought, "Either you
love your pride more than Bunny, or you love Bunny more
than your pride." And so, quietly, we had talked it over.

With no shadows between us, Phyll and I set out to enjoy
our holiday. I had not seen very much of Jennifer during the
eight years of her life, and this time together was a joyful one
as father got to know daughter, and daughter father.

One day Jenny was with me while I was playing golf on the
local nine-hole course. The grass was green and covered with
white daisies, and as I hit the ball Jenny would rush after it
over the daisy-strewn ground, fair hair flying, yellow cardigan
streaming in the wind. She was a picture of happy childhood
and it gladdened my heart to know that she was my daughter.

From "Tenisz" (Hungary)

"BUNNY" ASSUMES DON'S THRONE

Menzel, Riggs, Puncec, Henkel, Crawford, and Boussus do obeisance to the No 1 amateur of the world, as Budge leaves the scene with $75,000

John was five weeks old, and seemingly a healthy child. When he got hungry he yelled for his food and had an excellent appetite. On one occasion, however, he seemed to yell more furiously than usual, but not wanting to give in to what we considered his demand, we waited as usual until the appointed time for feeding. Suddenly John went limp. Fortunately we had a trained nurse with us. She called for a bath of hot water and taking John in her hands turned him this way and that to keep the breath of life in his limp and lifeless-looking body.

Slowly John recovered. He ate his meal and all seemed to be well. But a few days later it happened again. This time we hurried off with John to the local doctor. He advised us to take him immediately to a pediatrician in Montreal. We got hold of a car and drove, with Jennifer, to the city.

John was put in hospital. Phyll stayed with him and as there did not seem to be anything I could usefully do, and as we did not want to spoil Jennifer's holiday, I took her back to the country.

But our return to the country was short-lived. The very evening of our arrival the telephone rang and a friend told me that Johnny had had another attack. A chill of fear gripped me. I turned to the security I knew, I turned to guidance.

I sat down in a chair in the living room and I became aware of a light around me. The thought came to me to read in the Bible the story of the raising of Jairus' daughter. And then I wrote, "And at that hour the child was healed." I looked at my watch and noted the time. It was 9 p.m.

The next morning Jenny and I returned to Montreal and I hurried to the hospital. As I entered the ward, Phyll looked up at me with joy in her face. "He is much better," she exclaimed. "He suddenly got quite well last night."

I asked her if she knew what time it had been. She thought a moment, calculating from the times of Johnny's feeding.

"It must have been 9 o'clock," she said.

John left the hospital that day and never had another attack.

II

Phyll
Having spent my early life trying to be glamorous, I realised in Canada that I had to start all over again. I had to learn to

be a real woman instead of an artificial mannequin, to accept to be a wife and a mother not just a career woman. I realised I had everything to learn about how to create a sound family life and I do not know what I would have done had it not been for my daily quiet time. It was my life-line. Every morning I would wake an hour earlier for an unhurried time of meditation, and I was shown step by step how to bring up our children.

Jenny, as we called her, was very small in the early days in Canada. Perhaps because I had so much to learn God mercifully sent us a daughter who from the earliest age taught me as much as I taught her. To listen to God was as natural to her as sleeping and eating. I used to sit up in bed in the morning and write down the thoughts that came to me so I would not forget them. Jenny used to draw her thoughts before she could write. Often she would get her own corrective without my having to say a word.

One morning in the early days in Ottawa when things were not easy, I was wondering if I was crazy to bring up Jenny without all the material things I had had as a child. Then this thought came, "Nurture your child's faith. Teach her to care and serve others and you will give her the greatest heritage a parent can give."

Every evening I would spend unhurried time with Jenny before she went to sleep. We would talk over the day together, the good and the bad things that had happened. We played a game of five little men. Each finger on the hand was called Mr Honesty, Mr Purity, Mr Unselfishness and Mr Love and the thumb Jenny called Mr Obedience. Every night we would see how these gentlemen had got along during the day, whether they were standing up or whether they had fallen flat on their faces. I would go over Jennifer's and then she would go over mine. In doing so she came to realise that I had exactly the same difficulties and obstacles to overcome as she had. Because I was honest with her, she was able to talk over with me everything that troubled her including all kinds of fears and questions that I, as a child, had felt that I had to keep to myself.

I soon realised that I could not ask Jenny to live a quality of life I refused to live myself. When Jennifer was about six, for instance, I could never get her to bed on time. She dawdled and played around and I used to get irritated and in the end lost my temper, which only made her more stubborn. One morning I realised I had no authority in getting her to bed on time because I dawdled myself! That evening I told her about it and I asked her to help me. I have never seen anyone get into bed so quickly as she did that night and there was no more trouble.

I learnt that if I accepted the discipline of obedience to God I need have no fear of being firm with our children. Also we have always encouraged the children to tell us if they feel we need to be different on any point. This did not weaken our authority with them. It meant we had all accepted a higher authority.

Jenny was eight when her brother was born. She had always told us that she wanted a baby brother. So when I found I was going to have a baby I could not wait to tell her. I was away and wrote to her that I had a big surprise for her. As soon as I got home, she was excited to find out what the surprise was. When I told her, her face fell and she said, "Oh what a shame, I thought I was going to have a canary!"

After John was born, she began to be very silly and giggly. I could not make out what was the matter. Then one morning I realised that she was jealous. So that night I asked her what she really felt about her brother, not what she felt she ought to feel, and she burst out with, "Now everyone looks at him, and no-one pays any attention to me any more." We were able to talk it all out together and I told her how jealous I had been of my sister who was seven years younger and much prettier than me. I told her how people had come to our home and said, "Isn't she beautiful, so different from the other one!" We had a good laugh and decided that if she ever felt jealous again at any time, we could always talk it out together.

When the war was over and Bunny out of the army, I still continued living in Ottawa. Each summer I had been to the conferences at Mackinac, which had been annual events since the first in 1942 and continued to have far-reaching influence as thousands attended each year.

In 1946 I travelled to Mackinac with both the children. It

was a long, hot and dusty journey. It meant taking a train to Sioux Sainte Marie, changing en route at a place called Sudbury and then taking the car to St Ignace and the ferry to the island.

Jenny was eight and John only seven weeks old. As the train reached Sudbury Jennifer looked horribly sick and John was yelling his head off. I got out onto the platform, hot and weary. Again I began to question the kind of life I was living and its effect on the children. Was this a mad way to bring them up, moving from home to home and now making this hot journey to a conference where there would be hundreds of people?

Suddenly a voice seemed to speak over my shoulder, "There is a beneficent power always looking after your children." At that moment John stopped crying and Jenny's appearance changed from green to her normal healthy colour.

I went on my way content that however difficult the way might seem, I was doing what God wanted me to do and, as I did it, He would be looking after both me and my children.

III

During the 1946 conference as some of us began to think of the urgent needs of the reconstruction period, the conviction came that we should dramatise, in revue form, the great moral and spiritual heritage of America and Europe handed down to us by George Washington, Lincoln, St Joan, St Francis and a host of other men and women of faith throughout the ages.

It was one thing to have such a conviction. It was another to implement it. Many of those who had first created our theatre in the barn in 1942 had gone to Europe. Those who were left felt incapable of either writing or producing such a show.

When I was a sophisticated young actress I used to hear of the faith of Lilian Baylis of the Old Vic and had laughed about it. I had read an interesting book about her by Dame Sybil Thorndike in which she said Lilian Baylis used to get down on her knees and pray for what was needed. And she got it!

That is exactly what happened to us.

Bunny wrote the first scene about the heritage of America.

He read it to me one evening and I said, "This is marvellous. We must do it."

"But how can we?" he said. "We've got nobody here who can produce it." So, like Lilian Baylis, we got down on our knees and prayed for a director.

A few days later Nellie van Volkenburg Browne arrived on the Island. The wife of Maurice Browne, the producer of *Journey's End*, she was an avant garde director who was well known in America. She said, "Somebody has had the thought that I should come here for two weeks. I can't think why." So we said, "Would you sit down, and we'll tell you why." After listening to us she said, "This is very interesting. I would love to produce the scene, but you'll need music. Haven't you anybody who can write it?"

We said, "No, but we prayed and you arrived, so why don't we pray for a composer?" Three days later off the boat from the mainland came a man called Paul Dunlap. Paul Dunlap is a well-known musician from Hollywood who has done arrangements for some of the great films.

He said, "You know, I've had a very strange experience. All the way from Hollywood I've had a theme running through my head. I don't know what it's for. I'd like to write it down." So we said, "Get it down as quickly as you can."

We had the music and we had the director, and then Nellie Browne said, "What we really need is a scrim—so that the characters Lincoln, Washington, St Francis and St Joan could gradually appear from the past. We need yards and yards of black mosquito netting."

We were on this tiny island with only a few village shops. The stage manageress telephoned Detroit and Chicago, but they had nothing. Finally she sat down and thought, "What do we do?" The only thought she had was to go down to the village shop and buy a yard of black sateen for a blouse. So she went into a little shop and said, "Do you, by any chance, have any black sateen?" The man said, "I'm terribly sorry, I haven't. The only thing I seem to have is yards and yards of black mosquito netting. I don't know what to do with it." She said, "I know what to do with it! I'll have it all, thank you very much."

She was walking back with it under her arm and a man was walking beside her. He said, "Excuse me, but you're looking very worried. Can I help you?" She said, "I am worried. I've got all this black mosquito netting. I've got to put it into a huge frame and I don't know how to do it." He said, "I'm a sail-maker. I'd like to help you in any way I can."

That first scene was produced by the end of the week. It was the basis of a revue called *The Good Road*. Eventually it played in London at Her Majesty's Theatre. It went into Germany in the early days after the war and played in shells of burned out theatres. The hopeless and the faithless, the bitter and the dis-illusioned, caught a glimpse of a faith which could rebuild their shattered homes and lives.

Many other miracles made that revue possible. A song, 'The Whole World Is My Neighbour', with a haunting and lovely tune, was composed by two different people at different times. Neither knew the other was writing a song. Yet when they came together they found that one had written the verse and the other the chorus. They fitted like a glove.

Our leading man, Leland Holland, was a worker from Cali-fornia. He had been a shop steward at the Lockheed Aircraft Factory before he went into the Army. He fought and was wounded in the Battle of the Bulge and came to Mackinac after he was demobilised. He wanted to find an answer to the hell he had lived through. He was physically exhausted, and as he began to find new life coming back into his heart and mind and body he had the thought one morning to tell some of us that he had always wanted to sing but had been much too proud to say so. We found that he had a superb natural baritone voice.

We were also joined by Louis Fleming, a young radar expert, just demobilised from the Canadian navy. Immensely creative and highly skilled technically he and his wife Valerie have played an increasingly important role in the world-wide development of our theatre and films.

The Good Road had its première performance in the city of Grand Rapids, Michigan, at the invitation of its mayor, George Welch.

We opened in the local auditorium which seated 5,500 people

and was mainly used for skating, boxing, bicycle races and similar forms of public spectacle. Plays were seldom shown there, and the reason is understandable. The vast floor space is flat. From the back of the hall a telescope is almost necessary, while spectators in the galleries at the front can hardly see the stage at all.

This was a supreme test of the revue's effectiveness. If it could hold an audience in this vast auditorium, where sight and sound, however magnified, were most difficult, it could hold it anywhere.

As we walked back to our hotel Nellie van Volkenburg Browne said, "Frankly I did not think any play or revue could hold an audience of that size in that kind of auditorium. The fact that the revue did hold them from beginning to end shows its immense power."

We stayed several weeks in Grand Rapids only leaving to fulfil other engagements in Michigan and finally in Detroit. It was in Detroit that Bunny had news of his father's fatal illness and he returned to England.

IV

Bunny

It was seven years since I had been home. My mother received me as if it had only been a few days. She was older, of course, and her legs had grown stiff with arthritis. It was difficult for her to walk. Most women would have made an invalid of themselves, but my mother gave it little thought. She was unable to climb the stairs in the normal way, so she went up backwards. She had people other than herself to worry about.

There was my father. Seven years had worked a total transformation. I had left a man broad-shouldered and energetic, full of friendliness and optimism, always eager for the next game of tennis or the next game of golf, his eyes bright blue and sparkling and full of fun, believing if times were good, they would remain so, if bad, they were bound to get better. Now I found a little, wizened old man, his eyes closed in what seemed an almost permanent doze, his optimistic nature turned to a determined pessimism. His face which had been clean-shaven was now covered by a sailor's beard. His thick head of hair was snowy white.

He was dozing in one of the familiar armchairs which used to stand by the fireplace of our old dining room – one of the few pieces of furniture salvaged from our old home. He took no notice of me. An aunt of mine who had come to welcome me home tried to waken him. "Wolf, Wolf, your son is home." My father opened one disinterested eye, then closed it again.

It had been a hard time for my mother and sister. My father had had an operation for a prostate gland. In those days the doctors did the operation in two parts. After completing the first, they felt it was too dangerous to attempt the second. My father was condemned to what was for him a living death.

Active all his life, he was now confined to a chair. He had no inner resources. He could find nothing to do but sit and mope and complain and finally to give up altogether. My mother and sister had been models of patience.

And not only had they to endure the trial of my father's illness, but they had had to contend with the almost ceaseless attentions of the more sensational newspapers. While their American correspondents harried me in America, so their London reporters continually pestered my mother and sister. "It must have been very hard on you," I said to my sister one day. She looked at me surprised. "Oh, not at all. It didn't worry me a bit. I always knew you were doing the right thing."

During the next days I was able to help stir my father out of his endless lethargy and to talk over many things with him. For seven years I had not heard from him except for an occasional signature on a birthday card or a Christmas card. Whereas my mother and sister fully understood and were in deepest sympathy with all I had been doing, my father had been mystified.

One day, in order to try to understand his son's activities, he had called in a young man who lived in a house opposite our own. He was a minister of the Church. The young man had sat extremely uncomfortably by my father's bed. "Mr Austin," he had at last exclaimed, "I don't think I ought to talk to you. You see, you are not in my parish."

My father had shrugged his shoulders. So this was the type of man he supposed his son had become. He lost all further interest in my doings.

My father revived during my days at home, and we spent many happy hours together and became once more the good friends we had always been before.

v

It was strange to see my parents in a house different from the one in which they had lived together for almost fifty years and in which I had lived with them for twenty-five. It had been blown up in 1944. My parents had moved to a second floor flat in Upper Norwood. My sister told me the story.

Always, my sister said, there had been the alert first and then the guns–an engulfing sea of noise echoing and roaring in nerve-shattering waves. And then last of all would come the bombs.

But on this night there had been no alert. The roar and boom of the guns had not begun. Yet the bombs were falling.

Nanny met my sister on the landing on the first floor of our home. Nanny was very nervous. What was happening? Why were these bombs falling? Why had there been no alert? Why were the guns not firing? Why was there no sound of the planes?

My sister tried to give comfort to Nanny. She too was mystified. My sister was a fire-watcher. Should she go off to her duties–or back to bed to sleep?

Suddenly the sound of the bombs dropping stopped. My sister went back to bed where she was sleeping at the back of the house and Nanny back to the night nursery at the top of the house where first with Phyllis, then with Joan and finally with me she had always slept. But Nanny could not sleep. She was very much afraid. And when the bombs started falling again, she came downstairs to ask my sister what they should do.

My sister heard the second lot of bombs falling and she still lay in bed. She said the 91st Psalm over to herself. "But you have sheltered beside the Eternal and made the Most High God your home, so no scathe can befall you." She wondered if she should go on her fire-watching duty; it was difficult to know because she was not quite sure what was happening. What were these bombs falling? Where were the guns? Why had there been no alert?

But if bombs were falling her place must be at her fire-watching station. She got out of bed and dressed.

When she went out onto the landing Nanny was just coming down from her room at the top of the house. She greeted Nanny and thought it wise for her not to stay upstairs. It was safer on the ground floor or in the cellars.

My sister continued on downstairs, Nanny behind her.

And then it happened. Suddenly the whole house seemed to collapse around my sister. She sat on the little landing just at the top of the first flight of stairs. The tall stained glass windows behind her blew out and a curtain from the home across the road blew in and wrapped itself protectingly around her. The bannisters collapsed and bricks began to fall. But though some touched my sister, they never harmed her.

She carefully climbed down what remained of the stairs.

Mother and Dad woke up in the little room where they were sleeping on the ground floor. "Get my slippers," said my father.

Mother felt around. She did not know what had happened. She tried to find the matches but all she could feel was a strange substance which turned out to be the plaster from the ceiling that had fallen on the bed.

"I can't find any matches," said my mother.

"Get me my torch."

The torch could not be found either.

My sister joined them and helped them struggle out of bed. She found them their dressing gowns and helped them out of the house. The vicar was passing in his car wondering whom of his flock he could help. He picked up my father and mother and just as they were took them to a friend's home a mile or so away.

Suddenly my sister heard cries from the rubble. Half the house had been blown away and Nanny was mortally wounded, fallen with the house in which for forty-two years she had so devotedly, and so lovingly served.

It was Nanny's wish that when she died no one would have to bear the expenses of her funeral. And so for her funeral she had kept in a tin box in the kitchen money which was known as

'Nanny's burial money' or just Nanny's 'burial'. Nanny's burial had been a great financial standby in our family life. When funds were short money would be borrowed from it and you would hear mother ask: "Nanny, how much money have you got in your burial?" Nanny would name a sum. "May I borrow two pounds, Nanny?" Nanny would obligingly agree, "But don't forget to pay it back, Mummy dear. It's getting rather low."

And now when the time had come for Nanny to be buried my sister searched in the heap of rubble where the kitchen had once been. In the blast, the box in which Nanny kept her burial had been blown open and the pound notes which comprised it were strewn around. Patiently my sister collected them. And when her search was complete, she counted what she had found. The total exactly covered the expenses of Nanny's burial.

VI

During my first days at home I went down to see the site where our old home had been. The beech trees which flanked our front gate were still there and in magnificent leaf. But now there was no gate, and the path that led to our front door was no longer visible. The May tree that spread over the lawn in our back garden was now only a skeleton, charred by the blast of the bomb. And where the hedge and bay tree had once stood, which had divided the garden into two, sat a rather down-at-heel prefabricated house.

Across the road my grandfather's house still stood. But now it was sub-divided into flats. The monkey trees which had stood on the neat front lawn had disappeared, and the lawn and drive were no longer kempt. The wide gates we used to swing on as children had disappeared, too. The old stables were open to the public gaze. The well-ordered world of my grandparents was part of a departed age. I thought of their neat back garden. The lawn and shrubberies, the summer house, the tree-shaded walk, the mulberry tree from which we used to get the leaves to feed our silkworms, and the kitchen garden, succulent in summer when the raspberries and loganberries were ripe. All these were a memory, and Inky the dog, too, that fierce

Newfoundland which charged out from its kennel as you went in
the back way and terrified the tradesmen. I remember brushing
him one day, myself at his head, a friend at his tail. My friend
trod on his tail, and I received the bite. My knee still bears the
marks of Inky.

Yes, the old world I knew had gone. The blast of war had
done more than reduce so much of it to rubble. The whole
structure of that world had been shaken. It could never be the
same again. This was true not only of my world; it was every
world and all the world. Revolution was in the air, in some
instances a bloody one, in others quiet and in some instances
almost unnoticed.

A revolution was indeed needed. A new society had got to be
built world-wide. The old injustices, the old inequalities had
got to go. But what new society was to take the place of the
old? What was to be the basis of this new society? The bid of
Naziism for world domination had been crushed at enormous
cost. Was the philosophy of the master race with its use of
ruthless means to obtain its ends to be replaced by the philosophy of the master class, whose means to its end were also
bathed in blood? Was violence the only way to change? And
in the end, did violence change anything? "Revolutions," said
a French philosopher, "change everything except human
nature." And human nature unless changed put the clock back
again. The French Revolution guillotined a king and created
an emperor. It destroyed an old aristocracy and a new one
arose in its place. That would continue to be the pattern of
revolution until there was a revolution in human nature – the
birth of a new type of man who would create a new type of
world.

Was this utopian? Or was it the only reality? "To expect a
change in human nature may be an act of faith, but to expect
a change in society without it is an act of lunacy."

I talked to Mother about these things. One morning she said,
"Your work is needed. Isn't it time you went to Caux?"

CHAPTER ELEVEN

I

Bunny

CAUX stands on the steep shelf of a Swiss mountainside, looking over views of supreme beauty. To the left is the distant
Dents du Midi, its jagged peaks like a giant's teeth, as the name
implies. It stands a snow-capped guardian of the Rhone valley,
whence the Rhone river flows into Lac Leman.

Directly below Caux lies the lake itself, walled on its far side
by the mountains of the Haute Savoie. To the right, huddled
by the lakeside, are Montreux and Vevey and beyond, in the
distance, Lausanne. Far away where the lake bends out of
sight beyond the long line of the Jura, stands the unseen city
of Geneva.

The two main hotels of Caux are the Mountain House and
the Grand. The former, in pre-war days, was called the Caux
Palace and was a centre for winter sports. Its strange architec-
ture, with its towers and minarets, gives it an exotic and fairy-
tale appearance; and it is said to have formed the prototype
of the castle of *Snow White*.

Caux Palace was acquired by the Swiss MRA force after the
war to provide for Europe a centre for assemblies equivalent to
those at the Island House of Mackinac, and for this reason it
was re-christened Mountain House. It was found in a state of
great disrepair. During the war it had been used for refugees,
and for reasons known only to its frustrated inmates doors had
been pulled off their hinges and the lift shafts filled with rubbish.
When discovered, it was about to be sold to a company and
pulled down.

Those searching for the right centre in Switzerland came
across Caux Palace. For a building basically so fine, even
though requiring much restoration, it was remarkably cheap
but it was nonetheless a large sum, and any sum is large if
you have little or no money in the bank.

Moral Re-Armament is financed through sacrifice. There are
no easy funds. No great American millionaires or huge industries

stand as angels behind the work. Behind Moral Re-Armament stands the giving of those who believe that Moral Re-Armament must provide the basis of world reconstruction. They give till it hurts. Many have given all that they once possessed.

And now in Switzerland there were no ready funds for the purchase of the Caux Palace. One businessman gave a third of his capital. Others dug deep in their pockets, some giving all their savings. Many without money gave the service of their hands—carpenters and masons, plasterers, housewives, cooks. And out of its disrepair the Mountain House rose as a new building with a new look—and a new name.

Arthur Baker, the chief of *The Times* parliamentary staff, called Caux 'the headquarters of the hope of the world'. Not only did buildings and towns lie shattered in an exhausted Europe, but so did the spirit of man. Out of the concentration camps, out of the underground movements, out of the armies victorious or defeated, up from the rubble of broken houses and broken homes came men and women despairing of the future. Their hearts were often filled with dread; but far more dangerous were the bitterness and hate which are the seeds of future war.

These men and women flocked to Caux, the bitter and the hate-filled, the disillusioned and despairing, the men and women who were hungry not just for food but for the great realities on which they could rebuild their broken lives and broken lands.

And from Caux went forth, as those first post-war summers came and went, men and women with new light in their faces, new hope in their hearts and above all a determination not to rest until a new world had been built.

II

Phyll
I shall never forget the arrival at Caux. of the first delegation from Germany. They were the first Germans to be allowed out of Germany after the war and came with the permission of General Clay and Lord Pakenham (now Lord Longford) who was the Minister in charge of the British Zone.

I stood at the back of the big hall as they arrived. All my relations in France and Germany had suffered cruelly under the Nazis. As I have written my cousin Arlette died in the gas chambers with her two babies. Others lost everything they possessed, wandering without homes, food or money across Europe. One of my cousins was hidden for three years in Holland. I found myself feeling physically sick.

I went up to my room and looked out on the marvellous view from my window. There were the mountains, the Dents du Midi in the distance, the green carpet of the Rhone Valley and the wide stretch of the Lake of Geneva. The sun was shining and it was unbelievably beautiful and peaceful. "Why," I kept thinking, "when we live in such a fantastic world should men be so cruel to each other?"

Then as I thought of my family a great wave of bitterness and hatred towards those who had perpetrated such terrible things swept over me. The feelings were so powerful I realised that I was capable of exactly the same kind of cruelty towards the Germans as they had been capable of towards my people. I understood with extraordinary clarity that unless this cruelty and hatred could be cured, there would be a never-ending cycle of hurt, hate and revenge.

I in no way condone what is wrong. I hate the fiendish cruelty and brutality which made those appalling camps possible. But I was conscious that day that all of us have in our natures the seeds of that same cruelty and that only the power of God could control the forces in man which made these atrocities possible. I asked God on my knees to take that bitterness from me and when I got up it had gone. In its place was not a rosy glow of 'now I feel better', but a passionate determination to help bring a cure. I knew we could never build the future on hate, however justified.

It was some weeks later something happened which tested this experience. Some friends came to me and said, "A play is needed to go through the Ruhr in Germany, something that can bring a new spirit to that very troubled area. We know you are one who could help produce it." All the old feelings of bitterness started to well up in my heart again. Once more I went to my room to try and sort things out. I realised that if I wanted to heal the hurts and hates of mankind, here was the right place to start. I told my friends that I would do it.

The following day I met the Germans who were to be the cast, to start rehearsals for Alan Thornhill's *The Forgotten Factor* in German. I told them about my experience of the past few days. It was a time I shall never forget. One young doctor wept. He said, "Of course I realised what was happening was wrong, but I hadn't the courage to speak up. Had I and millions like me done so, it could never have happened." Another member of the cast who had been trained in the Hitler Youth told me how hopeless and disillusioned and lost he was when he realised the terrible consequences of the idea in which he had been trained.

A deep love for Germany was born in me. I do not forget the suffering of my people, I never will. Nor am I so starry-eyed that I ignore the fact that it could happen again. But I know now that there is an answer to it.

III

Bunny
Buchman made a bid to change the tide of German thought before the Second World War and failed. The headquarters of the Gestapo banned all Oxford Group literature from 1936, put spies in all meetings from 1937 and, in 1939, wrote the 126-page secret report on Buchman and his work which described MRA as "a force which preaches revolution against the National State and has quite evidently become its Christian opponent."

After the war, Buchman made another attempt to influence events in Germany and succeeded. At a time when no one else would welcome the Germans it was he who arranged for some two hundred of them to come to Caux. Among them were the future Chancellor, Konrad Adenauer, and all his family, and those who became heads of the trade unions, Minister Presidents of the various Lands and so on. Dr Adenauer, as Chancellor, said repeatedly that it was Buchman who first brought Germany back into the international family.

Adenauer was also impressed by MRA's work in the Ruhr

13(a). Lena Ashwell, Lady Simson

13(b). Joel and Frances McCrea

14(a). Bunny and Phyllis with Filipino Foreign Minister Serrano. Centre background
Rajmohan Gandhi

14(b). Rajmohan Gandhi at opening of new MRA centre at Panchgani, India

and its "unseen but effective part in bridging differences between the negotiating parties" in the Franco-German discussions associated with the Schuman Plan. In 1960, the German diplomat who, in the following year, was to 'become Ambassador in London, von Etzdorf, stated in the United States: "The most significant development in Europe since World War II is the new accord between Germany and France. For this, the work of Moral Re-Armament was largely responsible." Frank Buchman was decorated by the French Government with the Legion of Honour.

I was to hear the other side of this story in September 1953 when Robert Schuman, then the French Foreign Minister, came to Caux. With Frank Buchman's secretary, Morris Martin, I went to fetch him from Geneva where he was attending an international conference, and I acted as his ADC while he was at Mountain House.

Schuman had known Buchman for nearly five years. His interest was first kindled when an industrialist from Lille told him of the surprising effect of MRA in Northern France. Schuman, who was then Prime Minister, asked the industrialist to bring Buchman to meet him when next Buchman was in France. This meeting took place early in 1949. "We had barely twenty minutes," Schuman recalled, "but Dr Buchman's personality made a deep impression upon me".

In October that year the two men dined together with the industrialist in Paris. Schuman had had a frustrating summer. He told Buchman that he had long wanted to get out of politics. He would like to retire to a certain monastery and write. Yet he knew that he had a unique background which might enable him to play a part in ending the hatred between France and Germany. He explained that he had been brought up a German in Lorraine, served in the German Army in the First World War and then, when Lorraine returned to France, had become a Frenchman and served France in peace and war.

Buchman told him that certainly his place was in politics and at Schuman's request gave him the names of several Germans who had been to Caux and whom he could trust. Konrad Adenauer headed the list.

In January 1950 Schuman called on the German Chancellor

in Bonn. Already Buchman had seen Adenauer to prepare him and had written him:

"If we can get together and have a common mind under the guidance of God, then He can give the answer to the extremely difficult and seemingly insoluble problems which present themselves. All other problems are quickly settled when we have major agreement on that fundamental one. Foreign Minister Schuman is prepared to work on this basis. He realises your difficulties and is willing to cooperate to the maximum. I am sure you are more than ready to work with him."

At their meeting in January, Schuman and Adenauer came to know each other's minds and in May, in correspondence with Adenauer, Schuman first outlined what the world now knows as the Schuman Plan. Adenauer expressed himself in complete agreement with the basic idea and general tendency of the plan.

That same spring Schuman wrote a Foreword to Frank Buchman's speeches *Remaking the World*:

"If we were being presented with some new scheme for the public welfare, or another theory to be added to the many already put forward, I should remain sceptical. But what Moral Re-Armament brings us is a philosophy of life applied in action. It is not a question of a change of policy: it is a question of changing men. Democracy and her freedom can be saved only by the quality of men who speak in her name. This is what Dr Buchman expressed in simple and moving words. May he be heard more and more in all nations of the world by those who today still clash in fratricidal hatred."

As we drove towards Caux through the neat Swiss towns, through the vineyards with their ripening grapes, with brief glimpses of old castles in the hills and on our right the calm waters of Lake Leman, and as at last we drove up the steep road to the Mountain House with the view unfolding more and more breathtakingly, Schuman spoke much of his friendship with Frank Buchman and this visit to Caux which he had so long anticipated.

Frank Buchman was waiting outside the Mountain House to receive his guest and on a rise in front of it where the flags of the nations flew, a chorus from many countries in gay national costume sang their welcome.

It was quite late when Schuman arrived and he had had a tiring journey, but he was unwilling to miss a thing and immediately went into the theatre where a play was being performed. During the next days he attended the plenary sessions of the Assembly in the mornings and afternoons and further plays at night.

Then came the last meeting before he had to depart. He was not asked to speak, but as the meeting was ending he put up his hand and asked to say a word. He referred to the Foreword he had written to Frank's speeches:

"I had a sort of intuition which came to me through that book. I saw a new perspective opening before me. I caught a glimpse of what the life of Frank Buchman, past and present, must be like. I did not then know what he had been able to achieve nor of the massive support he had gathered around him. I had no means of knowing the enthusiasm with which he was regarded throughout the world. Now I know, and what impressed me more than anything else is how these things are translated in terms of international relations between countries."

He went on, "I leave here with a spirit noticeably different from the one in which I came here. I have been in politics for thirty-four years and during that length of time one learns to be sceptical. I am leaving with much less scepticism in my nature than when I came and at my age that is a considerable advance. I am accustomed to conferences, but they are very different from this. All others end in great disappointment–of a personal or of a general nature. Here there is nothing but satisfaction and a great hope. Thank you for giving me that hope. From now on we will never give up."

After the speech he walked the length of the platform and off to the side where Frank Buchman was sitting and in true French fashion kissed him on both cheeks. As he left the hall he said, "This is the greatest experience of my life."

IV

Phyll
The other dramatic production which emerged from the Caux Conference of 1948 was *The Good Road*, a European version of

the musical which we had created in America. After Caux it was invited by the Minister Presidents of the various German Lands to play in eight of their greatest cities. A force of two hundred and fifty set off in eight Swiss buses and numerous cars. They slept on floors, in kitchens or wherever there was space in those shattered cities and played in the old opera houses which stood gaunt amid the ruins. This was the first large civilian party to visit Germany since the war.

After Germany, *The Good Road* played for six weeks at Her Majesty's Theatre in London. There one evening I sat in the stalls with a woman who had played at Her Majesty's in its greatest years. Her name was Lena Ashwell. During the First World War she had pioneered entertainment for the troops, and afterwards her company, the 'Lena Ashwell Players', had taken great drama to the people in halls throughout the country.

When the curtain came down on *The Good Road* she sat quietly. Then she said, "You know, this is the vision Irving had for the theatre. This is what the theatre is meant to do for the world."

Some weeks later she came to Caux. At that time Lena was in her late seventies but she had the vitality of a woman half her age. I have rarely met anyone so energetic. It was hard to keep up with her. Her back was straight, her eyes were bright, a shock of white hair framed her still handsome face and her mind was as alert as a young girl's. She had been married to Sir Henry Simson, the gynaecologist who brought the Queen and Princess Margaret into the world. With Lena came her sister and faithful friend, Hilda Pocock. Lena was the elder of the two. Hilda did not have the physical charm of her sister but she was an indomitable old lady who had been a matron of a military hospital at Mafeking during the Boer War. She would often tell us of her meeting with Florence Nightingale. These two old ladies were like sturdy oaks with their roots deep in the great traditions of Britain.

Lena told us one day, "Secretly I was praying that God would take me—I could see no useful purpose for my life. Now I have asked God that He may give me long life for I've found a purpose greater than any before."

She spoke one day at Caux. "I was born on a battleship. It had been at Trafalgar and had once been Nelson's flag ship. That is how I think I happen to be a fighter, because you fight for your life at sea. This world needs fighters. It wants people who care about things.

"I fought my way into the theatre. I became a leading actress. I had the privilege of playing with many great actors, notably Henry Irving, Charles Wyndham and Ellen Terry. I knew Eleonora Duse and Sarah Bernhardt. Before Irving died I had a long interview with him which inspired me to feel the great mission of the theatre.

"I mention these things because I have the deepest feeling about the power of the theatre. I came to Caux because of the theatre. I felt that the new play, *Annie the Valiant* would enable people to realise the destructive and vicious influence of class distinction.

"I have only a small part in this enterprise. But I'm glad to have a share. It is a wonderful thing for me to be doing something in the theatre, through the theatre which brings so true and vital a message to my great country."

Today a portrait head of Lena stands in the Westminster Theatre and the star dressing room, which was equipped with the money contributed by members of her family, is dedicated to her memory.

v

We will never forget our last meeting with Lena. She had suffered a stroke and lost the power of speech. Her sister 'phoned us asking if we would come to tea with her. We imagined we would be sitting by her bedside, unable to communicate. When we arrived at her home in a London Mews we were shown into her living room. Outside it was cold and grey. Inside a warm fire burned in the grate, the tea was beautifully laid out with the best silver and in a wheelchair sat Lena in a beautiful purple velvet robe, with her white hair brushed off her lovely face. She looked like a Queen. Unable to speak she motioned for us to sit down and wrote on a pad the questions she wanted to ask us. She listened intently to everything we had to tell her, following our latest adventures with obvious enjoyment and laughing heartily at all our jokes. Then she handed us a letter she had just written to the Queen Mother. She felt all was not well with Britain. She feared for the future. She was writing her convictions. Like an old battleship whose days are numbered, she was sinking, but fighting with her last breath for the greatness of her country which she loved so well.

VI

Bunny

From London *The Good Road*, with a travelling force, went to America and after showings in New York, Washington, cities in the Mid-West and Canada, reached Los Angeles.

In Washington Ralph W. Page, a widely syndicated columnist, wrote:

"This inspired production has all the harmony, lilt and charm of the best professional musical comedies. But it also has the purifying and ennobling power of a great drama. It shows our ideal purpose of life not only as soul-satisfying but as hilarious entertainment.

"Wherever this revue is shown it plays to houses crammed to the ceiling with thousands turned away."

In Hollywood the interest of the film community was widely awakened and Phyll and I met many old friends and made many new ones.

One old friend we met again after a lapse of sixteen years was the film actress Frances Dee. She was one of the most beautiful girls I have ever seen, with a natural colouring which needed no make-up. We asked her to *The Good Road* when it was shown in Hollywood and she brought her husband, Joel McCrea, the hero of many a Western.

They loved it and we saw them regularly after our first meeting. They brought their relatives and friends to see the show.

Often they would invite us to spend the weekend with them at their ranch fifty miles north of Los Angeles, where we met their two sons, David and Jody.

It is a very simple ranch house built in the cleft of two hills with a verandah looking out over glorious unspoilt country. The 3,000-acre ranch is Joel's great joy and it was to make the money to buy such a ranch that had been the driving motive for his going into movies. It was the dividend of his success that he appreciated far beyond the fame that success brought him.

Joel owns many horses. One day he invited me to go riding. I viewed this possibility with a wary eye. My experience of horses was limited. Joel, being an understanding man, said he would put me on a quiet horse called Dollar and we would just have a quiet ride around the ranch and get up to no cowboy tricks. When I mounted Dollar I found Joel had been true to his word. Dollar carried me with solemn dignity while I admired the majestic sweep of the California ranchland.

After about half an hour, however, we came to a field which was full of horses grazing peacefully under the cloudless sky. Suddenly Joel decided he would cut out two work horses from the others and send them back with the ranch-hand who was riding with us. In a moment the peaceful scene became wild with horses galloping in all directions. Joel and the ranch-hand were charging to and fro and the air was rent with their shouting. A great deal of this was directed at me. I gathered that I was supposed to get myself out of the way and find a nice quiet corner of the field where I would be less mixed up with the proceedings.

Not able fully to interpret their instructions, however, nor knowing how to manoeuvre my horse, I just stayed put. And so did Dollar. I could not be more grateful to a horse. He remained totally undisturbed in spite of the wild goings-on of his brethren and when the stampede ended, there we were exactly as we had been, not having budged an inch.

We were to see much of the McCreas over the succeeding years and they remain our staunch and loyal friends. They brought many of their Hollywood colleagues to conferences on Mackinac Island and to our World Assembly Centre at Caux.

Today their son David is married and has a ranch of his own. Jody is in films. A third son called Peter has been born to them, the apple of their eyes and now sixteen years old.

Phyll

Not all our visits in Hollywood were pleasant ones. On one occasion I was hailed by an actor we knew very well by reputation. We were not even sure that we knew him, but he seemed to know us and was eager to talk.

He asked if we were connected with MRA. We said we were, so he said, "Why not come and have supper with us and we can talk some more." We thought it was very nice of him, took his address and said we would be along later.

We were greeted warmly by the actor and his wife and told that another couple would be along shortly. We admired his unusual and attractive living room and then settled in for a pleasant evening. We had hardly sat down when the assault began. Our friend, normally a pleasant-looking fellow, suddenly looked as if he were acting a character part of a villain in some Western. His eyes narrowed, his mouth was set, and I thought he might suddenly level a six-shooter at us. He started to tell us non-stop how much he hated MRA and proceeded to tell us a series of the most ridiculous, fabricated stories you could possibly imagine, but when we tried to protest he held up his hand in a lordly manner and said, "Wait a minute. Let me finish."

We let him finish and then tried to explain that he had got his facts wrong. He laughed meaningfully and said of course he happened to know the truth and we didn't.

I asked him if he had ever met anyone in MRA before. He said no, thank heavens he had not. Then where on earth, I asked, did he hear all this nonsense? From a friend who knew someone who knew for certain it was true, he said. "But," we went on . . . "No 'buts' " said the oracle.

He then proceeded to launch a vitriolic attack upon Frank Buchman. But we know the man, we protested, we have worked closely with him for many years. Would he like to hear our experience? He gave his wife an amused look. He shook his head. That was totally unnecessary. We had been duped, fooled. Whatever we said would not make the slightest difference.

At that point the other couple appeared. We hoped perhaps he could change the subject, but not at all. They had been brought in to reinforce our host's opinion. Not that they were allowed to say much, but at the appropriate times they gave the meaningful nod or wink or 'that's right' to underline a point he was making.

We could not quite make out why we had been invited because quite obviously our host had no intention of listening to anything we had to say. Several times during the evening I tried to tell him that I understood only too well how he felt, that the whole thing had maddened me and I, too, had passed on stories which were not true, not because MRA was wrong, but because it was right.

This started him off on another trend of thought. I gathered he had always been a remarkable person, a paragon of virtue, kind to his mother, loved by little children, generous and warm-hearted and had never said an unkind word about anyone. His wife and friends nodded in agreement.

We listened as patiently as we could. At last, when he paused for breath, we suggested it was getting late, we had a long way to go and perhaps we had better be on our way. "Wait a minute," he said. He rose from his chair; he was a tall man, over six foot. He walked towards me and seemed to tower over me. "One more question before you go."

"Certainly," I said, "if you will give me a chance to answer it."

"Why," he said, pointing an accusing finger and looking straight at me, "tell me why there are no Jews in MRA."

I took a deep breath and with some relish, I must admit, replied, "But you happen to have been talking to one all the evening."

CHAPTER TWELVE

I

Phyll

DURING this period of our life we were called upon to travel a great deal, so we felt the time had come for a more permanent base for the children. Jenny was already going to the high school in Mount Kisco and John had just started in a junior school in the neighbouring town of Armonk. A tiny cottage was lent us nearby in the lovely countryside of New York State near the town of Mount Kisco. In the spring the dogwood trees were in full bloom and when the autumn came the woods turned bright scarlet and deep gold. In an old tree in front of the cottage John and his father built a tree house in which he played all kinds of exciting games with his friends after school. Both children were very happy there.

They were looked after by Elisabeth, who had joined our family in 1950 and was to remain with us for ten years. Liz, as we called her, had been a children's nurse. Her father and mother had not been married. Unwanted, hidden by her mother's relations, beaten by a foster father, her childhood was a tragic one. When we first knew her she was a bitter woman. Though she was a genius with small children she would keep adults at arms length.

We received a letter from her one day saying that because our work now took us to many countries she would like to come and help look after our children. She wanted no salary, she said. It would be her contribution to the work we were all engaged in.

It was not easy at first. Though she was wonderful with the children, with us she was often jealous and possessive. We realised that at the root was the hurt and bitterness from her own childhood. But whenever we tried to talk about it she would lash out as if we had touched an open wound. Finally we felt we must somehow break through her defences and help her to find healing for the past. It was difficult and painful but at last the whole story came out and she was able to see not

only how cruelly she had been treated but how cruel she had
often been to people who wanted to help and befriend her. She
not only found forgiveness herself but was able to forgive those
who had hurt her. She lost her fear of being hurt again and was
no longer withdrawn. She was able to make friends as she had
always wanted to and she found that all that she had suffered
had given her a greater understanding and compassion for
others. She became so different it was hard to believe she was
the same woman. She cared for us as much as she cared for the
children and we as a family owe her a great debt of gratitude.

I always found it terribly hard to leave the children. This
time especially so, for we had just received an invitation to go
to Asia. It would mean being away for some months. We knew
Liz would take wonderful care of the children but it was a hard
decision nevertheless.

Both Jenny and John were more philosophical about it than
I was. They understood from an early age what we were out
to do and if we were undecided about leaving they would
encourage us to go. They used to say to us, "Most children
long to get away from home and their parents but for us it is
the greatest treat to be with you, so it is probably a very good
thing we don't see too much of you!"

II

All his life Frank Buchman had a deep concern for the Asian
countries he had first visited in 1915 – India, China, Japan and
Korea. In August 1952 he received an invitation from eighteen
leading personalities of India to bring MRA to their country.
"For", they said: "We are convinced that the true hope for
bringing lasting change in social and economic conditions and
for bringing peace to the world lies in multiplying such practical results as we believe to have been achieved by Moral
Re-Armament. The coming of a new incentive to industry, the
change of heart of capitalist and communist alike, the replacing
of mistrust, bitterness and hate between individuals and groups
with understanding and cooperation. We consider therefore

that such Moral Re-Armament of the nations is the need of the hour and the hope of the future."

There were Asian representatives in the room with Frank Buchman when this invitation was read out. There were also British present who thought they knew India well. They felt the time was ripe for a play to go with a force of perhaps thirty people.

Frank Buchman listened to everything that was said. His own impression of the men who signed the invitation was that if they meant what they had put their names to they would be capable of much bigger things. India would not be affected by men who were prepared only to do what was safe and possible. Russia and China were pouring in new ideas and men like a flood. His conclusion was we must give our best and do our best. We must answer the need that these men saw, not do the thing we thought we were capable of doing. It was decided to take three plays. The party finally numbered 200 – the casts of the plays, technical crew and representative spokesmen from many different countries and backgrounds.

An invitation from the Prime Minister of Ceylon and government, opposition, labour, business and social leaders quickly followed. Pakistan government members at Caux presented an invitation issued by Mr Jinnah before Pakistan became a separate nation.

There were no financial resources for this venture, which was estimated to take six months, though the Indian leaders promised to do everything possible when the force arrived in their country. As the plan was made known individuals spontaneously made gifts or approached others who had special interest in Asia. Retired British civil servants who would like to have joined the party paid for others who had no personal means. One lady who had just inherited a considerable legacy gave the entire sum for the expenses of the journey. Businessmen and workers took six months from their work to travel. Their companies and trade unions in some instances contributed to their expenses. When a KLM plane was chartered by the Dutch, the pilots asked if they could have a part by contributing their pay for the flight to the expenses of the journey. Others flew from London in a plane chartered by the British.

CHAPTER TWELVE

Before leaving for the East we made films of two of the plays
– *The Forgotten Factor* and *Jotham Valley*–under the direction of
Dr Paul Czinner who, with his wife Elisabeth Bergner, showed
constant helpful interest in the development of our films and
plays.

III

It would be quite impossible for me to give a complete picture
of all that happened on that journey, it would take a volume
in itself. But it was an experience that went very deep. It was
not until I went to Asia that I really understood the suffering
and misery of millions of people who had never known anything but hunger and poverty. I had never before seen anyone
die of starvation nor hundreds of men and women and small
children homeless, living and sleeping on the streets. For nights
I could not sleep. More than ever I wanted to give my life in an
attempt to bring an answer to the misery that I saw around
me.

Pictures crowd into my mind as vivid as the day they happened. An all too brief visit to Ceylon. Getting acclimatised to
the heat while rehearsing three plays. Playing eight performances a week–crowded receptions after the plays, the theatre
packed with people so that children climbed on to the stage
and sat by the footlights in order to see better.

Arriving in Bombay harbour as the sun set. The wonderful
hospitality of living in our first Indian home. A fiery press
conference, some for and some against us. Playing to Indian
audiences, the most intelligent I had played to anywhere in the
world, getting every shade and nuance, laughing, crying and
living into every moment with us–one of the most exhilarating
and rewarding experiences I have ever had in the theatre.

Then by train to Delhi, stopping off at Ahmedabad, break-
fasting at the palatial home of the owner of a textile mill, the
contrast of people living in wattle huts outside his gateway.
Lunching at Gandhi's ashram where he lived and worked until
1930, with young girls singing and dancing for us in the court-
yard–untouchables, re-named by Gandhi 'Harijans', 'children
of God'. Frank Buchman walking again down the road where

he walked and talked with Gandhi. "It was like a walk with Aristotle," Frank told us. "Think how one man alone with God can affect millions."

New Delhi–living in Jaipur House lent by the government, no longer a Maharajah's Palace but an empty building. The only furniture in our bedroom was two army cots, one either side of the room. The room was so large that when Bunny said "Good morning", I shouted, "What did you say, dear!?"

Nehru coming to tea there with Frank Buchman, whom he had known for many years. Tea in the beautiful gardens of the Vice-Regal Palace with President Prasad of India, an old fellow-fighter with Gandhi, talking to Frank Buchman that afternoon of his longing that the workers and villagers could be reached with a message that would re-inspire them and through them the nation.

The theatre packed again, with tickets at a premium. A talk Bunny and I had after the play with the governor of a vast state of sixty million people, an author and an artist. "I wish I could help you understand," he said, "that so many of the films and plays you send us from the West destroy every bit of respect we have for your way of life." And an official who told us, "If I had my way I would ban many films coming from Europe and America for in their wake come crime, delinquency and every form of immorality."

IV

We spent Christmas in Jaipur House. A giant Christmas tree was put up in the big hall, where we had supper after the theatre. Ambassadors and their wives, members of parliament, men from the trades unions, from every caste, class and background, came to those evenings around the tree. The chorus sang carols as the candles on the tree flickered out. 'Carol for East and West', written after the visit we paid to Gandhi's ashram in Ahmedabad, was one of the most beautiful. All barriers of class and cast seemed to melt away. There was magic in those evenings. There were no expensive gifts, no wrapping paper or ribbons, but the real Christmas spirit was in that bare hall. An Indian sitting next to me one evening said, "I used to think of Christmas as a drunken orgy. I begin to understand what it is all about."

We travelled by train to South India. Our carriages wooden benches and a bucket in the centre of the carriage containing a block of ice. A small fan blew on the ice which temporarily cooled the air as we travelled through the burning heat of the countryside. Thick dust came through the cracks of the doors and windows. We slept on hard benches, and as the trains rattled through the night, it felt sometimes as though one's bones would rattle to pieces.

Our first stop was Lucknow and our second was Hyderabad. There we gave several performances to the people of the city and one request performance for the Nizam. The evening we played for him and his family was an extraordinary experience. We had given a performance in the afternoon for the general public. After the theatre was emptied, soldiers arrived to search the place and took up positions at the gates with machine guns. Then members of the Nizam's own household arrived and once more searched the theatre. About a quarter of an hour before the curtain went up, cars and busloads of wives and children began to arrive. When I asked the chamberlain how many there had been in the party he said, "Five hundred. We don't often go out as a family because you see there are certain organisational difficulties!"

In Hyderabad we also gave a performance of one of the plays in a huge tent at the All-India Congress Party conference for the party workers who came from all over India for the public sessions. The audience was estimated at 15,000.

From Hyderabad we left for Madras. There had been a famine in the area. I saw people on the station platforms and in the streets dying of starvation. The extremes of wealth and poverty were dramatised in a most terrible way. They tore at your heart. One day outside a hotel I saw a beggar-woman with three small children foraging in a dustbin. She was carrying a small baby in her arms, another child clung to her skirts and another little naked boy was sitting by the dustbin with a golden paper crown on his head, some favour thrown out from a party the night before.

We opened in a small theatre to half empty houses. During

the last act of *The Forgotten Factor* a mob breaks into the employer's house to demand better conditions for the workers. Suddenly outside the theatre we heard shouts like those on the stage. They grew louder and louder, "Whites, go home, whites, go home." It was the same the following night, with pickets outside the theatre and banners across the streets. After the performance members of the cast and the stage crew talked with the demonstrators. We told them our plays were out to cure the things that they were demonstrating against, to answer the divisions of race and class and caste and to cure the hate and superiority which made those divisions possible. The following night the demonstrators were inside the theatre. We expected interruptions, but there were none. They began to bring their friends and by the end of the week the queues were so long that we had to move into a larger theatre. Finally we moved to an open-air theatre where we played to five thousand people a night.

Before we left Madras the South Indian Motion Picture Industry built for us a beautiful theatre on the largest sound stage of the Vauhini Film Studios. Queues began to form outside early in the morning. We gave two performances and still there were hundreds waiting to get in. Finally we were asked to give a third performance at ten o'clock at night.

From Madras we went to Bangalore. And from Bangalore to Calcutta where we stayed for several weeks, playing in a large theatre. One friend we made there was a labour leader from the Transport Workers' Union. He was a high-caste Brahmin and looked like a Roman emperor. He came again and again to see the plays and stayed talking with us afterwards. He told us that he had been jailed by the British before independence and that, after he had been let out, he had walked along the Afghan trails to Moscow, for there, he had heard, was the answer to the suffering of his people. He had met Lenin and become a convinced Marxist, though not fully satisfied with Russian Communism.

He told some of the cast, "This is not something the West brings to the East nor the East to the West, but a message man brings to man. When I first saw your plays I thought, you are not against Communism, you are way beyond it. You are re-

Worrell and Hunte, former Captain and Vice-Captain of the West Indies cricket team

16. Westminster Theatre production of *Give A Dog A Bone*, Peter Howard's perennial pantomime

assessing Marxism in relation to modern problems and moral values."

One morning he invited several of us to his home to meet his wife and family. He lived in Howrah, a poor area of Calcutta. In the small room where he lived and slept with his wife and entire family, we met with him and the many friends whom he had invited in to meet us. They asked us many questions. When two of us told them we had come from capitalist backgrounds, they asked us why we had left comfortable homes to travel the world. We replied, that like them we wanted to end exploitation and injustice but that we felt that unless we could change men, we would change nothing; we would merely replace one lot of power-hungry men with another. One young Marxist said, "But human nature can never change". I told him it was not true, that a very real change had happened in me. I realised it was just a beginning, but the whole aim of my life had altered. He replied, "If what you say is true, then I will have to rethink my entire philosophy."

In one city, living as usual with an Indian family in their home, I caught a fever. My temperature was between 104° and 105° for several days. I had shivering fits at night. As the temperature outside rose during the day, my temperature rose also, and I felt as though I were on fire. Lying in an empty room on a bed with no springs or mattress, but only a hard wooden board, I received a letter from a member of my family from her comfortable home in England. "Of course," she wrote, "you people are just selfish, travelling around living in the greatest luxury." It was the first time for several days that Bunny and I had a good laugh!

v

There followed the last stages of our journey–Kashmir, one of the hottest problems of the continent, with military permits required for entry and military checkpoints reminding us of the fighting that threatened at any moment to break out again. The journey by bus from Jammu to Kashmir, past paddy fields, farms and villages; the narrow roads with great precipices on one side, with certain death should the bus swerve a few inches. The Sikh driver who joyfully greeted his friends, taking both hands off the wheel. Finally the Banihal Pass, driving through a tunnel in the mountain and on the other side the Kashmir Valley, the majestic Himalayas rising in snow-capped peaks surrounding the valley below which was covered in spring flowers of bright yellow and blue.

A few days' rest in the heavenly mountain air after months of great heat. A visit with Bunny on my birthday across the lake to the famous Shalimar Gardens. Performances of the plays for the Prime Minister Sheikh Abdullah and his Cabinet, and for the Army and members of the UN Observation Forces keeping peace in that troubled area. The Prime Minister's verdict to Frank, "You have the answer to India and Pakistan. It takes patience but I think you can carry it through. I saw the answer in your plays. It is God."

On leaving Kashmir we set off on the final stage of our journey to Pakistan. The partition of India and Pakistan had been followed by terrible tragedy. Six million Moslems and 4,500,000 Hindus and Sikhs became homeless refugees. Some 250,000 from both sides were murdered in the Punjab alone. After those tragic days the boundaries were closed. No-one was allowed to cross the border by car, bus or train. In order to reach India from Pakistan or vice versa one had to travel by air or sea. Now for the first time we were told we would be allowed to cross the border on foot. Arriving by train at Amritsar, the great Sikh city, we went by bus to the Indian border. With porters carrying our suitcases on their heads we passed the armed Sikh guards, walked through the barren no-man's-land, passed the armed Pakistani guards and took buses to Lahore.

Reaching Lahore we went by train through the vast Sind desert with a temperature rising to 115°, to the fine city of Karachi.

We gave several performances of the plays in an open air theatre. Once more crowds filled the grounds. Those who could not get in sat on the rooftops and verandahs and climbed trees. Because the Prime Minister was present at the opening performance and because there had been a coup shortly before our arrival, armed guards were at the entrance to the stage and dressing rooms. In order to start each act we had to step over machine guns to make our entrances.

The story of *Jotham Valley*, the musical we gave that night, was based on the true story of two brothers in Nevada whose fourteen-year feud over water rights had been healed. The musical had been written several years before the Asian tour. At the time we were giving it in Karachi there was great tension between India and Pakistan over the waters of the Indus River. The quarrel over Kashmir was at its height between the two countries and there were threats by Pakistan that the waters of the Indus would be diverted.

After the first performance of *Jotham Valley* the Prime Minister spoke to us. He said, "I saw India and Pakistan as those two brothers on the stage tonight quarrelling over the water rights. Was the play especially written for this occasion?"

On our way home to Britain Bunny had a memorable visit in Istanbul with the Patriarch Athenagoras, a tall man with a flowing beard. On greeting Frank Buchman he said, "You are the modern St Paul. I know all about you. I have been following your movements closely."

We arrived home just in time to see the Coronation.

VI

Bunny

Frank Buchman's work was at all times built on people. Today the work in India has been furthered by those who met MRA during those six months of 1952–3.

In Delhi a young man from the university came to see the plays. R. D. Mathur was the Chairman of the Hindu College Parliament and the champion debater of Delhi. But he was more than a debater. He was a young man of action and had frequently risked his life in leading demonstrations against the British. But meeting MRA he realised the problems of his country and the world were not due to the colour of a man's skin or his racial background, but to his character and that the leadership India needed was of honest and incorruptible men. He enlisted in the battle and found his training with its forces in many parts of the world.

Today he is one of those heading up the battle in India, standing with Rajmohan Gandhi, the grandson of one of Buchman's oldest friends, the Mahatma. Mahatma Gandhi once said that MRA was "the greatest thing to come out of the West." Young Gandhi has devoted his life to make it indigenous to India and through India to China and the whole of Asia.

Tall and lean, he has many of the characteristics of his grandfather. He has his dedication and his courage. He has his selflesness. He shares with him his vision not only of an India free from British rule, but an India – and an Asia and a world – ruled by honest and incorruptible men under the direction of God.

He has founded a weekly magazine called *Himmat* for which each week he writes a fearless and blunt editorial challenging the leadership of his country to this concept.

He has wide support, not least from his other distinguished grandfather who is still living, Sri Rajagopalachari, who was the first Indian Governor-General of India. Recently Rajaji stated, "Amidst a world of murderous armaments there is a movement which aims at arming men with spiritual strength. This movement is christened Moral Re-Armament. If he (Rajmohan Gandhi) succeeds India will triumph, in spite of all odds against her – the involutions and complications of our economy, our difficult external politics and corruptions in our national life."

The Editor of Gandhi's paper is Russi Lala, who with his wife Freny were among others we met during the visit to India and are now working with Rajmohan.

In 1963 Gandhi led a 3,000 miles march on wheels across India to rouse "a revolution of national character". It started at Cape Comorin, the southern-most tip of India, and ended at Delhi.

Tens of thousands rallied to him on the route of his march. Many thousands of these were youth. To train them Gandhi founded a Roving College for a new India and organised eleven national camps in various parts of the country where the youth were trained from A to Z in a revolutionary answer.

Feeling the necessity of a more permanent base Gandhi found

and was given a piece of land in the Maharashtra hills at Panchgani sixty-three miles from Poona. 4,300 feet above sea level the land is blessed not only with superb views over the wide Krishna Valley ringed with mountains, but with an ideal climate. Here, thanks to gifts for the purpose received from all over the world, buildings began to go up—residence buildings, a meeting hall and a theatre. A distinguished Australian architect and a Bombay firm of consulting engineers have given their services free. The Harijans of Calcutta collected £3 11s. A Danish businessman sold his sailing boat. An Australian cabinet minister made a gift. The niece of Le Corbusier sold a painting. An Indian widow gave part of her capital: "I know," she said, "this is the only worthwhile investment I can make."

In January of 1968 the first Assembly was held. People came to it from all over the world and not least some 4,000 from the villages surrounding Panchgani.

The buildings are not yet finally completed. Side by side with their building goes forward the re-building of men; and back from this centre goes a stream of men and women, dedicated to the task of raising up a leadership of incorruptible men to solve the vast problems facing their own countries and the world.

CHAPTER THIRTEEN

I

Phyll

AT the end of a very strenuous summer at Caux Frank Buchman, then 76, was ordered by his doctor to rest. He invited us to join him at a small hotel in a town in the Tuscan countryside not far from the city of Florence. He told us when we arrived that he did not want to see anyone for some weeks. This astonished us because a 'rest' with Frank usually meant that the whole town was turned upside down and people from miles around came to see him from morning till night.

This time, however, it was different. For some weeks the only people he saw, apart from the hotel staff, were members of a Royal Family whom he had known for almost fifty years. In the many crises of their lives they had turned to him for counsel. Four generations counted him as their friend.

Apart from Dr Paul Campbell, his physician, and a young Englishman, Jim Baynard-Smith, we were the only members of his party. It was an extraordinary experience. I find it difficult to describe those weeks with him because he was, in fact, an extraordinary man and it would take someone far more skilled than I am to describe him adequately. Frank was not an easy man to be with. He had a way of seeing through you which was most uncomfortable. I believe it was why, although thousands loved him, there were some who hated him. He could read you like a book. If there was something one wished to hide or there was anything on your conscience, Frank was the last person in the world you wanted to meet.

Every day during our stay in Italy he would ask to see us. He did not have much physical strength but he would be thinking of people all over the world. Just as we had grasped the situation in one country, he would move on to people the other end of the world. One day he would be thinking of a Prime Minister or a President and the next day of a cook on the ferry boat to Mackinac Island, or of the old priest there and his dog. For once he did not have his secretary with him. Bunny, in a rash moment, said he could type a little. Without pausing for

breath Frank said, "Then take this down—Dear So-and-So."
For days and nights Bunny and Dr Campbell struggled to type
letters which he dictated non-stop!

He was a man in touch with the Holy Spirit and was therefore unpredictable. You could never follow a line with him or
try and reproduce the way he did things, because every person
and every situation was different and needed a new and
inspired approach. Joel McCrea said to me once, "Frank is an
old magician. He conjures things out of the air." For anyone
who liked a routine or the security of the known way this was
not the most comfortable way to live. He faced people and
situations with the greatest realism, often to my discomfort. I
found it more pleasant to live on the surface of things but Frank
dealt trenchantly with evil. He was a realist with faith, a man
who only saw and faced sin in himself and others because he
knew that Christ could cure it.

His heart was wide open to everybody. He got to know each
member of the management and the hotel staff and cared for
each one as though they were part of his own family. Mario,
the waiter who brought him his meals, was in tears one day.
His father had died. Frank ordered a car and was driven to
Mario's home in the village close by. Too weak to climb the
steep wooden stairs unaided, he had himself carried into the
living room. There he sat with Mario and his family for two
hours bringing faith and comfort to the bereaved widow and
her son. Mario became his devoted friend. So did the Communist dish-washer and another waiter who had suffered
cruelly during the war. Three times this man had been condemned to die in the gas chambers. Three times he had escaped.
For weeks he had known starvation and had lived on roots and
grass. After the war he too joined the Communist Party. Frank
and he had long talks together. He told me one day, "I have
never met anyone like Dr Buchman. I would be willing to die
for that man."

The manager of the hotel also became a close friend, so did
his old mother of ninety. Frank thought for that old lady in a
hundred different ways, as well as for the maid who did his
bedroom. One evening one of us had a birthday party. We
sent a piece of cake with a candle on it up to his room. When

we went to see him later in the evening we met the maid coming out of his room beaming. She was carrying a piece of cake with a candle on it!

When the school holidays came our children joined us. Our son, John, was nine at the time. He would sit quite still, a most unusual state of affairs for him, listening fascinated to everything Frank had to say.

When Christmas came and Frank's health had improved, more and more people came to see him. There was a large Christmas tree with candles and a crib in the room downstairs. Gathered round that tree for his Christmas party were the Queen and her family, the Communist waiter and dish-washer, the old lady of ninety, the small boy of nine, the lift boy of nineteen and many others. There was no barrier of rank or age. In those weeks he had created a family. It was in miniature the much talked of classless society. The whole thing fascinated John. He had never met anyone as old as the grandmother.

"Is that old lady really ninety?" he asked me.

"Yes," I said.

"Good heavens," he replied, "she looks younger than you!"

A month later when a Peter Howard musical play was given in Sesto San Giovanni, the workers' district of Milan, Frank invited all his friends from the hotel. They came by train to see the play–the manager and his wife and daughter, waiters, the chamber maid, the kitchen staff, the gardener, as well as the Royal lady and her lady-in-waiting. The chamber maid, overjoyed at seeing a friend again, put her head into the carriage and said, "Hello, Mrs Queen"!

I said to Bunny as we met the train and they all tumbled out, "that is a picture of Frank's life".

We asked Dr Campbell later, "How is it they all feel so at home?" He replied, "Because Frank treats everyone the same. To him everyone is a royal soul."

II

It was during our stay in Tuscany that Frank received an invitation to visit Australia and to take a small group with him. He invited us and our children to accompany him.

It was not an easy decision for us to make. A swelling had appeared on Jennifer's knee. We took her to the doctor and he prescribed treatment, but it did not respond. We began to get anxious. The doctor mentioned osteomyelitis. He advised a second opinion. On our way back to England we stopped off at the Nestlé Clinic in Lausanne. There she had many tests. Mercifully it proved not to be osteomyelitis, but the doctors could not diagnose the source of the infection. Her knee stiffened and she had to use crutches.

Jenny had finished her schooling: John had not. It would mean a big upheaval for him to start school in another country and with Jenny's leg causing us alarm, we were not at all sure it was right to make such a long journey. We spent wakeful nights wondering what was right. However, we knew from past experience that if we listened and obeyed we could find God's plan which would be the best for all of us. After praying a great deal about it, we felt it was right to go to Australia. It was a venture of faith.

On arrival in Melbourne we immediately told our host about Jenny's leg. He called in a young doctor who recommended a specialist. After a thorough examination the specialist diagnosed a very rare infection of the bone and told us that he happened to be one of the few world authorities on the disease. He had just written a paper on it. He had Jenny's knee put in plaster and prescribed the right drugs, and when the plaster was removed six weeks later, the swelling had subsided and the X-ray showed little damage to the knee. Had we remained in Europe it is unlikely that the infection would have been diagnosed and the knee might have been permanently damaged.

We had a similar experience over John's schooling. Our friends in Melbourne were unanimous that a certain grammar school, close to where we lived, would be the ideal place. But could we get him in? A friend whose son was already at the school said that he would enquire, but he came back to say that the school was full.

Once more Bunny and I prayed about it and asked for guidance. We felt sure it was the right school and that we should not take 'no' for an answer. So we went ourselves to see the headmistress of the junior school. She turned out to be a woman who had followed Bunny's career on the tennis courts for many years. Although there was no room in the upper school, she said they could arrange to take him in the top form of the lower school. The spirit of the school was so warm and friendly that John quickly settled down and after a few days he felt he had been there all his life.

It was my first visit to Australia. Bunny had been there on a tennis tour immediately after leaving Cambridge. We had many Australian friends in the tennis world. Jack Crawford and his wife Marjorie, Adrian Quist, Vivian McGrath, Harry and Nell Hopman and others. I had often sat in the stands with my heart in my mouth watching Bunny play some fierce Davis Cup contests against Australia. But off the courts they were delightful friends and a more generous and sporting crowd you could not hope to meet.

During the First World War we had had Australian soldiers billeted in our home and as a child I would listen to exciting stories of the outback and glowing descriptions of the Australian countryside. I was not disappointed. We loved Australia and the Australian people. We enjoyed every minute of our stay there. There is not time in this story to go into the details of the people we met and the places we visited. Working closely with Frank Buchman and the force of men and women with him, our days were spent in talking with the constant stream of people we met at conferences and receptions arranged in Frank Buchman's honour.

While we were in Canberra Frank was lent a house on the outskirts of the city by two young civil servants. It was a simple home with not nearly enough chairs for all the people who would gather at mealtimes to meet and talk with him. Benches were brought in and every available space was filled.

One man we had met at a reception asked if he could come and lunch with us as he would very much like to meet Buchman. He seemed ill-at-ease but gradually he told us the tragic situation in his home, how that very morning as he was leaving for work his wife in a fit of temper had attempted to run him down in her car. A week later we spent the evening in his home with his wife and children. They had decided to make a completely new start.

This was typical of men and women who left with hope and faith that the problems they were facing in their own lives or in the life of their nations could be answered.

After three months Frank invited us to go with him to New Zealand–from there to Japan and other Eastern countries, returning to rejoin the children later in the year.

III

Bunny

A huge concourse of people was at the airport in Tokyo to greet us. We were entertained to dinner at the Imperial Hotel, a masterpiece of the great American architect Frank Lloyd Wright. As we sat down I felt the room shake and the chandeliers sway. As no-one seemed to be alarmed I put it down to the result of twenty-four hours on the plane. I learned afterwards it was a minor earthquake!

Phyll and I were staying with Mr and Mrs Kichizaemon Sumitomo. He, a small, quiet, highly sensitive and retiring man, had been head of the great Sumitomo family, whose vast industrial empire employed five hundred thousand men. Now his empire had been split up and taken from him. In Tokyo he had been left two rooms in a house that he had previously owned. Phyll and I slept in one of them.

The Sumitomos were a gracious and charming couple, in no way bitter at their loss of fortune, but keen to rebuild Japan on new ideas. They spoke in quiet, almost inaudible tones as befits the well-bred Japanese.

Phyll and I loved Japan and the Japanese–their tradition of courtesy; their artistic sense which is expressed not only in their interior decorations, but in the streets of the old town hung with what we found to our surprise were Japanese lanterns! We were there for the May Day parades and were caught in a car in the midst of the well-known snake dances which, however, on this occasion were of a peaceful nature.

The President of the Japanese Lawn Tennis Association graciously gave a luncheon in my honour at which I met several old friends whom I had played against in England and one of their stars of former days, Mr Kumagai.

203

We met the Prime Minister, Mr Hatoyama, at his home. He admired Dr Buchman's work. When Frank complimented him he said, "No, no, you are the great one. You are an elephant. I am only a fly on your back!"

We met leading members of the Diet in a room in the Diet building, among them Mr Kishi who was later to become Prime Minister. It was a tempestuous time in Japanese affairs. Violence was threatened. The Liberal-Conservative party, the party in power, had introduced a bill the passing of which would immediately deprive the Opposition Socialist Party of fifty seats. Being in a minority in the House and therefore being unable to prevent the passing of the bill, the Socialists saw no other recourse but to violence.

As we met with the Diet leaders the atmosphere was tense. Only Buchman seemed fully at ease. He quietly told stories of how unity had been brought to warring factions in various countries he had visited. The atmosphere in the all-party audience began to relax.

At this point another member of the Diet entered. He was introduced to Frank as the 'bad boy' of the Diet, the man most violently involved in the current crisis. Immediately Frank's eyes began to twinkle. He told the new arrival how much at home he felt with bad boys. Once his own parents, Frank said, had sent him to a school in Grenoble to learn French. Unfortunately everything that he heard went in one ear and out the other. At the end of his time at that French school, he could only remember two French words, "mauvais garçon".

The Senate's 'bad boy' was amused. Having won his audience, Frank told how Robert Schuman once said to him, "Buchman, I want you to go and settle things in Morocco."

He told how he had gone to Morocco and how through a change in Arabs and French there had come a rapprochement of the divided Moroccan interests and a settlement with France.

That evening we were holding a meeting elsewhere in Tokyo. In the middle of it, Mr Hoshijima, a senior Diet member from the Government Party who was soon to be elected Speaker, mounted the platform. He said that after we had left the Diet Building, leaders of the two parties had convened a special meeting at which it was agreed that the offensive Bill should be sent back to Committee. "Violence has been averted," said Hoshijima, "and we owe that to you, Dr Buchman."

IV

From Japan we set out on our homeward journey. An early stopping place was the Philippines where President Ramon Magsaysay invited us to breakfast at Malacañang, the Presidential Palace. I was interested to see that Dwight Davis, the donor of the Davis Cup, had once been the Governor of the Philippines and had lived in the palace.

Hundreds of people were in the palace when we arrived, the common people of the country who were given free access to the President whenever they wanted to see him.

Magsaysay received us in a dining room, hung with massive chandeliers. He was a huge man, like an oak among saplings. He was a strong man, unwilling to suffer any sort of bribery or corruption in government, dismissing instantly any man found guilty of these crimes. Once, in a passion, pounding home a point to a colleague, he struck the wall with such violence that his hand went through it.

His courage was legendary. He brought peace to his country by winning over the Communist Huk rebellion in the South, not by arms, but by winning the men. He would fly into Huk territory to meet them and win them by his vision for the Philippines.

The Colwell Brothers, three gifted young musicians travelling with us, sang a song for him at the end of breakfast in the language of the Philippines, Tagalog. The President was delighted. He called for his aide. "Get the army," he commanded, "to record this song."

We told him stories of the work of MRA. He listened intently. At the end of breakfast he turned to Buchman. "Most people," he said, "load me down with problems. You bring me the answers."

V

Back in Australia at the beginning of 1957 we received a letter from Frank Buchman. He told us of a talk he had had with a leading Filipino journalist. This man had expressed the view that an interchange of convinced personalities between Japan and his own country was needed to overcome the hatred and bitterness left behind by the war. Frank Buchman asked if we would be prepared to go to plan with our friends in Japan and the Philippines how we could help the situation.

It was hard for us to leave Australia at that time. We had come to love the country; the work was advancing and we were making many friends. However, as the days passed it became increasingly clear that it was right for us to go. John was happily settled in school. We decided to take Jennifer with us. Our visits to these countries with Frank Buchman had given us many friends who would be helpful in the work to be done.

Before leaving for the East we decided to take the children on a holiday. A friend recommended Phillips Island, not very far from Melbourne. It was a beautiful spot, she told us, for a holiday. She had been there thirty years before and remembered staying at a small but pleasant hotel, the name of which she gave us. In our mind's eye we saw a charming building, not large but beautifully kept, with a carpeted front hall furnished with comfortable armchairs, a similar lounge, a quiet and shadowy dining room and comfortable bedrooms, with far vistas of the sea.

We rang through to the hotel and were delighted to find, although it was the height of the summer holiday season, that they had accommodation for us. Piling our belongings into a borrowed car, we set off with high expectations.

As we crossed the bridge from the mainland we were not disappointed. The Island is one of the last refuges of that delightful little creature, the koala bear, and as we drove along the tree-lined roads, we could see these little teddy bear like creatures in the trees.

We had some difficulty in finding our hotel. At last we came across a derelict-looking wooden bungalow, which had obviously not known a coat of paint for a great many years. It looked as if it might collapse at any moment. We went up to it to enquire the whereabouts of our hotel. To our horror we found that this was it! With sinking hearts we went inside. We came to the dining room and, though it was small and scarcely the room of our dreams, it did at least look clean. We called loudly to see if anyone was there and at last from behind the hatch leading to the kitchen, a forlorn-looking man emerged who said he was the owner. We asked if we could see our rooms.

Perhaps room is too flattering a word to describe the small cabins which were the bedrooms of the hotel. They were cramped and bedraggled and when we tested the springs, we realised that they had long ago collapsed with the onrush of old age. They sagged like hammocks, but they too, we were glad to notice, were clean. Hopefully we looked out of the windows for the expected vistas of the blue sea; instead our eyes fell on the wreckage of a Ford car rusty with long disuse, and a pile of slag. We looked at each other, we looked at the forlorn proprietor. In the face of every disappointment, we decided to stay.

Here in this funny ramshackle hotel, we enjoyed a marvellous holiday. Not far away, and even beyond our dreams, was a beautiful bay with golden sands. The sun shone, we bathed. We built huge castles on the sands with crisscrossing runways from top to bottom, down which we ran golf balls. We fished. We lay in the sun. We took trips in our car. And best of all we enjoyed the penguins.

The 'hotel', we found, was situated close to the nesting areas of penguins, little creatures about thirteen inches high. 'Close' is an accurate word. Two penguins had taken up residence under the cabin where our son and daughter were sleeping and spent much of their time making loud and complaining noises. At night, when darkness fell, the penguins came back from their fishing trips, well fed themselves and with food in their second stomachs to be passed on to their young. This return of the penguins had become a feature of the island. Searchlights had been set up and a charge of one shilling made to watch them come home. And hundreds of people gathered each night to watch them tumble out of the sea and waddle up the beach to their nesting holes in the dunes beyond.

We learned that the penguins, after feeding their young, and after a few hours rest, left again for their fishing trips in the early dawn. So one morning very early we got up to watch them go.

In the shadowy darkness, when the first light of day was beginning to break through, we could see them collecting in groups. When a certain number had gathered they would waddle off together towards the sea, while another group would gather out of the dunes to follow after them. Occasionally they would catch sight of us lying on the sand and would come over to see who we were. About a foot away from our noses, they peered into our faces. Reassured that at least we were not penguins and there was no need to wait for us, off they would trudge together to their day's adventure.

They were most endearing little creatures and your heart went out to them for their high courage. As they entered the water you knew that for the next sixteen or seventeen hours, far out to sea, they would be risking death from the sharks, their only defence their spectacular agility in the water. On the land they were weird, uncouth little birds, often falling over, their small legs finding difficulty in transporting their plump bodies, their wings of little help. But in the sea they were masters of their element, sweeping, diving, soaring, with a skill that surpassed even the fishes themselves.

We left Phillip Island well satisfied with our holiday, refreshed in body and spirit, with ourselves ready to go and John ready to see us go on our next journey to the East.

CHAPTER FOURTEEN

I

Bunny

PHYLL, Jennifer and I landed in Manila in February. It was hot as Manila always is. We were met at the airport and were driven to the home of a prominent labour leader and his wife who generously gave up their own bedroom for Phyll's and my use.

The following night we met together—the labour leader and his wife and other Filipino friends, people prominent in the life of the country. We told them we had received letters from Japan suggesting that an assembly for Moral Re-Armament should be held in the East and asking if we had any ideas as to where it might take place. Our Filipino friends said there was obviously only one place for such an assembly and that was in the summer capital of the Philippines, Baguio. The Philippines, they pointed out, were central in Asia, almost equidistant between Japan, Indonesia, Thailand, Burma and India beyond. And Baguio was, of course, with its beautiful climate and perfect hotel, the ideal setting in the Philippines. They would take us up to see it.

Soon we were on our way, driving through the burning countryside, slowly climbing into the cool of the mountain air. We found a delightful small town encircled with jungle-covered hills over which hung black clouds which mercifully never fulfilled their threat of rain and storm. Here it was beautifully cool, an ideal setting, indeed, for an Asian Assembly.

For such an assembly, we were told, sufficient accommodation could be provided and the hotel would cut their prices in half. We arranged that the assembly should take place at the end of March, and then, leaving the final arrangements in the hands of our Filipino friends, flew on to Japan.

Our Japanese friends were enthusiastic about the idea. The guilt of the war years hung heavily on responsible people in Japan. They had incurred the hatred of their Asian neighbours and they wanted not only to atone for the past, but to build new bridges of friendship with the nations they had wronged.

The Japanese are a dynamic people. They do nothing by halves. Those who had met MRA faced the wrongs they had committed towards other nations and were anxious not only to admit those wrongs and to apologise for them, but so to live that such things could not happen again. It was a dedicated group of Japanese who at the end of March met with delegations from Korea and other Eastern countries at Baguio.

Among those present was Senator Mrs Kato, the aristocratic wife of a fire-eating Socialist known as 'Fireball' Kanju Kato. She too was a Socialist and had been elected to the Senate with the largest majority of any Senator in Japan. With her was Mr Hoshijima from the Conservative-Liberal Party, a senior adviser to the Cabinet.

Their apologies had an atomic effect on the delegates of other nations at Baguio. Old hatreds began to drop away, old bitternesses to be healed.

One of those who responded to the Japanese apologies for the suffering inflicted during their thirty-eight-year occupation of Korea was Mrs Park Hyun Suk, a former Cabinet Minister, who had herself been deeply humiliated and whose husband had been bed-ridden for eighteen years as a result of Japanese imprisonment. She said, "Our past sufferings are meant to teach us how to build a new future. My bitterness towards Japan has been healed. I have lost my enmity."

At the conclusion of the assembly General Ho Ying-chin, former Prime Minister of mainland China and Commander-in-Chief of their five-million-man army at the end of the Second World War remarked, "More has been accomplished in ten days at this assembly than in ten years of post-war diplomatic effort."

It was a pebble dropped into the sea. The ripples spread. The following year the President of the Philippines visited Japan. Speaking to a joint meeting of the House and Senate he said, "The hatred between our two countries has been washed away in the spirit of understanding and forgiveness."

The new relationship between Japanese and Koreans born at Baguio was the first break in the bitter enmity stemming

from the Japanese occupation. It began a process which culmi-
nated in the treaty of 1965, and the Prime Ministers of both
countries have acknowledged the large part which MRA played
in the amelioration of feeling which made this possible.

At the end of the assembly Phyll and I stayed on for two
more weeks in the Philippines and then returned to Japan.

II

When we reached Japan we learned that Frank Buchman had
invited a hundred leaders of a youth federation to attend the
1957 assembly for Moral Re-Armament on Mackinac Island.
The federation, known as the Seinendan, consisted of 4,300,000
young farmers and factory workers from all over Japan. Its
headquarters was a gaunt building in Tokyo.

The president of the federation, Ninomiya, like many another
Japanese, had conceived a hatred of war and not without
reason. He had lived on the outskirts of Hiroshima. One day
he told us he had noticed a solitary American plane flying over
the town. It had been a perfect cloudless day and the plane had
shone like a silver bird against the blue of the sky. He had seen
something fall from the plane. Then a parachute had opened
which began slowly, quietly to fall towards the city as the plane
sped on its way.

The next thing he knew he was lying on the ground and all
around him was darkness and devastation. Fortunately he had
been far enough away from the centre of the blast to receive no
physical hurt. His home had been destroyed, but his wife and
child had escaped. After the devastation he went to the mountains. The one question in his mind he told us was how such a
terrible thing could be prevented from happening again?

When the war ended he saw in the new-founded Seinendan
an opportunity to train the youth in the ways of democracy
and peace.

But how to do it? What was the spirit that could give life to
the new framework of democracy created for them by the
Americans? For some years he was baffled. But now he thought
perhaps Buchman's invitation might provide an answer. When
Phyll and I arrived in Japan he invited us and other friends to

meet with the leaders of the Seinendan to arrange the details of their visit. The representatives were carefully selected, and late in May one hundred and two of them arrived at Mackinac. They were a rough, tough bunch and they exploded into the conference like a hurricane.

They were for the most part atheistic and Marxist in their thinking, and although happy to be visiting America, anti-American in feeling. Many reacted like Phyll on her first meeting with MRA. But gradually the fever died down, pulses returned to normal and they began to look on the world with new eyes.

They had been invited for a month. Many of them stayed on for three. They had straightened out their lives. Many had faced the callous way they had treated their wives whom they had often regarded as little better than beasts of burden. They had, in different cases, given up drink and drugs, promiscuity, and in some cases homosexual practices. They saw MRA as an idea that could raise up the incorruptible leadership needed to create the new Japan. But how to give it to their country?

One of their number had for several weeks been totally uninterested. He had decided on arrival that whatever was going on at Mackinac was a lot of nonsense. He dismissed as absurd all that was happening in the lives of those around him. He went to no meetings, but spent most of his time, when not eating, lying on his bed.

One day, however, it occurred to him that it was his attitude that was quite absurd. Why not attend the meetings? Why not find out what was going on? He did so and heard a great deal about God. This God could apparently speak to a man. He did not believe it for a moment, but he decided there was nothing to be lost in making an experiment. He tried it and a strange thought came into his mind – that he should write a play. Soon he made another experiment of listening and into his mind there came with astonishing clarity the play's outline.

The Seinendan members were gathered one afternoon in a sitting room overlooking Lake Huron, when this young man came into the room and told them of his experience. They suggested he should go away immediately and write the play while it was still fresh in his mind.

When finally he reappeared with the play complete we found that it dramatised in an impressive way the experiences of the Seinendan at Mackinac. Here, they recognised, was the means of putting before their countrymen the experience them themselves had found.

The play, called *The Road to Tomorrow*, returned to Japan and was soon travelling through the major cities of the country.

The cast, almost all members of the Seinendan, performed skilfully. Moreover, they acted at great sacrifice. Many came from small farms and the direst poverty. Being away from home meant to their families the loss of hands that scarcely could be spared.

But though the majority of the cast were members of the Seinendan, there was an interesting exception called Seki. He had served in the Japanese Army in Manchuria. He had been captured by the Russians and taken to a prisoner-of-war camp in Russia. As the long years passed and there seemed no hope of his release, a bitterness slowly corroded his heart.

One day, reading a Russian newspaper, he found an item that interested him. It gave him a glimmer of hope. It was an article on an ideology called Moral Re-Armament. He had never heard of Moral Re-Armament, but he determined that if ever he was released by the Russians, he would find out more about it.

Eleven long years passed, and Seki found himself at last a free man. Returning to Japan, he found that his wife and daughter had died. His son was on the dock at Yokohama to meet him, carrying a placard with the name Seki. He had only been three years old when the father had last seen him. Now he was fourteen.

Seki was reunited with his sister. She had married a young man by the name of Sohma. Remembering the article about Moral Re-Armament he had read in the camp, he asked his sister if she had ever heard of it. "I have been working for Moral Re-Armament almost since the day I last saw you," she told him.

III

In 1958 *The Road To Tomorrow* was invited to the Philippines and was performed in a theatre in the walled city of Manila.

It was here during the war years that the worst atrocities against the Filipino people were committed, when men were skinned alive and women and children bayonetted for fun. It was this part of the city, more than any other, that brought back to Filipinos the shudder of remembrance of things almost impossible to forget.

The atmosphere in the theatre on the first night was tense. One felt that violence could erupt at any moment. In the audience was the head of the Filipino War Widows' Association. She had lost all her male relatives—her father, husband and son—all killed by the Japanese. But she had never lost her Christianity and was determined that no bitterness should corrode her spirit. After the war she had made a special visit to Japan to convey her forgiveness to its people. Now this evening she had brought twenty-five members of the War Widows' Association in order to take action if any trouble should occur.

As it turned out there was nothing to fear. As the Japanese actors lined up before the curtain and each in turn apologised for his part in the wrongs the Japanese had committed; and as the play was performed, their sincerity and humility so won the audience that at the end of the play they swarmed up on to the stage. They wanted to meet the cast and to thank them for what they had done.

As Phyll and I watched the play that night I asked myself, is this what the theatre is meant to be? This was more than a play. It was a healing force. Where bright intellects and skilled pens in the West expose the ills of society like festering wounds, here was a play bringing healing to wounded hearts, a play which like the plays of ancient Greece was a purge, ridding men and women of the evil forces in their lives.

CHAPTER FIFTEEN

I

Phyll

IT was while the Japanese were at Mackinac that Muriel Smith came for a few days' visit, on her way back from Hollywood to London. She had sung the title role *Carmen* at Covent Garden and had made a great hit in *The King and I* and *South Pacific* at Drury Lane. She had made her name as the original 'Carmen Jones' on Broadway. She was on her way back to sing at Covent Garden again.

Muriel is a great artist. I do not use that phrase lightly. I have rarely heard a more beautiful voice nor seen a finer actress. But having achieved a great measure of success, she told me she would suddenly stop in her tracks and ask herself, why am I doing this? What is it all about?

She met and talked with the young Seinendan leaders. She was impressed by their honesty and especially moved by one young man who had faced the full implications of the terrible things he had done during the war. He told her that he wanted to find an answer to the cruelty which was latent in every human being.

At just that time the race riots erupted in Little Rock, Arkansas, and made front-page news in the newspapers across the world. Instead of going back to sing *Carmen* Muriel decided to stay and learn more.

Muriel is an American Negro brought up in Harlem. She and her mother had had a hard struggle. They knew what privation meant. Mrs Smith has often talked to me of those days, especially of the day when she could finally afford to buy Muriel a pair of stockings.

At the same time that Muriel was at Mackinac a blonde young actress arrived from Tennessee. Her name was Ann Buckles and she was beginning to make her name on Broadway and on television. These two actresses from totally different backgrounds, faced the things which had divided them and became friends.

Alan Thornhill and Cecil Broadhurst decided to write a

musical for them, based on the life of Mary McLeod Bethune, the great Negro educator. We had met Mrs Bethune when some years before she had come to Caux. She had told how she had founded the first Negro College, starting with only one dollar in her purse and the determination that her people must have the chance of a good education. She started with packing cases as desks, and baked sweet potato pies which she sold to buy ink, pens and pencils.

Caux was a great experience for Mrs Bethune. One day she spoke from the platform very movingly. In spite of having founded the Bethune-Cookman College and having become Adviser to President Roosevelt, she was always out to learn. "I have built a College and done many good things for my people," she said, "but often I have been too busy. I have failed my own son." She went on to speak of what it meant to be at Caux in a community where there was no elbowing but true equality. She ended by saying, "To be a part of this great uniting force of our age is the crowning experience of my life." So the play was called *The Crowning Experience*.

Bunny had chaired a meeting when Mrs Bethune was present and an elderly white Southern lady, whose family had owned slaves, had apologised to Mrs Bethune for the superiority of a family like hers. These stories were woven together in a musical play with Muriel Smith playing Emma Tremayne, a part based on the life of Mrs Bethune, and Ann Buckles playing the daughter of the white Southern lady.

When the production was completed we decided to open in Atlanta, Georgia. Bunny and I travelled to the South with Muriel. It was not an easy journey for any of us. None of us knew what kind of reception this play with an integrated cast would have in the Southern States. In Atlanta, we stayed with Muriel in the home of a gracious white Southern family and experienced real Southern hospitality. But we could not eat together in the restaurant, nor go to the cinema, nor even ride in a taxi together. It was a painful experience.

Many of the cast, white and coloured, were living in a hotel run by a coloured man. It was a hotel lived in normally only by coloured people. The cast had not been there long before a cross was burning outside the front door.

216

One sensed the passions, lying scarcely concealed, underneath the surface of this pleasant city and wondered sometimes at the patience of the coloured people, who lived under the oppression of an almost inhuman inequality.

We opened to a packed audience of 5,000 people in the Civic Auditorium. Lines in the play which seemed quite normal as we rehearsed them in the North, we realised were dynamite in the South. When the apology came from the white woman there was not a sound in the house. It was as though people held their breath. We did not know until later that there were fifty plain-clothes men in the audience and were interested to hear the radio announce with surprise that night that "there were no incidents in the Civic Auditorium this afternoon".

After the performance the manager of the Tower Theater, Atlanta, came to us with tears in his eyes. "I came in fear and trepidation," he said, "I leave in exaltation. You must have my theatre for as long as you would like to run *The Crowning Experience*." We accepted his offer and before it opened went to see him about the seating of the theatre. It was the practice of the Tower that whites sat in the stalls and the dress circle and the coloured people went through a side door to the peanut gallery. Before we could say what was on our minds he told us, "After seeing *The Crowning Experience* I have decided to alter the seating plans for this play. White and coloured will all come in through the same door, and there will be seats for both races in the stalls and dress circle."

When we moved to the Tower, the theatre was at first by no means full; only gradually did people pluck up enough courage to come. As I sat in the audience I marvelled at Muriel Smith's courage. She had to break through a wall of prejudice but by the end many were in tears as she sang in her deep rich voice, 'The world walked into my heart'. It would indeed have been very difficult not to have been moved by her performance. More and more people came including many leaders of the city.

A Negro leader said to me towards the end of the run, "This is the first time I have seen whites come into a theatre without superiority and coloured come in without fear." The wife of a minister told us, "For years in Atlanta we have been listening to the tick of a time bomb waiting for it to explode in our city.

Now we are listening to the tick of the Holy Spirit. You
have come to us at the right time."

Drew Pearson, in his nation-wide newspaper chain, described
the effect of *The Crowning Experience* in Atlanta, where integra-
tion was being calmly and wisely achieved, and continued,
"Behind what happened in Georgia is the even more amazing
story of how dedicated people from all walks of life are organis-
ing to find a solution to the problem that our political leaders have
been unable to resolve – the explosive challenge of Little Rock."

A leading Negro lawyer, Colonel Walden, added, "After the
visit of *The Crowning Experience* Atlanta will never be the same
again." A big claim? Perhaps too big, but it was how he felt.
A new climate of trust had been created in the city and it is a
fact that soon after *The Crowning Experience* left Atlanta the buses
were integrated without trouble, the parks were integrated and
ahead of most of the rest of the South, there was token integra-
tion in the schools. Some years later President John Kennedy
sent for Colonel Walden to ask him about the work done at
that period.

I was in the room when Muriel Smith was speaking on the
phone to Sam Goldwyn, who was offering her a leading part
in the film of *Porgy and Bess*. "No, Mr Goldwyn," she said,
"*Porgy and Bess* will not give a true picture of my people to
the world. Come and see *The Crowning Experience*. In it is the
kind of spirit that the whole world needs."

II

Bunny

After our time in Atlanta, we made *The Crowning Experience* into
a film. Part of the filming was done in California and on arriving
in Los Angeles I went to call on my old friend, Don Budge.

Don is a big-hearted man and he welcomed me warmly.
"Gee, Bunny, it's good to see you," he said. "We must have
a game."

I explained that I had scarcely played at all since he had
wiped me off the court in the 1938 Wimbledon Final, and that
I was totally out of practice. He brushed my objections aside.
"Nonsense," he said, "I'll get hold of Jack."

I looked at him apprehensively. "Jack?" I queried. "Jack who?"

"Jack Kramer," said Don blithely. "And we'll get hold of old Gene."

Gene turned out to be Gene Mako, who with Don provided the greatest doubles combination of the 'thirties.

I again expostulated with Don, but he would take no refusal, so a few days later I found myself walking onto the court with Jack Kramer to play against the mighty pair of Budge and Mako.

Kramer at that time was the king of the pros and if I were to venture a ranking list of all the world's great players, I would put him close to the top. For years Pancho Gonzales was considered the world's greatest player. Yet in a series of matches between Pancho and Jack when both were at their best, it was Jack who was the winner.

It was with this Jack, then, that I found myself on court. Playing two sets together we held Budge and Mako to a draw, one set each. Considering the fact that I had played no top-flight tennis for some eighteen years, I played remarkably well. Was it some form of inspiration or some subconscious memory from long ago? Whatever the reason, it encouraged me to accept another game with Jack, Don and Gene. This was my mistake. The next time I was hopeless and for all Jack's genius, Don and Gene beat us with ease.

In the coming days Phyll and I saw much of Jack and his wife Gloria and their five little boys. And they have remained good friends over the years since, years when Jack turned the tennis world upside down, skimming the cream from the amateur ranks and creating a group of magnificent pros known then as 'Kramer's Circus'.

It has always been my hope that Jack, highly gifted as an organiser, as well as a player, and with daring pioneering qualities of character will one day head the circus of those revolutionaries who are out to upturn the world.

III

Phyll

While in America I had the news that mother was ailing. I came back to England to be with her. Although the doctors assured me her condition was not serious I had a growing sense that she had not long to live. I helped to look after her through what proved to be her last illness.

My sisters and I would take it in turn to stay with her. In the evenings when I was alone with her we would pray together. One night she suddenly asked me if we could say the twenty-third psalm. "Yea, though I walk through the valley of the shadow of death, I will fear no evil." Every word went to my heart.

Another time when she was very weak, she asked me to say with her the prayer of St Ignatius Loyola:

"To give and not to count the cost,
   To fight and not to heed the wounds,
   To toil and not to seek for rest,
   To labour and not to ask for any reward
      save that of knowing that we do Thy will."

Mother had not been a woman of great faith. But during the war, and later when my father was so ill, she had been helped by a young minister at the church near her home in Sussex. All that she had learned from him and through talks with Bunny and me seemed to come back to her during those last days.

One morning when I telephoned the nurse told me not to hurry in as she was in a coma and would not know if I was there or not. But I had the strongest feeling to go nevertheless. When I arrived she was fully conscious. She opened her eyes and said, "I'm very afraid."

I asked her why. She told me she had had a terrible dream of a great black bird hovering over her. I told her how well I understood her fears and how much the ninety-first psalm had helped me: "You need not fear the terrors of the night." I read it quietly to her. She went into a deep peaceful sleep. The doctors told my sisters and myself that she might linger for days, even for weeks.

We were planning for our son, John, to finish his schooling in England. One day we went to visit Bunny's old school at Repton. We stayed overnight, but in the morning I had the thought to hurry back. "I have a feeling that Mother may go today," I told Bunny.

CHAPTER FIFTEEN

We drove through a heavy thunderstorm and arrived in a downpour. It was like night in Mother's room when we arrived. She was breathing with great difficulty. Gradually the storm abated and suddenly the sun came out. A pool of light lit up her bed. She gave a little sigh and stopped breathing. It was all over. She lay there as if she were asleep like a small child.

It is a sobering experience to see someone so close to you depart from this world.

As I sat by my mother's bedside and watched her life flicker out, I realised how precious life is, how much we need to make every moment count. And yet I was more certain than ever that this life is only the beginning.

CHAPTER SIXTEEN

I

Bunny

ON August 8, 1961, a few weeks after Phyll's mother, Frank Buchman died, aged 83 years, in Freudenstadt. Thousands gathered there to say goodbye to the man who had meant so much to their own lives and to the life of the world.

Frank often used to say, "It takes great faith to believe you'll see your loved ones again." But of the after-life he had no doubt. He sometimes spoke of his experience in Saratoga, America, in 1942. He was desperately ill, and at one moment it seemed he had slipped away. The doctor gave him up for dead; but he awoke. "I saw the outstretched arms and they were wonderful," he said. He would speak of this experience and the glories of the world to come when he felt it would help a doubting faith.

That illness greatly lifted his spirit, though it almost totally eclipsed his physical strength. Before he had been a man of iron, able to work long hours without tiring, dynamic and quick-moving. I was once walking and talking with him when suddenly I found he had disappeared. Eventually I saw him thirty yards ahead of me. He had spotted a friend and had moved with lightning speed to greet him.

After his illness his brain remained unimpaired. His memory was as prodigious, his thought as quick as before. But physically he had to be helped everywhere he went—helped in and out of chairs, in and out of cars, trains and aeroplanes. He never let this affect him. He travelled as much and as widely after his illness as before, though often in great pain, especially in the cramped accommodation of aeroplanes.

For a man once so strong and physically independent, it must have taken great humility to accept without a moment's protest or complaint his physical incapacity.

I watched him travel for thousands of miles in Ceylon, through India—often in the hottest weather—through Pakistan, Iran, Turkey and back to Switzerland. At night he would drop into bed totally exhausted, only to rise again in the morning prepared to give every ounce of his limited energy.

In Italy one night he gave a reception for his many friends in Rome. Afterwards I was with him. He was sitting exhausted in a chair. "Well," he said, simply like a child, "I've done what I was told. Now I'm going to bed."

"Unless you become as little children, you cannot enter into the Kingdom of Heaven," said the One who was Frank's Leader. It was with the simplicity of a child but with the wisdom of a statesman that Frank followed Him all through his life.

He always disclaimed leadership. "I have been wonderfully led," he would say when anyone praised him. "It is not I who lead, it is Christ." And he carried out to the letter the injunction of Jesus, "He who will be greatest amongst you must be the servant of all."

II

In these last years Peter Howard was much at Frank Buchman's side sharing his responsibility, and after Buchman's death, much of the weight of the work naturally fell on his shoulders.

Phyll and I knew Peter for more than thirty-five years. We had heard of him first as a rugger international and captain of England and later as the hard-hitting political writer for the *Express* newspapers. One day we heard that he had become engaged to one of our dearest friends in the tennis world, Doris Metaxas of France. Doë, as Peter called her, had a rare grace and charm, and a forehand drive of unusual power for a woman. Her face lit up radiantly when she smiled and she was a woman of wide Gallic culture. We looked forward eagerly to meeting this controversial *Express* writer.

Then we met him. It was at the Stade Roland-Garros in Paris during the French Championships in the early 'thirties. He was not at all what we had expected. We met a dynamic and highly original character with immense humour and with a fearless glint in his eye. We were immediately won by him. He was unlike anyone we had met before.

I next saw Peter in the Members' Stand at Wimbledon. The day before, in a moment of pique, I had given my racquet a kick and it had flown to my great embarrassment onto the lap of a lady in the crowd. The *Daily Mail* had headlined: "Bunny Austin loses temper and match". This amused Peter and he chortled with delight.

In the following years we often saw the Howards playing tennis at the Melbury Club. Tennis was not Peter's game, but he played it with a mischievous subtlety and sense of strategy that frequently bamboozled players of far greater ability.

Then in 1939, after war had broken out, a vague message reached me that Peter Howard would like to see me on the subject of MRA. I wondered what Peter had in mind. Was it a genuine interest or would I be fodder for one of his slashing *Express* articles? I was not to know. Before seeing him I left for America.

Eight months later, in August 1940, the news came that Peter and Doë Howard were themselves engaged in the work of MRA.

Books which he wrote began to cross the Atlantic to us in America – *Innocent Men*, *Fighters Ever* and *Ideas Have Legs*. This last I used to give to my Army friends. They would return it two or three weeks later very much the worse for wear, and I would learn that, having read it themselves, they had lent it to a friend, who had lent it to a friend, who had lent it to a friend, and so on. These three books sold over 800,000 copies in Britain alone.

Then, with the outbreak of peace, Peter Howard followed his books to America and fell in beside Frank Buchman, beginning the long years of training, with the hammering, the chiselling, the planing and sandpapering that equipped him at last to take full responsibility with Frank for the work of MRA on a global scale.

In 1952 Peter turned his powerful pen to the writing of a play. It was the first of many, all of vast originality and coming burning from his pen. Their birth was rapid only because the gestation period was long. His plays were the fruit of profound thought and emerged as the result of intense mental wrestling with the issues of our time.

By 1961 he had written a dozen plays which had been played in as many languages all over the world. In that year it was decided to put on two of them – *The Hurricane* and *The Ladder* – in double bill at the Westminster Theatre.

CHAPTER SIXTEEN

It was at this time that Phyll and I became associated with the Westminster and a new and fascinating chapter in our lives began.

The Westminster had been acquired in 1946 "as a living memorial to those men and women of Moral Re-Armament who gave their lives in the armed forces during the war". More than two thousand people had contributed towards the purchase. Service men and women gave their gratuities. Miners, textile workers and other trade unionists, housewives, industrialists, business and professional men all had a part. From the beginning it was a real theatre of the people and the audiences at the first play, *The Forgotten Factor*, like those that have followed down to this day, had a far higher proportion of workers than those in any other serious London theatre.

In the next fifteen years the theatre was at times leased to other managements. Now, in 1961, it was decided to keep the theatre under our own management. Ever since then professional casts have played to audiences paying West End prices in what J. C. Trewin describes as "one of the most up-to-date and elegant theatres in London". The productions–from tragedy to pantomime, from high-spirited musicals to the drama of ideas–have offered entertainment and much more besides. They have presented a theatre of humanity and hope and of constructive ideas.

III

Phyll
With the production of John Osborne's *Look Back In Anger* in 1956, there had come a theatrical revolution. Everyone in his senses welcomed the new burst of British playwrights, many of them from a working class background, who brought a new excitement to the London theatre. But, as Harold Hobson wrote some years later, "Man cannot live for ever on antagonisms. The need for assertion is sooner or later imperative." Later he was to add, "Where has all the goodness gone? . . . The licence our stage has arrogated to itself goes beyond the limits which any decent society would permit . . . the theatre is too exclusively conscious of evil. Our dramatists, especially our

225

ablest dramatists, are bosom pals with what is vile and disgust-
ing, but they are blind to the goodness in the world."

We at the Westminster feel the need to make such assertions.
We do not think that life is a meaningless bad joke, or that God
is dead. We believe that there are solutions to problems. We do
not shrink from reality, but reality is not all evil. The sordid, the
violent, the cruel, the perverted, are certainly aspects of reality.
But they are a fraction of it. There are vast areas of reality
which many writers today never touch–the reality of courage,
of loyalty, of staunchness for a cause, of sacrifice for conviction,
of love and comradeship, of heroic endurance, of patience in
adversity–aspects of reality which are far more relevant to the
world in which we live. We believe that the good can be more
exciting, more interesting and probably more shocking than
evil has ever been.

This conception ran counter to the current theatrical trend.
Once more we found ourselves in a battle.

The chairman of the Trustees, Kenneth Belden, with whom
we work very closely, had dinner one night with a dramatist
who has several successes to his name. He told Ken that after
the first night of his latest play he ran into one of the London
critics. "I like your play," said the critic, "but I'm sorry, old
boy, we shall have to destroy it."

"Why on earth?" asked the astonished playwright.

"Because," said the critic, "it is against our modern trend."

A well-known theatre columnist came to see me at the Westminster one evening. He had known me in the old days and
was keen to hear more about what Bunny and I had been doing
in recent years. "Personally," he said, "I think what is being
done at the Westminster Theatre is magnificent."

"Then, of course, you will write about it in your column,"
I replied.

He shifted uneasily in his chair. "Er, no, no, I couldn't
possibly do that," he said.

I asked him why not.

"Well, people would laugh at me," he replied. "Besides,
what would Kenneth Tynan think?"

This fear of a trendy clique may be one reason why we have
to break through a blanket of silence thrown over us by some

of the London critics. One critic said he would not set foot in the Westminster Theatre because the plays there are 'propaganda'. Yet he puts both feet in theatres where propaganda plays by Brecht, Shaw, Wesker, Weiss, Hochhuth and a host of others are being performed. In fact a large proportion of modern theatre is propagating some idea or other, often against God and for a distorted way of life.

In answer to those who accused Peter Howard of writing propaganda plays he wrote in a preface to one of them: "Why should drama in favour of pessimism, promiscuity and class war be called art and plays in favour of faith and decency be called propaganda?"

Yet in spite of meeting much unfair opposition the Westminster Theatre flourishes. In the last resort it is the public who decide.

IV

In the production of *The Hurricane* I played the part of a planter's wife whose trusted cook turned out to be, by night, a revolutionary leader. Muriel Smith played the cook, a part based on a true story in Kenya. *The Ladder* dramatised the conflict in a man between his calling to serve his fellows and his determination to climb to the top. I played the hero's mother, a possessive woman ruthlessly trampling on his scruples and scheming for his success. The choice before him was powerfully dramatised.

One evening a young miner from the Rhondda sat in the audience. He had got fed up with his wife and job, had left home and found work in London. That evening he had been talking to two men in a café in Hammersmith and had come with them to the theatre. *The Ladder* so struck him that he came back to see it again. He decided he must go back to Wales to his wife and child. Next day he went, but when he got there he could not summon up the courage to face his wife. He took the train back to London without seeing her.

Next morning he realised what a fool he had been. Once more he took the train. This time he went straight to his home. His wife opened the door. "I've come back," he said. He went in to see his small son who was in bed. As he talked to him he asked, "Do you love me?" "I don't know," said the little boy. "You walked out on Mum and me."

The first days were not easy, but two weeks later he came to the theatre to see me with his wife and son. A second honeymoon had begun which has lasted to this day.

While Joan Littlewood in Stratford East and Arnold Wesker with his Centre 42 rightly felt the need of a Theatre for the People, the Westminster Theatre has become the People's Theatre, not in theory but in fact. Men from the mines, from the docks and shipyards, from the railways and motor industries, from all over Britain, bring their wives and families. By train and coach, the people pour into the Westminster Theatre. At the same time diplomats from both sides of the Iron Curtain, men from management, students from schools and universities in Britain and abroad can be found discussing the plays until midnight. The Westminster has become a theatre for the people in the truest sense, not just for one class or age group but for men and women of every age and background who want to be entertained certainly, but who are concerned also in finding solutions for the vital issues of our age.

Many theatres today seem to mistake avant-garbage for avant-garde and, like small boys who love to shock Mum and Dad, are pathetically preoccupied with presenting the public with a very adolescent and one-sided view of life. The Westminster Theatre is avant-garde in the sense that it looks to the future. It dares to discuss the deeper issues which motivate the hearts of men and sends people out of the theatre, not only having been entertained, but with faith and hope that something can be done to make this tired, sick old world a better place to live in. It is the kind of theatre I had dreamed of being part of all my life.

v

Bunny

When *The Hurricane* and *The Ladder* were playing at the Theatre Royal in Brighton, I telephoned Fred Perry, who has a home in Rottingdean, and he and his wife Bobbie came to see the play.

He invited us back next day to see their home and meet their little daughter, Penny.

I first met Fred in 1929 at the Dulwich Covered Courts where I often used to practice. "Hello," said Fred as we shook hands, "I'm the table tennis champion of London, Middlesex and the world!"

When I watched Fred play, the table tennis influence was immediately noticeable. He had transferred unchanged on to the court the strokes he played on the table, the flicked forehand, the stabbed backhand. And though he was wild at that time, there was no mistaking his great promise. He had the indefinable hallmark of a champion, the potential skill, the strength, the confidence.

Sport can seldom have thrown into such close teamwork two personalities more diverse than Fred and I. In 1935 I wrote of him:

"Fred Perry is greater than many of his contemporaries give him credit for. He has all the attributes of the champion: great strength, great stamina, a well-nigh perfect technique, and, arising from this, confidence in his powers. And he has more. He has a genius for the game which enables him to do the right thing at the right moment, to pull out the great shot in the crisis, to win matches when from a spectator's point of view he appears to be playing badly and it seems impossible that he could win.

"Surely no man who has ever played tennis, not even excepting Borotra, has covered a tennis court with such terrific speed. Has anyone ever seen Perry unable to reach a drop shot, or get back to a lob which has fallen over his head?

"There is nothing spectacular in his speed of foot. He does not appear to be moving fast. But without apparent movement he is everywhere in the court at once, and he covers the net so swiftly that he is seldom, if ever, passed.

"My matches alongside Perry in the Davis Cup form my happiest lawn tennis memories. The Davis Cup for me is synonymous with Perry.

"I have been glad to have played in the same team with so great a player, and I am only sorry that the days which are passed cannot come again."

When Fred turned 'pro' and our paths diverged, I seldom

saw him. One occasion was in California at the time of our great meeting at the Hollywood Bowl. Fred had been there, seen the vast crowds and begun to wonder what 'The Rabbit' as he always called me, was up to now. I met him afterwards.

"Say, Rabbit, what's the racket?"

I explained to him as best I could. I had never any doubt of Fred's affection for me, but I also knew I was something of a mystery to him. "Bunny and his bloody Shakespeare," he used to say. I enjoyed poetry and often visited the art galleries of the European capitals we played in and generally behaved in what was to Fred an odd manner.

The war parted us for years and I did not see Fred until I met him again in Florida where he was tennis 'pro' at a luxurious millionaire hotel at Boca Raton. Phyll and I were together. He greeted us warmly. And then as we walked into the palatial hotel he looked at us with a grin, "Not a bad little joint, eh?" he said.

The only blots on Fred's success story were his marriage troubles. But when I met Fred in his home at Rottingdean all these were behind him. He had married an enchanting wife –gay, full of life and with an irrepressible sense of humour about herself and Fred and life generally. She was as fond of Fred as Fred was of her and of their daughter, Penny.

In 1966 I saw Fred at the Runaway Bay Hotel in Jamaica where he is Sports Director. He invited Phyll and me for the day and we played golf together, going round the course in an electric cart: Rockefeller Golf, Fred called it. Fred spends five months in Jamaica at the pleasantest time of the year. He is at home there, a friend to and a friend of Jamaican and American alike. The other seven months he is in England broadcasting for the BBC and ITV and keeping an eye in both places on Perry's Sportswear.

For all his success as a tennis player, for all the money that has come his way, Fred's road through life has not been easy. But in these last years he has sailed into calm waters. He has made enemies, but he has the gift of being always himself and his generous spirit wins him a legion of friends.

Phyll
The Hurricane, the first of many of the Westminster Theatre
plays to be filmed, was shot in Africa and America. After completing the film I received a cable from Peter Howard asking me
to play the lead in his new play *Through The Garden Wall* at the
Westminster. With me in the cast were Oliver Johnston, Bryan
Coleman and Richard Warner. Bryan and Richard were to stay
with us at the Westminster for three years without a break.

Through The Garden Wall is a comedy about two families who
live either side of a wall. The Allways and the Stones represent
symbolically the so-called Free World and the Communist
World. Dr Gold, who was called in by both families, does not
accept the wall as an inseparable barrier. He realises that it
exists only through the hatred and prejudices of the two families
and he walks right through it.

Aggie Allways, the Western mother whom I played, is a
dominating woman who entirely controls her husband and son.
One scene is between the husband and wife when Aggie tells
her husband how, after a talk with Dr Gold, she has faced her
bitterness against her mother-in-law and realised she had taken
out her frustration on her husband and son. The effect of that
scene on many married couples was one of the most extraordinary experiences I have ever had in the theatre.

People I had never met came round to see me in my dressing-
room. One night a married couple from behind the Iron Curtain stayed late into the night talking with me about the
divisions in their family. Another night I received a card from
a delightful Jewish pair who run a successful wholesale dress
business. They said they would like to give me a new summer
dress. Of course, I was delighted. When I asked them why they
should give me such a generous present, the husband said, "For
twenty years I've longed to tell my wife that she was exactly
like the part you played tonight. At last I've had the courage
to do it!" Another man told me, "I am a Jew, my wife is a
Gentile. All our married life there has been a wall between us.
Since we saw that play it has disappeared."

Another night a woman shop steward from a factory in the

Midlands came to see me. She had come to the theatre rather unwillingly on a coach party. She told me she was unhappy and had decided to leave her husband and go off with another man. Her son was doing badly at school and had constant headaches. Everything was in a mess. She said, "Tonight after watching your scene I realise it was my fault. I'm going back to have an honest talk with my husband and see what we can do for our boy." She came back to see me some weeks later. Her family had been reunited, her son was doing better at school and she had begun to bring a new spirit into the factory where she worked.

Another night a leader of the unemployed came round to see me. He sat with his head in his hands and said, "How can we break down those bloody walls between management and labour?"

I could tell countless stories about what has happened through men in industry seeing the plays at the Westminster Theatre. Just one other example:

In 1962 the secretary of the mineworkers in a pit in Northumberland came to see the play *Music at Midnight* by Peter Howard and Alan Thornhill. His pit was in a critical condition. A thousand families depended on it for their livelihood, but it was threatened with closure because it could not pay its way. Only 1,700 tons of coal were being raised each day, and it was losing 39s. 6d. a ton. The miners' secretary was impressed and moved by the philosophy of the play. He decided to apply it in his pit. Instead of maintaining a state of running warfare, he called together every element in the pit to cooperate to raise production, reduce absenteeism and improve quality of work. By the time *Music at Midnight* reached the Theatre Royal, Newcastle-upon-Tyne, on its tour a few months later, he was able to invite some of the cast down to the coal face on the day when production reached 2,500 tons a day. Some months later it topped 3,000 tons a day, and the pit is still in production. Not only did one thousand men retain their jobs but the pit was able to employ men from a neighbouring pit which had been damaged by fire.

VII

It was Bryan Coleman, who played opposite me in *Through The Garden Wall*, who introduced us to Henry Cass. A short, stocky man with a warm heart and quick intelligence, Henry immediately invited confidence. He had a blunt manner and spoke his mind. We knew where we were with a man like that. We took to him right away.

Henry Cass started in the theatre as an actor. Later he became a director and made his first success as a director at the Croydon Rep, when several of his productions of Ibsen's plays were transferred successfully to the West End. Following his time at Croydon Lilian Baylis invited him to be the director at the Old Vic, where he remained for two years. He worked closely with Bernard Shaw on his play *St Joan*, and did a particularly fine production of *Peer Gynt*, as well as the many Shakespeare plays of those two Old Vic seasons.

Later he enjoyed equal success in the West End and after one triumphant first night received a standing ovation as he entered the Savoy grill for supper.

In the midst of these successes he went one evening to check up on a murder play he had produced which was enjoying a long run. As he watched it he became horrified. "What have I done?" he asked himself. "This play is teaching people to commit murder and other crimes." He went home that night to re-think his responsibility as a director towards the public; and, although he continued to make films and direct opera at Covent Garden, he retired from play production.

Cass had been out of the theatre for some years when Bryan Coleman brought him to lunch with us. He has been our director at the Westminster ever since. He is a perfectionist dedicated to the theatre and to the very heart of what the author wants to say. The bigger the challenge the more he grumbles and rumbles to begin with, but enjoys wrestling with the problem to be overcome. And his best work is done at what he first considers an impossible task.

He shows a great humanity at auditions. Casting a play is not easy. The theatre is an overcrowded profession. Often at auditions when Henry, Bunny and I see actors and actresses every fifteen minutes throughout the day, it is a heartbreaking business. Some are so nervous that you know they are not giving you their best. Some have not had work for many weeks. I know from experience the fear that grips you before an audition, waiting to hear if you have got the job, the elation if you get it, the familiar message if you do not: "I'm sorry, but we will keep in touch." Henry is sensitive and understanding. No matter how good or how bad they may be he treats each actor or actress with the greatest consideration. One actor told our stage manager, "Usually I feel like cattle at a show, but in this theatre I feel like a human being again." Another actor told us, "I felt my dignity had been restored."

From the first Henry Cass has understood what we were out to do. He met criticism and misunderstanding from old friends when he came to us, but this, too, he regards as a challenge to be faced gaily and fearlessly. One evening, speaking to a group of students, he made the following speech:

"The theatre of Shakespeare, the theatre of Shaw, Ibsen, Chekhov, Galsworthy – and I would like to include Robert Bolt – all men of ideas, these kept the theatre at its best, kept it alive, creating a great excitement. I think excitement is the word. You have got to have it in the theatre – plays where an evening's entertainment does not finish with the fall of the curtain.

"Now at the Westminster you have such a theatre, an original theatre. Although I work in it, although I am the producer there at the moment, I am detached from it if you know what I mean. I can see it, I think, for what it is.

"It is dedicated to the task of showing the public that people can think right as well as wrong. Peter Howard says, 'I write plays to give people a purpose. The purpose is clear. The aim is simple. It is to help all who want peace in the world to be ready to pay the price of peace in their own personalities. It is to enlist everybody everywhere in a revolution to remake the world. Neither more nor less.'

"Now I put it to you. Is this dedication to be encouraged or discouraged? Is this a theatre with new ideas? I had a strange experience at a rehearsal of Howard's play *Mr Brown Comes Down The Hill*. I found that often I could not take the goodness of those people committed to Moral Re-Armament. Nor could I take the goodness inherent in the play. I had to run away from it. I had to hide from it. I still have to hide from it. But I always realise in spite of running away and hiding from it that it is I who am wrong.

"Now perhaps some of the critics run away from it as I run away from it, often out of fear. Life after all is very much easier if it just jogs along. The theatre is very much easier if it just jogs along. Why bother about anything?

"But the Westminster Theatre does bother and I must take off my hat to it. It bothers all the time with extraordinary energy and with a faith which moves mountains. It is absurd to do anything but to salute their effort and give them all the encouragement they deserve because they are working not for their own aggrandisement, not to make a fortune or their personal success, but they are devoting all their lives and energies to the good of mankind.

"Is not that a new thought in the theatre? In a town like London which has some forty theatres, is not there a place for at least one theatre which shows that life is not merely a series of dull negatives, but a place where hope runs high, where people can learn how to fulfil themselves and to enrich their lives by a full understanding of what it is all about? This, in my opinion, is what the theatre at its best can and should do."

VIII

Bunny

On February 25, 1965, Phyll and I were preparing to go out to tea with two friends. The telephone rang. It was our friend Roland Wilson. "Peter Howard is seriously ill," he said. We detected something ominous in Roly's voice which made the word 'serious' even more serious than its face value.

"How serious?"

"It's a question of his heart."

I put down the phone quietly. The news was difficult to take in. Peter ill? We had never known Peter ill. He was a giant of a man, capable of immense labours with a body toughened in the rough school of rugby football. Encouraged by the knowledge of his physical strength, yet knowing that something must be seriously wrong, we kept our tea date. When we returned the avalanche fell. Peter Howard was dead.

The news was impossible to grasp. For twenty-four hours we went around numbed, unable to believe it.

235

People all over the world were as shocked as we were by the news of Peter's sudden and totally unexpected passing. He died in Lima, Peru. The President of Peru and the Lord Mayor of Lima, as a tribute to his life and work, arranged that he should lie in state in Lima City Hall. At 8.30 in the morning crowds gathered at the main entrance and all day long hundreds filed past to pay their last tribute to this remarkable man. Messages from high and low, rich and poor, from every station in life and every political colour, began to pour in to his widow and family. Presidents sent messages, Prime Ministers, former Prime Ministers, the Secretary-General of the United Nations, Cardinals, Bishops of both Catholic and Protestant Churches, and revolutionary students.

It was as a dramatist that, in the last years of his life, Phyll and I worked most closely with Peter. Some said his plays were the most brilliant plays they had ever seen and would be re-membered long after many current dramatists were dead and gone. Others disliked them intensely. It was very difficult to view them dispassionately, because in a most uncomfortable way they viewed you. He wrote in his preface to the play *Mr Brown Comes Down The Hill*, "The doctor, the black man, the harlot are not real in themselves. They are parts of every human heart. They are bits of you and me walking and talking before us. Like or dislike them, it is ourselves we survey."

Gabriel Marcel, the French Catholic philosopher in an article in the weekly *Les Nouvelles Littéraires* wrote, "The many drama-tic works Peter Howard produced were for him very often the most effective means of reaching and renewing the inner life of the individual. In this sense his work can be compared with that of Brecht, for both it is a matter of forming a new type of man, one being Marxist and the other trained to the dictates of a Christian conscience."

Egon Karter, director of the Komedie Theatre in Basle, said of him, "Peter Howard has shown how a real theatre of the people can be created. He has left behind the psychological drama of Ibsen and Sartre and has made the stage a platform, not for a discussion of self-realisation, but to hold up a mirror in front of man so that he sees himself clearly. It is a shock therapy for the human reason and the human heart. He speaks a language that is understood everywhere in the world. The power of his plays lies in their truth."

Across the Atlantic, the Hollywood *Citizen-News* on its entertainment page wrote, "Peter Howard was beloved by many, hated by others. On one hand he was defended with intense loyalty, on the other he was attacked with bitter vengeance. He was an idealist who hammered away ceaselessly at everything he believed destroyed man's dignity, his honour and his initiative. He let the chips fall where they would. Thus we pay tribute to Peter Howard for all he contributed to mankind and salute those who would choose to follow in his footsteps. The theatre will miss him for his dynamic plays. The world will mourn him for his ideological passion."

Yes indeed we would miss him. Life around Peter was always gay, humorous, profound, original and intensely interesting. His warmth of heart and depth of understanding made him a rare friend. It was hard to believe that we would not see him again and even harder to understand why he should have gone so soon. As I write that sentence I hear him say something we often heard him say in his lifetime – "Remember 'My ways are not your ways, nor your ways My ways,' saith the Lord."

IX

Four years ago the Trustees in consultation with Peter Howard had begun to plan a new development around the Westminster Theatre. As time went on it had become increasingly clear that greater facilities were needed: an enlarged foyer, a snack bar, a restaurant with excellent food at reasonable prices, kitchens, a library, conference rooms, a cinema and first-class dressing rooms for the actors who serve the theatre so well.

After the death of Peter Howard it was decided that the new building should be called the Westminster Theatre Arts Centre and should be dedicated to his memory.

Once more it was a venture of faith. When Kenneth Belden signed the contract for the building operation to begin there was no money in the bank. With the squeeze and the freeze and the economic crisis in the country it seemed an impossible task to raise the money needed. Yet by the time the Arts Centre had been completed every bill had been paid. More than fifty countries contributed. The people of Wales donated the Welsh slate, the Sudanese Government gave leather panels for the foyer from their tanneries in Khartoum. From Lapp craftsmen in their tents in the Arctic Circle to Pueblo Indians in New Mexico, people had been at work to help the Arts Centre forward. Up and down Great Britain courageous and imaginative work was undertaken by trade unionists and businessmen, farmers, teachers, housewives, students and even small children who made jams and sweets to sell in aid of the Building Fund. Phyll and I decided to give a part of our legacy, believing it to be an investment for the future of our children.

In November 1966 the Arts Centre was opened by Rajmohan Gandhi, a close friend and fellow-worker of Peter Howard. Rajmohan came specially from India for the opening ceremony.

He said, "As an Indian and Asian I feel profoundly thankful for this Centre. Through the films and plays that it will create, the Centre will woo, challenge and inspire millions in my part of the world, as in every other part, towards a way of life that will solve our problems. A revolutionary answer is needed. The weapons released by the Centre will strike every corner of the world."

CHAPTER SEVENTEEN

I

Phyll

WHEN in 1961 Bunny became a Trustee of the Westminster
Theatre and I became a member of the permanent company and later went on the Council of Management of Westminster Productions, we felt the time had come for us to have
a home of our own—or rather a house to put our home in. Both
Bunny and I had been left legacies and so we started looking
for a house. We try in our family to find a united mind on our
projects. It is not always easy!

Having lived in Hampstead all my early life, I returned there
like a homing pigeon. I found a house with which I fell in love
at first sight. When I took Bunny and the children to see it,
there was a deadly silence. Bunny liked the view but nothing
else. Jenny said, "Mum, you don't mean you really *like* this
house." John made it quite clear it was not even worth considering.

Then the three of them found a house that they all raved
about: it had a small garden and everything they wanted.
I went along to see it and thought it terribly depressing and
impossible to run. For some time we continued looking all over
London, but we could not find the right house.

Then one night before we went to bed, Bunny said, "Let's
pray and see if God really wants us to have a house and, if He
does, where He wants us to have it." Next morning we were
all clear it was right and that the house needed to be somewhere
close to the theatre where we both worked.

The following day I had occasion to phone an estate agent
who had taken us to see a house which had been too big and
too expensive. "Do you by any chance have anything much
smaller, close to the Westminster Theatre?" I asked. He replied,
"As a matter of fact, I think I have what you're looking for. It
is five minutes from there and has just come up for sale today."
The moment we stepped inside the front door, all four of us said
unanimously, "This is it. This is where we're meant to live."

An old friend of ours had told us, "When you find the right house, all your furniture will fit like a glove." Our furniture had been in storage for twenty-four years. Everything fitted as though it had been made to measure and everything matched perfectly.

To find a wallpaper which we all liked for the dining room was something of a problem. I would come home with one I thought was enchanting. John would take one look at it and say, "Ma, you're slipping." Bunny found a striped one with gold spots which we both liked very much. The children were polite about it, but we could see that they could not stand it. John said he would go mad counting the spots. We looked at every kind of wallpaper, with spots and without spots, with patterns and without patterns, until suddenly we came on one and all said, "That's it."

We moved into our new home on my birthday. It is the first home of their own the children have ever had. Every day we appreciate it more. It's funny the things that strike you after not having had anything for so long. I kept saying, "Isn't it nice to have our own teaspoons."

When we were unpacking we found all kinds of interesting things—old photographs, scrap books with newspaper cuttings from our early life and many fascinating letters. One letter was from Baird, the pioneer of television, thanking Bunny for being on the first programme ever televised. He wrote, "As you know, the present is the first occasion in history that TELEVISION, that is the actual and instantaneous transmission of vision, has been demonstrated as a definite and practical achievement for a series of performances in a public place of entertainment. The science of TELEVISION is obviously in its infancy, but when, as it is certain, it develops, we are sure that you will feel satisfaction at having been one of the first to be so presented." The letter is dated July 31, 1930.

II

Because we now have our first home in twenty-four years it does not mean we are settling down to a quiet cosy life. That is not for us. It is the continuation of the work to which we have

DIRECTORS:
THE RT. HON. LORD AMPTHILL, G.C.S.I., G.C.I.E.
SIR EDWARD MANVILLE. [CHAIRMAN]
LT.-COL. GEORGE B. WINCH.
F. R. A. SHORTIS.
JOHN LOGIE BAIRD. [MANAGING DIRECTOR]

133, LONG ACRE,
LONDON,
W.C.2.

CODES : A.B.C. AND BENTLEY'S.
PHONE : TEMPLE BAR 5401.
[PRIVATE BRANCH EXCHANGE]
TELEGRAPHIC ADDRESS :
"TELEVISOR RAND LONDON."

31st July, 1930.

H. W. Austin, Esq.,
Sunnyside,
South Norwood Park,
S.E.25.

Dear Mr. Austin,

On behalf of myself and of the Directors of Baird
Television Limited, I beg to offer to you our sincere thanks
for assisting at our demonstration of TELEVISION at the
London Coliseum.

As you know, the present is the first occasion in
history that TELEVISION - that is, the actual and instantaneous
transmission of Vision - has been demonstrated as a definite
and practical achievement for a series of performances in a
public place of entertainment.

The Science of TELEVISION is obviously in its infancy
but when, as is certain, it develops, we are sure that you will
feel satisfaction in having been one of the first to be so
presented, as we ourselves are honoured by your acceptance of
our invitation to be Televised.

Yours very truly,

J.L.B/DR

Letter from John Logie Baird

given our lives. Our son and daughter stand with us. No parents are more fortunate than we are. John and Jennifer are not paragons of virtue, far from it, but they are wonderful friends and very good to us. We have never forced them to live as we do. They have always been free to choose which way they would go.

For Jennifer in some ways it has been easier than for John. As I have said, ever since she was a child she has had a faith in God which was as normal to her as breathing. From the time when, at eleven years old, she decided entirely on her own to care for people as much as she did for dogs and horses, her life has been filled with people of all kinds and descriptions. She could never understand a small, selfish concept of family life. Sometimes when we had been away we would suggest a picnic with just our immediate family. Jenny's face would fall, "Only us?" she would say, disappointed. And we would end up with a large party.

Now in our home this has become a family joke—"I hope you don't mind, Dad and Mum, but there will be four extra for lunch," or "There is a student I met from the Middle East who has nowhere to go, or I've invited two Israeli girls who know very few people in London."

One young student from a Middle Eastern country was a great friend of Jenny's. Whenever we thought we would have a quiet evening, Jenny would suggest that we had this girl for dinner. "But, Mum, she lives in one room. We must have her in and give her a good meal."

One night watching the nine o'clock news on TV, we saw to our horror that a bomb had been thrown into the garden of the girl's home and that her three young brothers had been killed. Another friend who knew her felt Jenny was the one to break the news to her. This Jenny did. The night before the girl left to rejoin her parents she came to spend the evening with us. "Jennifer's friendship saved my life," she said. "We have got to raise up a leadership in my country that can answer hatred." This girl was an Arab—Jenny is half Jewish.

John is very different from his sister. He is the brains of the family. He devours books on philosophy at a rapid rate. On a holiday in Jamaica he would swim out to a raft with a book on philosophy in a sponge bag and sit reading Kierkegaard, Teilhard de Chardin and Spinoza. Intellectually he knew MRA was right, but he was not sure he wanted to live it. We left him entirely free to decide. Finally he came to us and had an honest talk. "With the world in the hell of a mess it is, it's pointless to live a selfish life," he said.

III

Bunny

One of the joys of being in Britain has been the chance to see something of our oldest friends. Among these we have always counted Daphne and Tommy Browning. Daphne is the daughter of Sir Gerald du Maurier, the actor-manager whom we had first met when Galsworthy's play *Escape* was being filmed on Dartmoor with Gerald in the lead and Phyll playing the part of the 'lady of the Moor'.

Gerald and his wife, Muriel, lived an arrow-shot from our old home at the top of Hampstead Heath and on a great many Sundays we went to lunch in their beautiful house, Cannon Hall, and to tennis afterwards.

Gerald was a great practical joker. One day he had invited an American actress who had a high opinion of her tennis. Gerald told her that he had that afternoon a young English player whom he considered had great promise and he would be grateful to get her opinion of him. When the game started the actress gave her expert advice to the young player, and when the match was over Gerald asked her what she thought of him. "Oh," she replied, "I think he shows great promise." "He should," said Gerald, "his name is Bunny Austin."

One day in mid-week Gerald came to see us at our flat. He had an old schoolfriend coming to lunch the following Sunday, he said. His friend was an awful old bore. His daughters Angela and Jeanne could not stand him. Would we please come along and help him out? We said we would be delighted.

The following Sunday we arrived a little ahead of time and found Angela and Jeanne in old clothes looking thoroughly bored. At last the door opened and the dreaded guest arrived. "Mr Gary Cooper," announced the maid.

Gary Cooper at that time was the film star idol of every flapper in England. But it was too late for the two girls to do anything to improve their appearance and it was a long time before they were prepared to forgive their father.

Angela and Jeanne were always at Cannon Hall on our Sunday visits. But Daphne, the third daughter was always away. We were keen to meet her. We heard she was writing—short stories of a strange nature and a novel called, *The Loving Spirit*. We were told she lived at Fowey, Cornwall, and were shown intriguing photos of her dressed in fishermen's clothes and smoking a pipe.

One summer's day we were invited to tennis at Cannon Hall and met at lunch a strikingly handsome man in a grey flannel suit which he wore with the cuffs of the jacket turned up. We learned that he was a major in the Coldstream Guards and were not surprised: he was perfectly cast for the part. His name, Gerald told us, was Browning.

One evening a few days later we were visiting Gerald in his dressing room at the theatre and asked him who exactly the guardsman was. "Believe it or not," said Gerald, "he came to ask the hand of my daughter Daphne in marriage."

"Are you glad?" we queried. "Glad!" exclaimed Gerald, "I'm delighted."

With the announcement of the engagement Daphne at last came up from her beloved Fowey and we met her for the first time. In the succeeding years Daphne and Tommy became two of our best friends and we referred to each other as the As and the Bs.

Soon after their marriage Tommy was promoted in rank and Daphne, up till that time more used to fisherman's clothes than setting a fashion, found herself the colonel's wife. They were posted to Egypt.

When war broke out I went down to see Daphne and Tommy where he was posted in Kent. He was out in the fields when I arrived. I went to greet him. Now he was a general and he looked every inch the part as he stood in the fields in his general's uniform. "Well, Tommy," I asked. "What do you think of it all?"

"I wish I were a farmer!" said Tommy ruefully.

He was the simplest of men and totally without side. He told me then of his fears and his memory of the First World War when he had been a young subaltern. "I have seen myself in and out of trenches all night," he said.

Daphne wanted to know what she should do. She had thought of becoming a flying nurse. I suggested that her greatest contribution might be through her pen. She responded to this and later, as I have already told, wrote a book of stories of how ordinary people, all engaged in the work of MRA, helped build morale both on the home front and in the forces in the early days of the war. The book was called, *Come Wind, Come Weather* and sold over 800,000 copies. Tommy later raised the British Airborne Division and went on to be Chief of Staff to Lord Mountbatten in South-East Asia. He was in command of the airborne landing at Arnhem, where Peter Howard's brother, John, lost his life.

Daphne was one of the first to greet me on my return from America in 1947 and very soon the As were able to take up again their friendship with the Bs, though we had of course corresponded during the war years.

Both remained warm supporters of the work that Phyll and I were doing though as Daphne was now living in Cornwall in the house which had been the inspiration of her novel *Rebecca* and hated coming up to London, she was difficult to see. But Tommy was always available, first at Clarence House where he was Comptroller of Princess Elizabeth's Household and later at Buckingham Palace where he worked with Prince Philip.

Phyll and I last saw Tommy in 1963 when we were on a holiday in Cornwall, staying at a hotel not far from Falmouth. We motored over for lunch one Sunday. It was our first visit to Menabilly. It was November and as we arrived it was real du Maurier weather. It was a grey, cold day. The trees of the park which surrounds Menabilly were bare and gaunt against the rain-threatening clouds. The wind moaned through the trees and all the characters of Daphne's books seemed to be riding with it.

We went inside. The house, except for the drawing room, was sparsely furnished. But the welcome of the Bs to the As was as warm as ever.

We sat around the fire in the drawing room after lunch. We talked of this and that, of the state of the country, of Mr Wilson and of the Tory Government, then still in power but with its fortunes waning. Tommy saw very clearly into the heart of things and his judgement was as sound as ever, but even then we felt the waning of his physical strength–which had never been the same since his titanic efforts during the war. It was not long afterwards that we heard the news that this best and most loyal of friends had gone, leaving an aching void in his wife's life and a great sense of loss in our own.

IV

When for the first time for many years I saw my old friend of Davis Cup days, Pat Hughes, at Wimbledon, his first remark to me was, "Bunny, the lawn tennis world is a shambles." He referred to sham amateurs or 'shamateurs' as the phrase is to-day. And he was in a position to know: it was his job to pay the players competing in the Dunlop Tournaments.

Many people felt that the state of affairs could not continue. One of these was Herman David, Chairman of the All England Club. In the spring of 1967 he gave a healthy shock to the lawn tennis world by calling its amateurism 'a living lie'.

Then in the autumn of 1967 the Council of the Lawn Tennis Association took the bold step of abolishing all the distinctions between amateur and professional and calling all players simply 'players'.

Interviewed next day by Miss Ann Batt of the *Daily Express*, Mr Eaton Griffith, Vice-President of the LTA, was reported as saying, "Just sickening it was, the way shamateurism went on. I knew so many cases of famous players who flew under the colour of amateur but were quietly collecting £300 for a week's play. Well, it wasn't right. It wasn't HONEST."

Then followed a lively situation. The International Lawn Tennis Federation which controls the game was outraged. This was no way for a lawn tennis nation to behave, they declared. Unless Britain mended her ways and obeyed the Federation rules they would be outcast and isolated. Her players would be banned from competition outside of Britain and foreign players would be banned from competing inside Britain.

But though some members of the press got highly alarmed at this point and shouted for the British to retract and go slow and like good boys work through the Federation (which they had been trying to do for years), the LTA remained unmoved. At a general meeting they voted overwhelmingly to back the bold decision of the Council.

Gradually their firm stand began to pay off. The Swedes rallied to their side proposing an Extraordinary General Meeting of the ILTF to discuss the question of Open Tennis. Then two of the great lawn tennis powers, Australia and America, came into the arena backing the Swedish initiative.

Following this the *Daily Express* wrote an excellent leading article under the title, 'Giving the Lead': "When Britain decided to end shamateurism and open Wimbledon to professional players there were gloomy forecasts that we would be isolated.

"Now, suddenly everyone who matters is in favour of Open Tennis. The Australians, Americans and Germans give their blessing. The International Tennis Authority will have to face the facts and agree to the British plan which it originally denounced.

"By their willingness to stand alone the British tennis chiefs are winning.

"That is leadership. It is something we could do with in fields other than tennis."

I echo the *Daily Express* leader and applaud the honesty and sense of the men who have faced the reality of an untenable situation. It is obviously no longer possible to control the number of those who profit financially from so-called amateur sport, for it is no longer possible in the tough arena of international competition to excel and not get paid unless you have private means. The demands are too great.

Sooner or later this situation will have to be faced in athletics. The situation now is the same as it was in tennis. The athlete simply cannot attain world standing unless he is subsidised. After the Winter Olympics at Grenoble a well-known ski-equipment manufacturer from Austria openly admitted that he had employed a great amateur Austrian skier for fourteen years. "He is my expert," he said. "I pay him just over sixty pounds a month."

But while I applaud those who make it possible for dishonest amateurs to become honest pros, does the matter end there? It seems to me the real issue facing sport today is not whether a man is an amateur or a pro but the spirit in which the game is played.

Today there is an enormous emphasis placed on winning, and individuals and even countries will sell their souls for a silver cup or a gold medal. Winning is the whole emphasis in sport. An enormous amount is wrapped up in it. Not only the fame, but the fortune of those taking part. For a club it means bigger gate receipts. For a country a boost in its national prestige.

Now don't get me wrong. I am all for winning! It was the objective of the whole of my tennis life. But too often the determination to win gets out of hand. Major sport becomes minor war.

v

One who realises this and believes something can be done about it is my friend Conrad Hunte, former vice-captain of the West Indies cricket team who made the final throw in the now-famous Test Match during the West Indian tour of Australia. He hit the stumps from ninety yards away to run out the last Australian batsman and bring about the only tie in Test history.

Conrad met MRA in Australia. He says, "I have always yearned to solve the social and economic injustices of our people and create a society of peace and prosperity for all. But as I advanced in my career as a sportsman I saw more and more clearly how inadequate I was to tackle this task. It would take more than cricket to solve the common problems of the countries I visited. I needed a force in my own life deeper and more revolutionary than anything I had yet experienced.

"In February 1961 I found what I was looking for. It was at Melbourne, at the end of the Fifth Test Match with Australia. I saw a film *The Crowning Experience*. This was a turning point for me.

"I have talked much of cricketers being ambassadors of unity but I was divided by hate and fear from my own father. I wanted our politicians and businessmen to be honest but I used to cheat on my income tax and expense accounts. I put these things right because I believed that a dishonest and hate-filled man could not build a sound society. I began to learn how to cure the divisions in the hearts of men. Divisions of hate, fear, selfishness and greed."

There is little need to describe Hunte. As a great opening batsman he is known to thousands who have seen him on the cricket field and millions more who may have followed the Tests on TV. They have seen him rock-like at the crease with every now and then a superb on-drive or a flashing four through the covers. Hunte has played in forty-four Test matches. When he retired from first-class cricket in November 1967, *The Guardian* wrote: "He made himself the West Indies' most reliable opening batsman for a decade. Like all great players he triumphed as much by character as technique."

After meeting MRA Conrad Hunte continued to play cricket–in the Lancashire League and for the West Indies. He topped the averages in the Test matches against England in 1963 and against Australia in the Caribbean in 1965.

In 1968 a damaged knee forced Conrad to retire from the game of cricket. But he is continuing his wider battle to bring the spirit of true sportsmanship into every area of life. I quote in part from a speech he made at the West Indies Students' Centre in London recently:

"There are 800,000 West Indians in Britain. Their numbers understandably give concern to the Government and to the people of these islands. It necessarily brings new situations and new challenges to all of us. It is not a matter of the colour of a man's skin. It is a matter of the character in his heart. It need not be a problem of so many more mouths to feed and heads to shelter, but it could be a glorious opportunity of so many more brains to put to work, hearts to care and wills to engage in doing the job that needs to be done in this country and in the world.

"I believe we could, if we so decided, create here in Britain a multi-racial society varied in its colour, diverse in its culture, with many languages and one common purpose valid for East and West which would be a pattern for the Common Market countries, the Communist countries and the non-Communist countries of the world.

"For one thing I am particularly grateful–Britain taught the West Indies how to play cricket. Together we can show the world how to live."

Life is not always easy for Conrad. In his native Caribbean he is worshipped as a hero. In Britain he has been admired and applauded for his cricketing skill. But in the crowd he is often just another coloured man. He is heir to the insults that the coloured people in Britain too often suffer.

One evening he came to see me. He had lost some of his usual buoyancy. He had just been insulted. A casual passer-by had turned to him, "You bastard, you bloody bastard. What the hell are you doing here?"

Conrad had smiled and gone on his way. But the insult was like a barb in his soul. The pain was deep. Fortunately he was able to tell me about it. He knew he could turn to God and find healing and forgiveness for the man who had insulted him. He could renew his determination to fight in Britain and across the world for a new humanity between the peoples of the earth.

For without this Conrad knows what will happen. The coloured people will not lie down for ever under insults. Pain leads to bitterness. The bitterness to hate. And hate to the desire for revenge. And there are those who are waiting to fan that desire and to turn it into violence.

Conrad says: "Neither white power, red power nor black power are the answer. But there is a power available and adequate to answer all men's needs–for food, faith, employment, housing and human dignity. Men living by absolute standards and by a common commitment to listen and obey the voice of the Living God will be able to get us out of our difficulties into a world of plenty, peace and unity for all."

VI

Some time ago I heard indirectly that my membership of the All England Lawn Tennis and Croquet Club, which I had enjoyed for many years, had been taken away from me. Foolishly perhaps I did not give this much thought at the time. My championship days were over, I was playing very little tennis, seemed unlikely to be in England during the Wimbledon championships and so if I was removed from the membership of the All England Club, I was not unduly concerned. Moreover I innocently believed that whatever the reason for my suspension of membership, the matter would ultimately be put right without my having to do anything about it.

The years went by and one day I found myself in England at the time of the championships. I saw my old friend Herman David, the chairman of the Club, and he immediately got me tickets for the centre court. I was invited to the members' tea enclosure and was moved by the warm reception of my old friends. Apparently the word had gone round, "Bunny's back", and one after the other they came to the members' enclosure to greet me.

Once more I went abroad and it was not until 1961 that I found myself back again at the time of the championships, with the prospect this time of being in England on a more permanent basis. Again I got in touch with Herman David and he kindly got tickets for me. "Of course, you'll have to pay," he said. I did not feel this unreasonable, although the commissionaire, as I picked up the tickets at the gates, said, "Good Lor', Mr Austin, I wouldn't have thought *you* would have to pay"!

It was at this time that I began to think seriously about membership of the All England Club. No one seemed to be taking any action on my behalf, so I decided to take action myself. I rang up Herman David and asked him to lunch. He replied by asking me to lunch in the City in the board room of the Diamond Development Company, of which he is chairman.

After lunch he told me that he had anticipated that I would want to talk about my membership and had looked up the facts in the minutes. I had lost it, he told me, because I had failed to pay my subscription during the war. I had, he said, been written to many times and had never replied. I told him I had no recollection of receiving any letters and asked him what he would advise. He suggested I write and apologise for my failure to pay my subscription and apply for re-election. I asked him if he would support me. He said he would but added, "It will be very hard to fight it through. There are some who do not want Moral Re-Armament in the All England Club."

Taking Herman's advice I wrote the letter as he had suggested and received an acknowledgement. Six months and one week later I received another communication informing me that my letter had been placed before the committee and enclosing a form of application for re-election. It required that I should have a proposer, a seconder and two supporters. I wrote to Herman David asking him if he would propose me. He replied that he was proposing two others that year and was forbidden by the rules to propose a third. He agreed instead to second me. I then asked another old friend of mine, R. K. Tinkler, with whom I had won the schoolboy's doubles championship some time back in the dark ages, to propose me. He agreed, saying that I had been out of the club too long.

I now needed two supporters. One of those I asked has important business connections with the Club. I had known his father well and had played with the racquets manufactured by his firm. He had visited our centre at Caux and had returned brimming over with enthusiasm for the work. During the championships of 1961, he had made me tell everyone I met about it. However when I asked him to support me he became dubious. He wrote that I was a controversial character, that some did not approve of my war record, that others did not want MRA in the Club, and he felt he could not risk the Club's business goodwill by supporting me, unless I was prepared to state that my desire to rejoin the Club was entirely a personal and individual matter not connected with my work.

I wrote back apologising for being any source of embarrassment to him and saying I would rather like to come to Wimbledon now and then, perhaps to play some tennis and meet and talk with people I like. I also said, "I suppose some members of Wimbledon are like myself members of the Church of England. Others like yourself are Catholics. If any club I belonged to tried to extract conditions from Catholics, Anglicans or Jews, or to limit their liberty of speech before joining, I would instantly resign from such a club. It would smack to me of Hitler." And I ended by saying, "Naturally I'm sure you did not mean to cram any gag into my mouth, or shackle me in any such way at all, but if you ask me why I want to join Wimbledon, it is as I have said for the same reasons, neither more nor less, that other players want to join. In my case there are no trading motives involved."

By return came a charming note saying that he was afraid he had hurt my feelings and that he had that day written off to Wimbledon supporting my application.

And so, my application form complete at last, I sent it in. That was seven years ago. And there the matter rests.

One day during the championships of 1965 a journalist from the *Daily Mail* rang me up. He said he had been speaking to the All England Club and had asked them why I was not a member. Was it, he had asked, because I was in America during the war or because of my identification with Moral Re-Armament? They had replied that these were not the reasons.

"Do you know the reasons?" he asked me.

"Your guess is as good as mine," I replied.

"Well, I think it's a damned insult," he said.

Insult or not, this matter seems to me to go far beyond my personal relationships with a tennis club. The All England Club are entitled to do as they please. If they want to elect titled people; if they want to elect sons and daughters of committee members, and keep others on a waiting list for years, and if they do not want to re-elect me, it is their affair. But only to a point. The reason for rejecting an application for membership is important. If it is on account of a man's religious convictions it is dangerous. The very essence of sport and the hope it offers to the world comes from the fact that it is above discrimination. Will we begin to apply this discrimination to Jews, Catholics or those of different coloured skins? Where does it end?

Whoever they are who want to keep me out of the All England Club seem to be a powerful coterie and their power seems to extend beyond the All England Club itself. For during the last six years I have been in England, I have only been invited to one lawn tennis function – to the fiftieth anniversary of the Frinton Lawn Tennis Club.

Three years ago during a visit to the championships I went into the dressing rooms to see a friend. The following day I received a letter from the Club's secretary informing me that I had been seen by a committee member where I was not entitled to go. It was a nice letter and I felt the secretary wished he had not been told to write it. In ending he said, "I'm sure you will appreciate we must stick to our rules and that any variation of them causes confusion and embarrassment among the stewards."

I could not help thinking that perhaps it would be more embarrassing and confusing to the stewards to find that I was not a member of the Club – a Club where I had played with some success in fourteen championships, where I was the last Englishman to reach the final and where I had for three years helped successfully to defend and hold the Davis Cup.

Phyll

It was April, 1966. John and I were sitting on the verandah of a bungalow in Jamaica. A flock of green parakeets were chattering in a nearby tree, causing Dick, the old parrot in his cage on the front porch, to complain loudly, shouting at the top of his voice and throwing his tray around in a frenzy of frustration at his own captivity. Bright yellow Saffron Finches descended on the lawn by the pool and humming birds with long green tails hovered like helicopters over a flowering hibiscus.

Bunny and I had accepted a very generous invitation from our friends the Kerr-Jarretts to be their guests in Montego Bay. Accompanied by our son, John, we had one of our rare holidays together. We had spent some wonderfully happy weeks swimming in the clear blue water, snorkling and watching the tropical fish of all shapes and sizes and colours swimming around the coral reefs in the bay. We visited friends and stayed with Minnie Simson, Lena Ashwell's sister-in-law, in her home high up on a hill looking over beautiful valleys, watching droves of white egrets flying home as the sun set.

For the final weeks we had been loaned the low white bungalow of the son of our host, Ian Kerr-Jarrett, who was in England with his wife and children, much to the sorrow of the parrot who missed his friends and called the name of the youngest daughter ceaselessly in a deep mournful voice, "Sarah, Sarah, Sarah". The bungalow, situated on a hill in the middle of a sugar estate, was completely isolated. There was not a house to be seen for miles around.

Up till then it had been a heavenly holiday, one of those rare gifts, and then suddenly it happened. We were coming back from the beach up the long drive through the cane fields, a road lined by tall palm trees. It had always been completely deserted. We were rounding a blind bend leading to the house when the cook's brother who had been visiting him came racing down the hill on his motor bicycle. He seemed to head straight at us. Bunny swerved to avoid him. We left the road and hit a tree.

We had been lent a small Volkswagen by our host. It was completely smashed. John and Bunny dragged me out. We were bruised and shaken, but when we took a look at the position of the car it was an even greater shock. It was right on the edge of a ravine. Had Bunny swerved one inch further to the left the car would have toppled over into the ravine below.

Bertha, the old housekeeper left behind by our host to look after us, came running down the drive. She lifted her hands to Heaven when she saw the position and state of the car and said, "The heavens opened and saved you."

The man on the motor bicycle was mercifully unhurt except for a small cut on his knee and so a disaster was averted.

A few days later, possibly from shock, Bunny picked up a virus and became very ill indeed. Day and night he could not stop coughing. To make matters worse a storm came up and a fierce wind blew incessantly, sending currents of dust swirling round the bungalow. We were very isolated. At nights there were strange creaking and scurrying noises on the roof. Suddenly the dogs would start barking and whining and then would bay at the moon.

One night in the distance we heard the drum beats as the Rastafari came down from the hills for a celebration in the town. Three years before, we had been told, a family had been murdered in a house just beyond the hills we could see from our window. It was eerie and frightening with Bunny so ill. I was glad when daylight came.

While John and I were sitting on the verandah, Bunny was sleeping. His temperature would not go down. John said, "It has been a difficult time, Ma, but your marriage vows said, for better or for worse. This is for worse."

My mind went back to our wedding day when we made those vows. So much had happened to us in the thirty-six years of our marriage. When we started out we were young and immature. In a court of law we would most certainly have been called incompatible. We not only came from totally different backgrounds but in a sense we had nothing in common. It was no wonder we had run into difficulties.

I thought that evening of the people we had been to for help when things were difficult. I thought of the doctor who told me I would never be happily married because of some of the things which had happened to me in my childhood; of the Church dignitary with whom we had been staying for the weekend, how after breakfast one morning when we told him things were not going too well between us, he had looked embarrassed, coughed, got up from his chair, gone to the window, murmured something about everything would be all right and had changed the subject; of a popular preacher and his wife who suggested that in our case divorce might be the best way out.

I thought with gratitude of those who had not been afraid to give us help when we needed it. Of Annie Jaeger, whose understanding and compassion had helped me to face the things in my nature which had made me so difficult to live with. Of Frank whom I had persecuted, who had helped us so much and who became my best friend.

I was grateful, sitting on that verandah, for these true friends and others who helped us to stick to those marriage vows: "For better for worse, for richer for poorer, in sickness or in health, till death us do part." That has been so much our experience. Sometimes it has been for better. Sometimes it has been for worse. We have had money and we have had no money. We have had good health and bad health. We have found that the Marriage Service is one of the great statements of true love in the human experience. It has not always been easy but in sticking together we have learned what a rich and wonderful institution marriage can be and what love really means.

As I thought of these things there came back into my mind a poem Bunny wrote me for an anniversary:

> "*Many the lines of love that men have sung,*
> *And many the lives lie wrecked upon its shore.*
> *Many the tears and pains that it has wrung*
> *From those who once had murmured 'I adore'.*
> *For love is not a surge of shallow waves,*
> *Nor storm of passion beating at your door.*
> *Love is not lust of getting, no nor craves*
> *Its satisfaction in desire for more.*

Love is the sea itself, an endless tide,
Forever flowing in a heart at peace;
Now ebbing, now in flood, as deep as wide
As the wide earth, its rhythms cannot cease.
For in the heart of loving man and wife
God is enthroned and He gives love its life."

II

Bunny
This is only a small part of our story. Nor is it the end.

The present fills us with anguish. War stirs our emotions and rouses our passion or compassion. Earthquakes, floods, riots, poverty, hunger, death tear at our hearts. We ask what can we do?

The future rushes at us, full of new challenges. We are told that after landing on the moon, our goal is the planets. There is talk of flying to the stars in capsules, in which men and women will procreate, the children reaching earth for the first time fully grown.

Already human organs are being transplanted and the scientists talk of freezing people and then unfreezing them fifty or a hundred years hence when a cure for their diseases has been found.

Amidst the anxieties of the present and the vast developments of science the question still remains, will we learn how to live together on our teeming earth, wife with husband and husband with wife and both with their children? Will we learn to build a classless society? Will the races find an answer to prejudice and hate? Will bridges be built between the ideological and geographical East and West? Will we find global unity in a way of life superior to any we demonstrate today? In short, will man learn to modernise himself or will he still follow his historic road to violence and destruction, this time perhaps to final extinction?

These questions are not academic. The answers to them mean life or death. They rest with each one of us.

Only our human nature—which God can change—stands between us and the answers we want to find and the world we want to see.

257

Permissiveness has been tried. It has not worked. The world is ready for a new way. We in Britain can give a lead once more.

Sir Arthur Bryant writing in the *Sunday Express* of February 11, 1968, quoted a letter he had received a few years ago from a Norwegian. The Norwegian had written, "We have always looked to England as a counterbalance against all the evil that exists in the world. . . . You give us the faith that there is still a pivot point in the world worth fighting for."

Sir Arthur goes on to say, "So the end of her comparatively brief period of global ascendancy does not mean that Britain's mission in the world is finished. . . . She cannot by pleading penury withdraw into an inglorious isolation without betraying those who look to her for leadership. . . .

"In the grimmest moment of the last war Churchill told the boys of his own school: 'Never give in, never, never, never, never—in nothing great or small, large or petty—never give in except in consideration of honour and good sense. These are not dark days, he told them, these are the greatest days our country has ever known.'"

One man rallied Britain in those days—refused to accept defeat when all seemed lost. His indomitable spirit inspired the nation and called it to what he described as its finest hour.

Will a million men and women with such a spirit rally us today? We can, if we will, shift our country and our civilisation above the tragic divisions of race and tribe, class and creed and demonstrate how life is meant to be lived—how through a God-led unity all hands can be filled with work, all stomachs with food and all hearts with an idea that really satisfies. We can make the coming years the greatest Britain has known and once more save ourselves by our exertions and the world by our example.

INDEX

INDEX